MY FATHER'S BOOK

The true story of a Japanese Prisoner of War based on the secret diary hidden in his RAF cap

Islands of South East Asia & The Spice Islands

8th March 1942 to 16th August 1945

Elizabeth Carter

First published in 2025

ISBN PAPERBACK [978-1-7384234-0-8]

ISBN HARDCOVER [978-1-7384234-1-5]

Created in conjunction with The Book Shelf Ltd:

Editor - Ameesha Green
Typesetter - Kyle Albuquerque
Cover designer - Niall Burgess

The spellings and names of many of the places described in my father's manuscript have since changed and I have used both the old and new where possible. A list of names and places can also be referenced at the end of this book.

Important Disclaimer

Please note that my father's manuscript was written by him in his later years and was based on a diary he kept during the war under extremely challenging conditions. As a result, some names, places and details may be inaccurate. To preserve the authenticity and integrity of his experiences, I have chosen not to alter his original diary entries or type-written manuscript.

This book discusses historical events involving Japanese prisoners of war, including wartime captivity, treatment, and post-war experiences. Every effort has been made to present these events accurately and respectfully, based on available historical sources and research, but there may be errors or omissions. It is also important to note that the spelling and naming of many locations have changed since the period described. Where possible, I have provided both the historical and modern names. A list of names and places can be found at the end of the book for reference.

Readers should be aware that the content may include descriptions of violence, suffering, and other difficult topics reflective of the era, and these may be upsetting. These depictions are not intended to glorify, excuse, or vilify any individual or group, but to provide an honest account of historical realities.

Certain terms and expressions that were commonly used at the time - such as the word "Nips" when referring to Japanese soldiers - are now recognised as derogatory. These terms have been retained in the text to reflect the historical context in which the diary and manuscript were written but their inclusion does not imply endorsement or approval.

I acknowledge the sensitivity of the subject matter and extend respect to all individuals affected by these events, their descendants, and all who seek a deeper understanding of this chapter of history.

Dedicated to the memory of my father

Thomas William Henry Orton and tens of thousands of British service men

who suffered the brutalities and atrocities as Japanese Prisoners of War

for three-and-a-half years during World War II.

March 1942 – August 1945

Contents

PREFACE

My father was a courageous man who defied the brutal Japanese military throughout his three-and-a-half-year captivity as a surviving Far East Prisoner of War during World War II. Evidence of his defiance and bravery was borne out of his courage and determination to conceal a small handwritten diary in the waterproof lining of his RAF cap throughout his captivity, something I admired him for throughout my childhood and adult years. A brave man who risked vicious consequences should his secret have been discovered by the Japanese or Korean guards.

My father was a member of the ground crew (some say the "unsung heroes" of the RAF!) and many years after his release, it was always his absolute desire to write a book to record and raise awareness of his experiences as a Japanese Far East Prisoner of War. Although, throughout our childhood, we were aware that he was an Ex-Far East Prisoner of War, my father never talked about his experiences, he never mentioned places such as the islands of **Haruku** or **Muna**, names that today fill my mind with visions of wretchedness and despair. For many years, prior to his death at the age of 84 years, he would spend many hours burning the midnight oil at his home typing a manuscript with just two fingers! A proficient typist he certainly was not but due to his strength of mind and sheer determination to finally share his experiences, his roughly typed manuscript has become his legacy. Passing away in February, 1998 he left behind his unfinished manuscript along with items of his treasured archive material, including the actual diary, his own personal notes on many photographs, maps and press cuttings, plus my mother's collection of personal letters and telegrams. These letters and telegrams were posted throughout their courtship, their marriage in Birmingham in January 1941, my father's posting in the Far East, imprisonment, release, journey home and activity following those difficult years. It soon becomes apparent to any reader of these letters that Joan and Tom were just an ordinary young couple clearly so much in love during an incredibly difficult and turbulent time that was to become such a major part of our history. My father had meticulously kept his collection of documents, including 1940's Newspapers, Far East Prisoner of War Bulletins, British

Red Cross letters, Air Ministry letters, maps and photographs. Irreplaceable World War II documents that will benefit future generations in their studies of the tragic but fascinating history of World War II both in the city of Birmingham and the Far East.

Many of the letters written by my mother to my father were either returned to her as 'undelivered' by the Air Ministry or they did not reach their destination but this did not deter her; she continued dutifully writing letters to her newly-wed husband on an almost daily basis. At one point she was notified that he had been reported "missing, assumed dead". One can't even begin to imagine what a devastating effect such letters must have had upon those loved ones left behind, such as the letter from the British Red Cross informing her that her husband was now a "Prisoner of War with the Japanese"! Such unexpected and devastating news surely would have triggered an overwhelming sense of relief, sheer frustration and feeling of helplessness. It becomes evident in Joan's letters that the impact of having to bear the load during these difficult times became too much for her and she was referred to a convalescent home for a short period in Clevedon, North of Weston-Supermare, Somerset. I believe this period of respite was perhaps to aid her recovery from a possible nervous breakdown or other psychological issues that could have emerged following the uncertainty and trauma of losing her newly-wed loved at one point without trace. In addition, she had to face the heart-rending consequences of her father attempting suicide, being admitted to a psychiatric hospital and his tragic untimely death due to cancer.

My mother, Joan was the middle one of three daughters and lived with her parents in Alum Rock, Birmingham during the war years. Her home was dangerously close to the Spitfire Aerodrome factory. My father, Thomas William Henry Orton was born in Sutton Coldfield, Warwickshire, as it was known at that time (now West Midlands).

Tom and Joan first met during World War II in the Spring of 1940 on Hodge Hill Common, Castle Bromwich, Birmingham and they married after a fairly short courtship in Birmingham in January 1941. As a newly-married young couple they were soon to be parted just three months later in March 1941 as Tom was to board the troopship SS "Duchess of York" in Liverpool bound for Singapore. Separated for almost 5 years, Tom and Joan became so reliant upon their precious letters, telegrams and cables as these became their only form of communication during what was to become a traumatic and unsettling period in each of their lives.

Many of the memories and experiences detailed in this book have been taken from the secret diary my father kept hidden in the lining of his RAF cap and his roughly-typed manuscript. I understand he was asked to hand the diary over to the Government upon his return from the Far East but I am unsure as to the reason why, or, how long they retained it.

Following my father's death on Friday, 13th February 1998, I decided to fulfil my father's dream by building upon his manuscript and getting his treasured book published to ensure that this immensely important part of our history is kept alive ... Tom's legacy!

I am not an experienced or professional writer, I grew up as a child of an Ex-Far East Prisoner of War, witnessing at times his violent and angry rages towards his wife and children. Such behaviour has left an indelible mark and very mixed emotions; feelings which emerged after embarking upon this project. I now consider it an honour and a privilege to have been given the opportunity to work on such an enthralling heart-rending part of history, which thanks to my father's detailed account and valuable archive material, has enabled me to put this book together. This book is intended to reach out to readers, not only to raise awareness but as a special tribute to my father and all those who suffered alongside him, also to their wives and families who endured pain and suffering throughout the inexplicable and difficult war years and the years that followed World War II.

My mother continued in her almost daily pursuit to write to my father even during periods of silence at which time she would write regularly to the British Red Cross and other government bodies in desperation for some news. She received a stream of letters written by my father prior to his captivity, from April 1940 to 1st December 1941 but then came the SILENCE! until the day he was finally allowed to write his first letter on 14th September 1945 on a piece of "Nip" Officer toilet paper. The Japanese had surrendered in August 1945 and they were now free men.

Letters from the British Red Cross and the Air Ministry to my mother confirm my father being reported to be a prisoner of war at the hands of the Japanese, followed by a report that he was missing, followed by another letter of apology stating he was in fact confirmed as a prisoner of war! These letters are a fundamental part of this book as they illustrate Tom and Joan's turbulent journey through the years prior to, during and after World War II; a short courtship of eight months, a wedding in January 1941, my father's departure overseas into the unknown in March 1941, his captivity in March 1942, his release in August 1945 and finally his homecoming.

My father describes in his manuscript about how at the time he was issued his RAF Cap, he would not have envisaged that he would be married wearing the cap; captured wearing the cap; spend three and a half years as a prisoner of war wearing it and finally be freed wearing that very same RAF cap.

During my research it became evident that the Japanese Prisoners of War were advised not to talk about their experiences when reaching home; advice that is quite the opposite of that given today, whereby psychotherapy and counselling sessions are now so freely available and encouraged. We question whether our family life would have been perhaps less challenging had our father been given the necessary support to help him adjust and prepare for his future role as a husband and role model to his children.

As a fit and healthy twenty-seven year old my father embarked upon a ship from Liverpool to Singapore, returning years later a very different and troubled soul, having spent three-and-a-half years as a prisoner of war at the hands of the brutal Japanese. This traumatic experience surely had to have a huge psychological impact on any man but you try telling this to a mother and her four young children as they are growing up with a man who at times appeared so cruel and bad-tempered. I had little or no comprehension of the unbelievable brutality and atrocities my father had endured and witnessed during his captivity or that his pain and suffering did not come to an end upon his release. Throughout the remainder of his life, he was subjected to psychological trauma and the manifestation of the tropical diseases he acquired whilst prisoner.

It was my father's absolute desire for someone, somewhere to one day pick up the mantle and take the time to put all the pieces together and publish his treasured work.

EPIGRAPH

These Far East Prisoners of War were servicemen, they were our fathers, our brothers, uncles and grandfathers and I wish to dedicate this book as an act of respect and devotion to all those brave men that suffered brutal atrocities at the hands of the Japanese during World War II. The Children of the Far East Prisoners of War and future generations deserve to know their story, will live on in our history books and that they will never be forgotten.

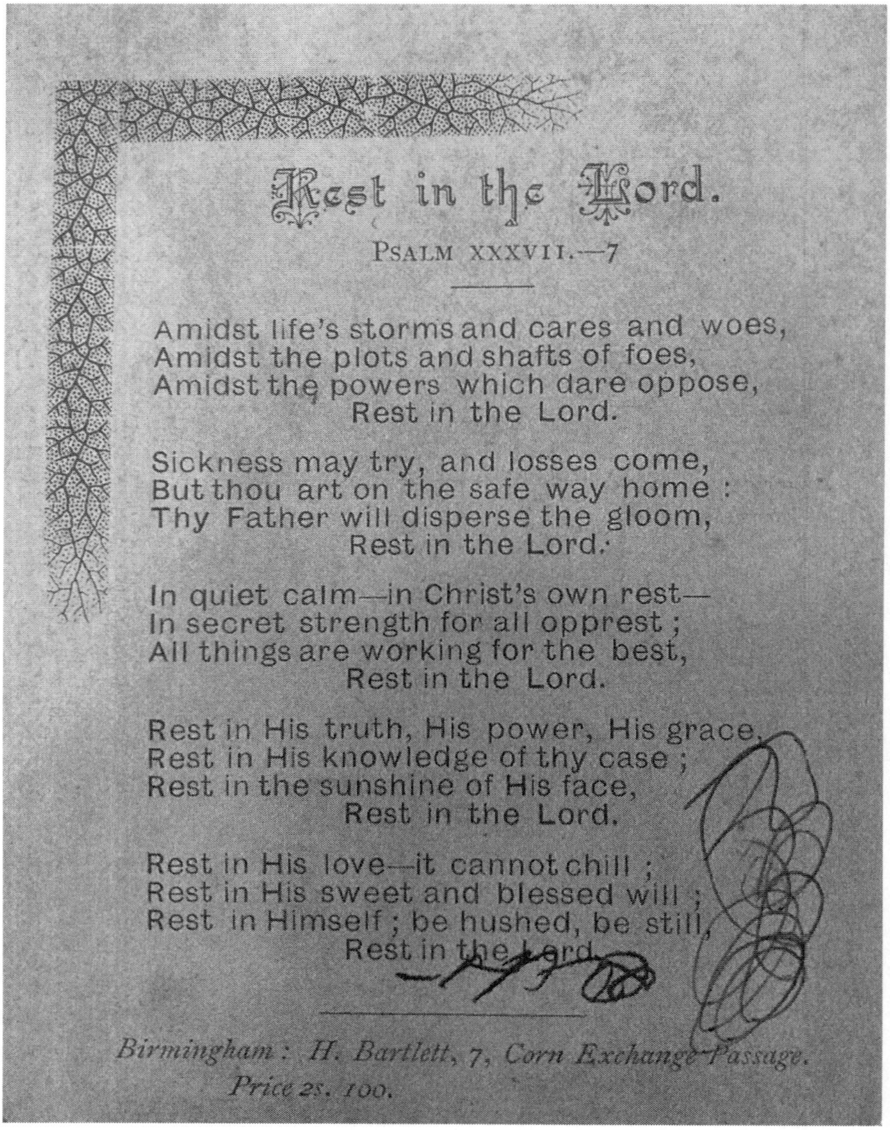

Rest in the Lord.

PSALM XXXVII.—7

Amidst life's storms and cares and woes,
Amidst the plots and shafts of foes,
Amidst the powers which dare oppose,
Rest in the Lord.

Sickness may try, and losses come,
But thou art on the safe way home :
Thy Father will disperse the gloom,
Rest in the Lord.

In quiet calm—in Christ's own rest—
In secret strength for all opprest ;
All things are working for the best,
Rest in the Lord.

Rest in His truth, His power, His grace,
Rest in His knowledge of thy case ;
Rest in the sunshine of His face,
Rest in the Lord.

Rest in His love—it cannot chill ;
Rest in His sweet and blessed will ;
Rest in Himself ; be hushed, be still,
Rest in the Lord.

Birmingham : H. Bartlett, 7, Corn Exchange Passage.
Price 2s. 100.

A small card found alongside my father's secret diary.

Chapter 1

A TRAGIC ERA IN OUR MILITARY HISTORY

Here is a fairly brief explanation of circumstances that led up to 'the Fall of Singapore', as there were many aspects that may have contributed.

Singapore was a vital part of the British Empire which was seen as a strategic British Naval base by the Japanese. "The "Fall of Singapore to the Japanese" took place on **15th February, 1942**, which has gone down in history as Britain's worst defeat in World War II and recorded as a total embarrassment for the British military.

Japan attacked British, Dutch and American territories in Asia and the Pacific. The British Army, Navy and Air Force personnel (my father being one) were sent out to the Far East to reinforce existing personnel in Singapore, however, it all went tragically wrong, even though many of the Allied forces were initially able to escape southwards to **Java**.

The Japanese military used a combination of speed, ferocity, savagery and surprise which led to many Japanese prison camps being set up scattered all over the Far East. For a long period of three-and-a-half years the Japanese Prisoners of War were subjected to gruelling slave labour, vicious punishment, torture, starvation and disease. Not to forget, the thousands who were murdered at the hands of the Japanese.

Tell us more?

Singapore is an island at the southern end of the Malay Peninsula. Prior to **1939**, it was home to a sizeable military base set up to protect Britain's other Imperial possessions in the Far East.

Following Japan's surprise attacks on "Pearl Harbour" (US Naval Base, Hawaii) and the British Colony of Hong Kong in **December 1941**, it was considered that Singapore would become the next obvious target but it is alleged that the British military command in Singapore believed that any attack by the Japanese would be defendable.

It was strongly believed that the Japanese would attack from the sea and not through the jungle and mangrove swamps of the Malay Peninsula, which turned out not to be the case. They had in fact got it all so totally wrong as the Japanese didn't attack from the sea but through the jungle and mangrove swamps. A tactic which caught the British military totally unaware and completely unprepared!

The Japanese attack on both "Pearl Harbour", Hawaii and Hong Kong in **December 1941** and Singapore in **February 1942** had a devastating effect on the British and American military. There were many casualties and the RAF lost the vast majority of front line planes on Singapore.

On February 8th, 1942 approximately 35,000 Japanese soldiers attacked Singapore. The Japanese decided to speed up their advance on Singapore by also using bicycles. What an incredibly simple and basic means of transport? The Japanese soon captured, tortured and murdered many thousands of Allied soldiers alongside the local natives who had helped the Allies. The brutality of the Japanese soldiers shocked the British.

How did it all end?

It all ended with the use of atomic bombs on Hiroshima on **6th August 1945** and Nagasaki on **9 August 1945** by the United States of America.

On August 15th, 1945 Emperor Hirohito made a radio speech to the Japanese public. **Japan had surrendered** and the prisoners of war were to be liberated, however, this did not happen overnight and it was discovered that some Japanese even continued to kill prisoners after the surrender.

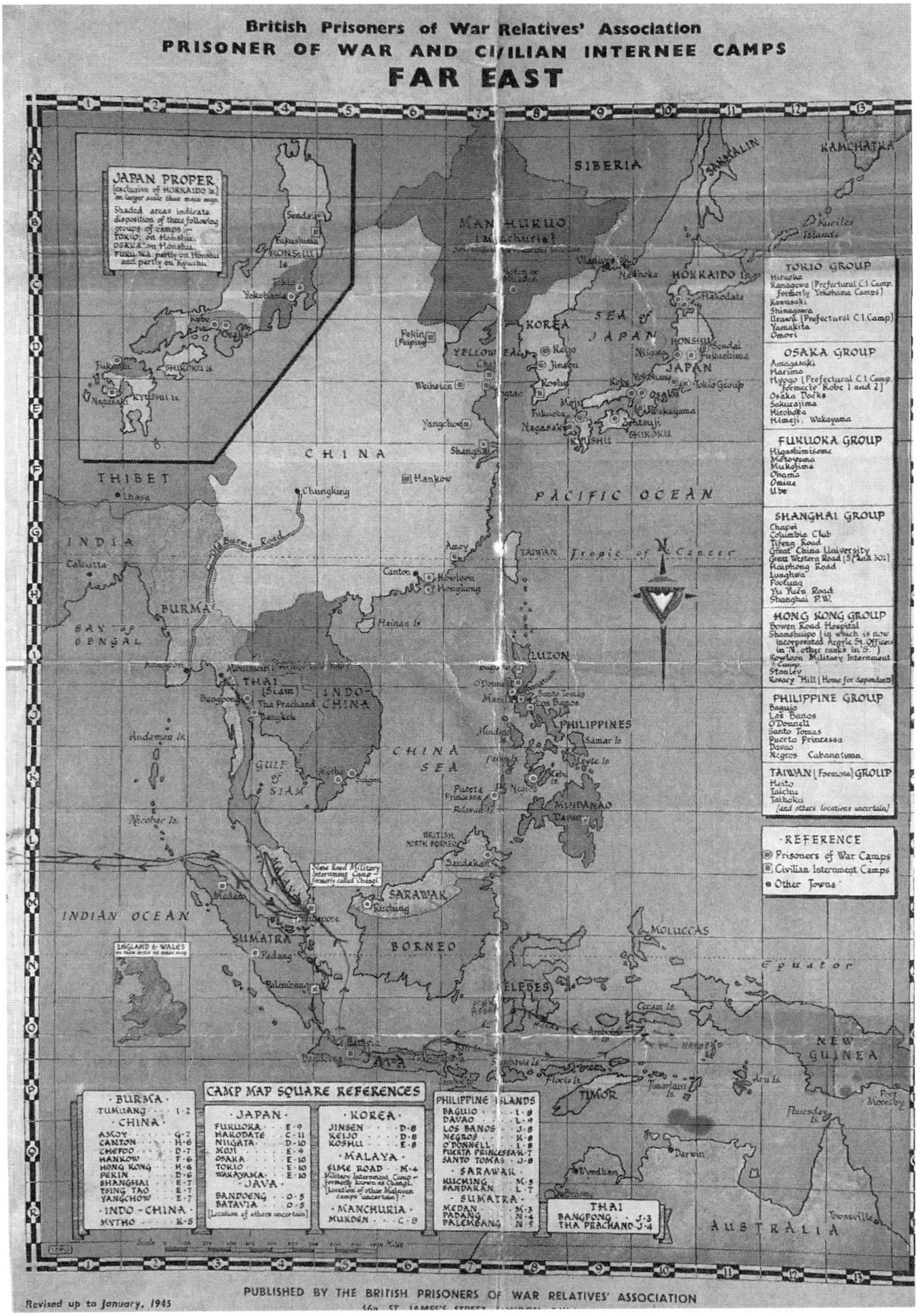

MAP OF THE FAR EAST ISSUED BY THE BRITISH PRISONERS OF WAR RELATIVES ASSOCIATION showing Prisoner of War Camps (this clearly shows lack of information available at that time)

ISLANDS OF SOUTH EAST ASIA (formerly The Dutch East Indies) - The Dutch East Indies became the United States of Indonesia in December 1949. Tom mentions **Sumatra** and adjacent islands, including the Moluccas (**Spice Islands**)

THE SPICE ISLANDS are situated in the East Indonesian Archipelago between **Sulawesi** (previously Celebes) and Papua New Guinea (previously New Guinea). They are made up of approximately 1,000 small islands. Many of these islands are mountainous, some low and swampy, some with active volcanoes. The climate is tropical with many rain forests. They were discovered by early traders due to the aroma of the spices, however, after the atrocities during World War II, they sadly became associated with the "odour of death".

JAPANESE PRISONER OF WAR CAMPS - Tom's Far East Prisoner of War Liberation Questionnaire was completed upon his return to "Blighty" - Block 104, RAF, Cosford. Dates are approximate and not confirmed.

Camps:

JAVA – Jaarmarkt

JAVA – Lyceum Camp

JAVA – Darmoc

Haroekoe – (Pelauw Village)

AMBOINA ISLAND – Weijami

MOENA ISLAND – Camp Raha

CELEBES – Bajoa, Watampone (one night – rice barn collapses)

MACASSAR, Celebes – Tap Marine Barrack PC – War is over

BATAVIA, JAVA – Cycle Camp

Chapter 2

"THE COURTSHIP and THE LETTERS" (TOM and JOAN)

25 May 1939 – Tom joined the Royal Air Force (Service No. 849112)

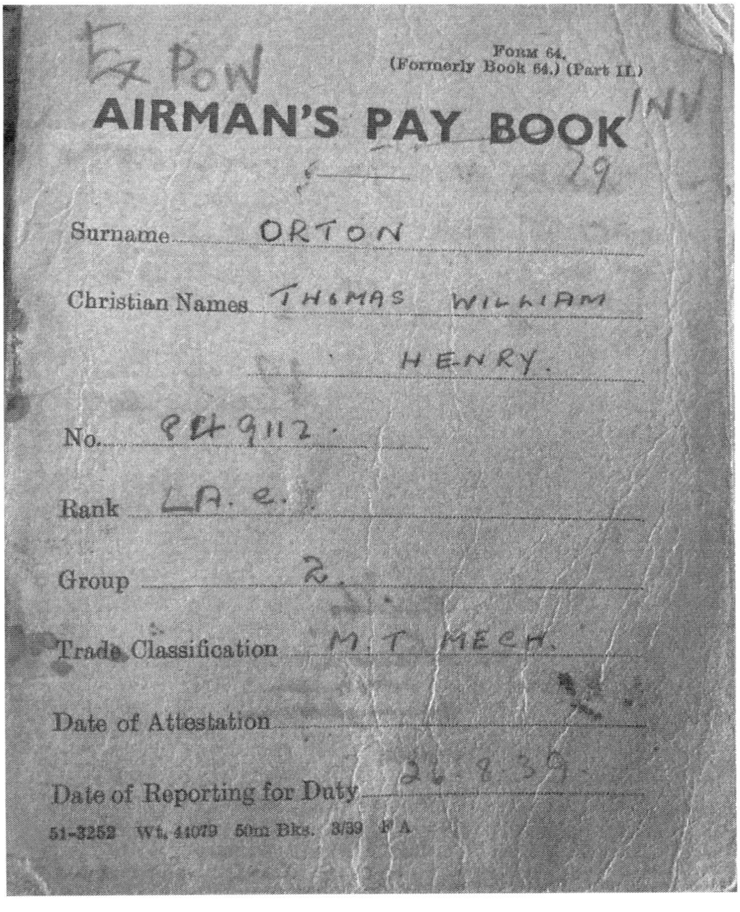

Ex POW

FORM 64.
(Formerly Book 64.) (Part II.)

AIRMAN'S PAY BOOK

INV

29

Surname ORTON

Christian Names THOMAS WILLIAM HENRY.

No. 849112.

Rank L.A.C.

Group 2.

Trade Classification M.T. MECH.

Date of Attestation

Date of Reporting for Duty 26.8.39.

51-3252 Wt. 44079 50m Bks. 3/39 P A

April 1940 - Hodge Hill Common, near Castle Bromwich in Birmingham was to be their first encounter, my mother Joan Olivia Mills and my father Thomas William Henry Orton. Not entirely sure of the event, or circumstances surrounding their first meeting, I believe it may have been some sort of fair or meeting place. I do remember quite clearly my mother saying that Tom looked very smart in his RAF Uniform and being attracted to this handsome chap with beautiful piercing blue eyes, she asked him the time! This moment was to be the beginning of a lifetime of uncertainty down a long rocky and difficult road with many twists and turns.

The letters I am about to share with you describe how Tom spent his early months in the RAF in World War II here in England and latterly in the Far East as a Japanese Prisoner of War right through to the surrender of the Japanese and Tom's journey home to his patient loving wife. Throughout this time Joan was living through not only the torment of not knowing the whereabouts of her new husband, or whether he was dead or alive, but having to survive the terrible conditions of the Birmingham Blitz. Tom hears the worrying news of the relentless bomb attacks and air raids on Birmingham and encourages Joan in his letters to travel across Birmingham to stay with her mother-in-law in Sutton Coldfield for safety.

At a glance, the letters between Joan and Tom appear to amount to just small talk but it is clear from these narratives that Joan and Tom innocently, and some might say naively, believed that the War would not last. This is what makes the letters so fascinating to the reader today. Tom and Joan were just an ordinary couple, along with thousands of others, who would be the victims of a long and extraordinarily troubled life due to the war. They were remarkable people with strong beliefs and their positive, optimistic and upbeat attitude shines through in these personal yet informative letters. It also comes to light from the letters how many different addresses Tom was located at around the country, which give an indication of how much the RAF personnel were moved from camp to camp leading up to and during the early part of the War. The earliest letters talk about Tom going overseas but reading on through the letters, this posting overseas did not in fact happen until 12 months later. It's also fairly evident throughout that Joan and Tom were both determined to raise one another's spirits, trying not to focus on what was really happening around them! The years of separation passed so slowly for this newly-married couple but their love clearly blossomed with every letter.

Tom & Joan during courtship in 1941.

Letter from Tom to Joan:

Royal Air Force,
Whitehouse Common,
Sutton Coldfield
(Tom's hometown)

27 April 1940

My Dear Joan

Just a few lines to let you know that I have been moved up here and we are at present standing by to go overseas, what country I do not know yet. We may be going tonight (Friday) or tomorrow. Really, we ought to have some leave before we go but at present it seems as if we shall not get any but I will do my utmost to get over to see you if I can. I thought I would write to save you going all the way over to Stechford tomorrow, so I hope you get this letter in time.

I am so sorry about it all dear but you will always be in my thoughts and I will write as often as I can, every day if possible. If you do happen to miss any letters from me on account of any trouble with the post you know where my home address is. You can always pop over and see my ma, 84 Coles Lane, Sutton Coldfield. Anyway, you can write to me as soon as I get settled down. I must say that I shall miss you terribly but things will not always be this way. Don't forget if I can possibly get out before we go, I will come and see you. I have had to take the old motorbike home so I can easily call for it and brazz over. Thinking of you always.

All my love Tom xxxx

The beginning of World War II - Tom far right

Tom

Tom back left with comrades

Letters from Tom to Joan: RAF CARDINGTON

(2 miles south of Beford. 3 sections: Balloon Units, Recruit Units and Gas Plant. Almost 300,000 recruits passed through the gates of RAF Cardington during W.W.II)

A.C.I. T Orton 849112
"B" Flight A Mobile Squadron
Royal Air Force
Cardington
Beds

Postmark 27th April 1940

My Dear Joan

I am stationed down here in Cardington, how long for I do not know. Some say we are going over the water tomorrow and some say different. It is a very nice place and very interesting. I think we have got to have some rifle or revolver practice this afternoon so I shall be quite busy.

If you write to me straight away, your letter will reach me alright and I would very much like to hear from you. I reckon it is a bit tough not getting any leave don't you? But still darling duty must be done. This place will be closing down for Whitsun so if it does happen that we are still stuck here you can bet your life I will be over to see you. I have been looking over the hangars where they used to keep the R100 and R101, they are massive buildings.

Don't forget to write to me as soon as possible

With all my love Tom xxxxxxxx

Tom centre back row

A.C.I. T Orton 849112
"B" Flight A Mobile Squadron
Royal Air Force
Cardington
Beds

Wednesday, May 1940

My Dear Joan

I have just got your very welcome letter so I am writing straight back to you to show you how glad I was to receive it. Really darling you should not get depressed on account of me being away from you because you know that no matter how far I am away, I still love you with all my heart. Get that straight honey but it is so nice to think someone loves you so much as to cry over you. I certainly had a big lump in my throat and I can tell you I felt a bit down in the mouth when I left but I feel better now that I have heard from you.

We are still stuck in the same place and how long for I do not know. I think it was all a lot of phooey about going abroad straight away. Anyway, if we are here much longer, I hope to get some leave and then I shall be able to see you again. We have been living in tents ever since we arrived here, having to shave and wash in cold water at 6.00 am. There is a picture house in the station so I go to watch a film now and again because the nearest town is about 3 miles way.

There is one thing I would like and that is a photo of you. Don't think that I have forgotten what you look like but you know I would like to look at you now and again.

I will write in my next letter to ma and pa about you going over to Sutton, I am sure they will be very glad to see you. The weekend after I left our kid brother Ray came over from the Navy so I just missed seeing him. Goodbye for a bit my love.

Yours, always yours Tom xxxxxx

Tom 2nd from left back row

A.C.I. T Orton 849112
"B" Flight A Mobile Squadron
Royal Air Force
Cardington
Beds

Postmark 6th May 1940

My Dear Joan

I am being moved from Cardington tomorrow (Monday). We have had orders to be ready for 11.30 a.m. and I think we are making for somewhere on the South Coast. I will let you know my new address as soon as I get there as I really do enjoy hearing from you. You are always in my thoughts but things will not always be like this and I am longing for the day when I shall be with you for always.

Well, I think I am getting better at writing letters don't you? Please write to me as soon as I send my new address. I can hardly wait. Goodbye my love.

Your loving sweetheart Tom xxxxxxx

Letter from Tom to Joan (Postmark 7th May 1940 - RAF SHEERNESS – Isle of Sheppey

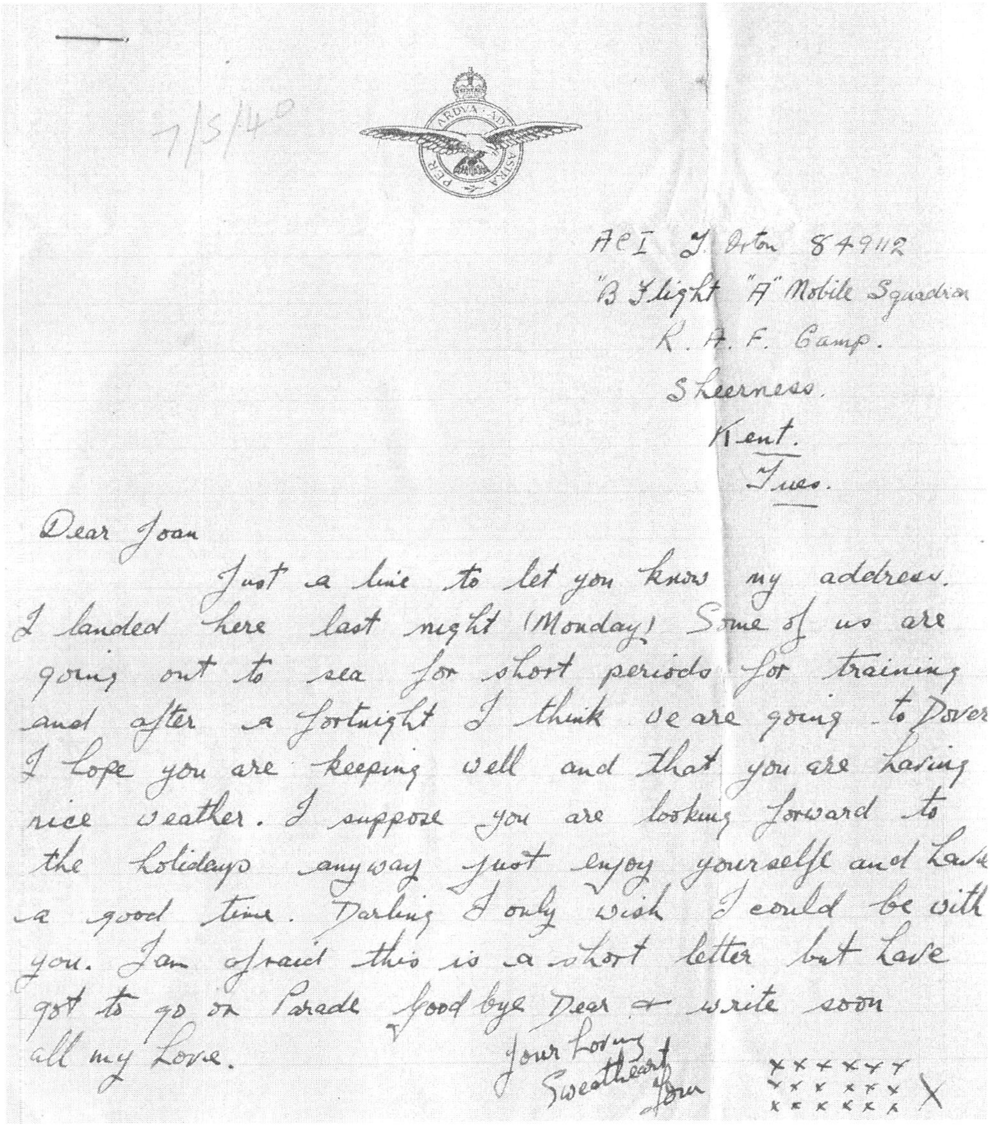

7/5/40

PER ARDUA AD ASTRA

AC1 T. Orton 849112
"B" Flight "A" Mobile Squadron
R.A.F. Camp.
Sheerness.
Kent.
Tues.

Dear Joan

Just a line to let you know my address. I landed here last night (Monday) Some of us are going out to sea for short periods for training and after a fortnight I think we are going to Dover I hope you are keeping well and that you are having nice weather. I suppose you are looking forward to the holidays anyway just enjoy yourselfe and have a good time. Darling I only wish I could be with you. I am afraid this is a short letter but have got to go on Parade good bye Dear & write soon all my Love.

Your Loving
Sweatheart
Tom

XXXXXX
XXXXXX
XXXXXX X

NEWS HEADLINES ... 10th May 1940 - "Winston Churchill becomes Prime Minister"

Letters from Tom to Joan: RAF DEAL - Kent

A.C.I. T Orton 849112
"B" Flight R.A.F
Deal
Kent

Postmark 14th May 1940

My Dear Joan

I do not know whether you have written to the other camp as I was moved down here to Deal on Saturday so your letter may be delayed. I hope you are well and had a nice holiday. I received a letter from ma a few days ago and she would very much like you to go over any Sunday.

We had an air raid over the last place (Sheerness) and the Jerry planes came within a hundred or so feet of our boats at 5.00 a.m. ... a bit of action for the first time! This place is about 8 or 10 miles from Dover and we have to go out to sea for the same distance. Maybe we should have joined the Navy instead of the R.A.F!!

I should be getting some leave soon but on account of this new development, I shall have to wait a bit. I am longing to hear from you, so please write to this address. With all my love.

Your every loving sweetheart Tom xxxx

Tom – Deal, Kent

A.C.I. T Orton 849112
"B" Flight Royal Air Force
Deal
Kent

Postmark 18th May 1940

My Dear Joan

I got your most welcome letter this morning. I do hope your hand is getting better and fancy them cancelling your holidays! Please do not think I have forgotten you, if you do happen to miss a letter from me, there will always be one on the way. Wherever I am I shall always write to you, I only wish I could get some leave so that I could see you again. As you say it seems years instead of weeks and I am looking forward to the day when I can be with you again. I only hope you still feel the same. I do not think we shall go far from here but if I am moved, it will only be to Dover 8 miles away, so your letters will be sent on to me.

Your ever loving sweetheart Tom xxxxxxxx

A.C.I. T Orton 849112
"B" Flight R.A.F.
Deal
Kent

Postmark 27th May 1940

My Dear Joan

Thank you so much for the parcel received this morning and for the one I received last Saturday. It is so good of you and I feel so grateful. You've no idea how much I look forward to your letters. It is so tough being apart but as you said we must keep our chins up. If only I could get a couple of days leave it would not be so bad.

I am sorry I have had to write in pencil but I am part of a guard just outside Deal. We are guarding a "Spitfire" that had to make a false landing. As if it would run away! I am sorry to hear you are still having your hand attended to and hope it will soon heal. Ma has asked me for your address to write to you. I hope you don't mind. Sorry to hear you are working long hours and weekends.

I am your ever loving sweetheart Tom xxxxxxxxx

DV

Guarding Spitfire Nr Deal, Kent – lst Spitfire shot down over the channel, managing to belly land 1940

A.C.I. T Orton 849112
"B" Flight R.A.F.
Deal
Kent

Postmark 28th May 1940

Dear Joan

I am so very glad your hand is getting better. I had a letter from ma yesterday but she did not mention whether you had been over to Sutton. I was offered 24 hours leave today but I may as well stay in camp as wander around for 24 hours with nowhere to go so I gave my chance to a chap that lives not far from here.

We had another heavy air raid last night, talk about deafening, our ears were ringing for hours after. Bombs dropped right alongside our boats but I was watching from the sea front. After we got in, we could not go to bed until about 2 in the morning - they were going at it hammer and tongs. I am doing my best to keep off the boats so that I shall be one of the first to get some leave. I am longing to see you and feeling quite jealous of George, being that he can speak to you and I can't!! Remember me to him and tell him to join up and get some real service in, he will laugh his eyes out.

You are always in my thoughts… the gramophone is just playing Faithful Forever.

Your loving sweetheart Tom xxxxxxxxxxxxxxxxx

Tom's parents (Elizabeth & Tom Orton snr)

A.C.I. T Orton 849112
"B" Flight 956 Squadron
Royal Air Force
Deal
Kent

Postmark lst June 1940

My Dear Joan

I hope you received the little present I sent you and that you are not working too hard at the Fort Dunlop. It is so tough for us to be apart but still each day that passes brings us nearer to the day when I shall be with you again which I am sure can't be all that far away. I had some snaps taken yesterday and I will send you one as soon as they are developed. I have still got your photograph pinned up over my bed in the barrack room. Goodbye for just a little bit.

Your ever loving sweetheart Tom xxxxxxxxxxxxx

p.s. Remember me to your Ma & Pa

Tom Far left

Tom – Deal, Kent

RAF PATCHWAY

(North of Bristol, also came under the command of the RAF Filton station commander)

T Orton
c/o 15 Southsea Road
Patchway
Bristol

Postmark 7th June 1940

My Darling

Sorry I have not written for a few days but I have been standing by to move since last weekend. I have arranged to have my letters sent to this address so as to get them sooner than if they were sent to the camp. It seems ages since I last heard from you but there are a lot of letters that have not been delivered to us yet from headquarters, hence the reason I have given you this address.

The weather is scorching and the heat is terrific here! We are living in tents again about 5 or 6 miles from Bristol and they do not know what an air raid is, so it is a bit different to the other joint.

Hoping to hear from you very soon.

Tom xxxxxxxxx

T Orton
c/o 15 Southsea Road
Patchway
Bristol

UNDATED

My Dear Joan

I am so sorry I did not ask you what kind of ring you wanted, just like me to forget a thing like that! You can let me know any time and I will have a scout round the City to see where the best are sold. It will be 2 to 3 weeks before I can get there so there is no hurry.

I have given up smoking for good and I find that I feel a lot better in myself as well as my pocket. I am trying to save every penny I can. I am hoping we will be able to meet soon as they are continuing to give our chaps the 24 hrs so far. In the meantime, I suppose we have got to be content with just writing to each other. I look forward so much to reading your letters. It is very nice to hear that from your Ma and Pa, I am sure my people feel the same about you. Anyway, I'm happy you're happy and we shall be happier still when we are together.

Yours for always Tom xxxxx

T Orton
c/o 15 Southsea Road
Patchway
Bristol

Postmark 27th June 1940

Darling

Thanks for the letter, I hope you enjoyed the concert and that you did not have to rush away like the last time, remember?

Yes, I have given up smoking for good. Nice work if you can do it but you can't save money and spend it can you dear? Have you had any air raids yet? This place is getting as bad as Deal, he has been over 3 nights in succession, so some of us have gone short of our beauty sleep.

I think the next time I come over, I will be able to get a lift as I know a driver who comes down here from Brum every day. Will you give me the gen on the ring in your next letter.

I am yours <u>Forever</u> my Darling Tom xxxxxxx

RAF PUCKLECHURCH

(North of Bristol under the command of the RAF Filton commander)

A.C.I. T Orton 849112
Royal Air Force
***Pucklechurch*
Nr Bristol

Postmark 4th July 1940

My Dear Joan

I have been moved down here from Kent but do not think this will be my permanent address as I may be moved again tomorrow, so please hang on before you write again. There may be a letter of yours at Deal so I suppose it will follow me. I think it is too bad being mucked about like this but we have just got to make the best of it. I hope you got your present and the photos I sent you. I will write as soon as I get to this other address which I don't think is very far from here. I am glad we are not stopping here as it is right in the countryside, 9 miles from Bristol and buses only come half way. I will write the moment I get to the next joint they dump me in so expect a letter say in a couple of days.

Cheerio for a bit dear. All my love Tom x

Tom second from right

c/o 15 Southsea Road
Patchway
Bristol

July 1940

Darling

Just a few lines to wish you very many happy returns for Monday.

I managed to get your ring o.k. I am sure you will like it but I would prefer to give it to you personally, ideally on your birthday on the 7th. I have tried to change my day for the 7th but without luck so far. Anyway, it will be one of the days this week so I am sure you will forgive me for keeping you waiting another few days. I will let you know definitely which day it is.

I have been very worried about you! Today is the first day I have heard from you since I returned and I am glad you are now working less hours at Fort Dunlop, you certainly deserve a good weekend's rest after working all week. Roll on my 24 hours so that I can be with you again. I am really looking forward to this one!

Have you had many air raids lately? He still comes over here almost each night, although he came in the day time either Wed or Thurs and dropped one right onto one of the lorries holding one of the bladders round the drome. Thankfully there was no one in the vehicle as it was blown into little pieces and part of the road which is about eighteen inches thick was absolutely heaved up. Two of the chaps are in sick bay and the "B" was fetched down before he got many miles away. Still enough of this, let's look forward to when I come home, I am counting the hours. God Bless you and take care of you. .

Yours for always Tom xxxxxxx

T Orton
c/o 15 Southsea Road
Patchway
Bristol

Postmark 12th July 1940

My Darling Joan

I received your letter this morning and your other letter just after I had written to you so you see there is a delay if they are sent to the camp.

I am so glad you enjoyed yourself in Sutton. As you say my old man is a bit of a case and I would have loved to have seen you brazing along on the old triumph, I bet it was a bit hard having no pillion seat though! Thanks for the gen about brother Ray coming home for 10 days. Lucky devil, still he needs it if he is going back on-board ship. I hope you will go over to Sutton pretty often to see my folks. I received a letter this morning from Ma saying they really did enjoy your company. I have just got Ma an allowance through. I have been saving in the post office savings bank so I am sending my bank book home and Ma will put so much in each week, I can't get at it then to draw any! Have you received my little present, or have I missed another letter?

I only hope with all my heart that the fortune teller was right saying that I should see you for your birthday and I will do my utmost to make it. I am constantly thinking of ways to get over to see you but don't worry I will get over somehow.

Your Ever Loving Sweetheart Tom xxxxxxxxxxxxxx

***ps. Don't put RAF by my name when you put my address, as it is better if you put just the plain address.** Goodbye my love xxxx*

c/o 15 Southsea Road
Patchway
Bristol

Postmark 15th July 1940

My Darling

I got back o.k. although just a bit late. I did so much enjoy coming over, you do not know how happy I am when we are together. I hope you did not think badly of me when I said you need not buy me anything, it's just that I think in times like these we should save our coppers for other times and I hope those times will soon come. When I return here after even a short time with you, I always have a lump in my throat for a day or so but then, I try to think of the times when we shall be together for always. I enjoyed my time with your Ma and Pa very much on Friday night. I hope you don't work too hard at the Fort, after all work will always keep and I am looking forward to the day when you won't have to. Roll on another 12 days, what do you say?

I am yours for always Tom xxxxxxx

Joan & Parents

c/o 15 Southsea Road
Patchway
Bristol

Postmark 24th July 1940

Dear Joan

I have just arrived back at camp in reasonably good time. They tell me that we may be on the move again, where to, I do not know but hope it will be nearer home so I should wait a couple or three days before you write to me. I will let you know my new address as soon as I get there.

I was so glad to see you again, you don't know how much I enjoyed my 24 hours. I think that even if I was at Lands End, I would get over to see you somehow. All that I am waiting for now is my next leave so that I can come and be with you again.

I am now going on duty so I must close now until I can find out definitely what my new address will be. Goodbye for a bit, and God Bless you. I am always thinking of you.

I am yours For always Tom xxxxx

c/o 15 Southsea Road
Patchway
Bristol

Postmark 25th July 1940

My Dear Joan

I have some real good news ... I shall have my 4 days from Aug 2nd - 6th. I am the only one left here of the original lot, all the other chaps have been posted to Avonmouth. I am rather glad as it is quite handy here for getting home and as far as I can gather, I am stopping here, for a time anyway. I do feel quite bucked that we are having our leave at the same time so we can both look forward to a good time together can't we my love? I really thought I was leaving here when they said we were all going (perhaps they can't do without my valuable knowledge, ahem!) I do hope you are looking after yourself. I am just going on telephone duty for the night at the Vicar's House I told you about. I shall sit there and think about the good time we shall have. Always thinking of you my loved one.

With all my love Tom xxxxxxxx

c/o 15 Southsea Road
Patchway
Bristol

Postmark 27th July 1940

Darling

Thanks so much for the parcel. I got home o.k. from your house Sunday night as I managed to get a lift right into Sutton. I have just had some good news, I am having 4 days leave 11th to 15th August but will still carry on with the 24 hrs in the meantime, so I shall soon be with you again my dear. Tell your Ma that our Ma was sorry she was not in on Sunday evening but she hopes to meet her soon.

I have just arrived back in camp (6 p.m.) only 2 hours late, so I reckon I have done very well. I was the first one to try hitch-hiking and being as I did it o.k., they are all going to try it.

I hope to have your ring in a few days and I am counting the days until I can be with you again. I was so glad to hear you say that you would always wait for me, which I am sure won't be for as long as we think.

From your Ever Loving Tom xxxxx

p.s. Remember me to your Ma & Pa

Joan

c/o 15 Southsea Road
Patchway
Bristol

Postmark 30th July 1940

My Dear Joan

I have just arrived back and writing to you straight away. I am sorry you were so upset when I left you at the station and I do hope you feel a little better by the time you get this letter. I can honestly say I felt the same but perhaps I didn't show it. As soon as I got into Bristol, I had your name tattooed under the emblem on my arm so you see Darling, I am now branded for life! This made me over an hour late but I was determined to have it done straight away. I walked into camp as bold as brass, handed my pass in and no-one said a word! Have you mentioned the ring to your Ma and Pa? I do hope they are in favour. I shall do my best to get over again as soon as possible. I feel so very lucky to have you say you will wait for me forever but it will not be for as long as we may think. Will you go over to see Ma pretty often? I can't explain but it will make me feel so much better and you know that you will always be welcome.

Remember me to your Ma and Pa and tell them that I am very glad to have met them. I shall have to close now, although I feel at the moment that I could go on writing to you all night.

Your Loving Sweetheart Tom xxxxxx

c/o 15 Southsea Road
Patchway
Bristol

Postmark 31st July 1940

My Dear Joan

Thanks so much for your letter received this morning. I hope you like your new job, although as you say it is a bit mucky. One thing you can say is that you are doing a job of national importance.

I saw the sergeant this morning and he said my leave was still o.k. It is very nice to think that I shall be with you the day after tomorrow, so I am waiting patiently for the time to roll by. This is all I can write for the moment as I am due for kit inspection so cheerio for a bit. All my love.

Your loving Husband (to be) Tom xxxxx

Tom & Joan are now ENGAGED

c/o 15 Southsea Road
Patchway
Bristol

UNDATED

My Darling

It is very nice to hear that you are getting some things together. You bet I will keep my eyes open for anything we shall need. I will bring those sheets with me when I come over again sometime next week. I feel quite honoured to think we have towels with our initials on! I am sure, if we persevere, we shall have a home together in no time.

One of our chaps has had his discharge through this morning, as he is going back to his civvy job, lucky devil! We are just giving him a send-off, I think he works at the G.E.C.

It has been pretty quiet here for a day or so and we are taking advantage of the rest. I should get my 4 days a bit earlier, now that this chap is leaving us. Hoping his replacement will automatically come on the end of the rota. Some of our chaps pull my leg when I say I don't care much for going out at night now I am engaged! Anyway, all I look forward to now is coming home to see you my Darling.

From your loving Husband (to be) Tom xxxx

p.s. My last letter was posted in Sutton by a Corporal home on leave

NOTE NEW ADDRESS:
T Orton
c/o Mrs Betteridge
13 Southsea Road
Patchway
Bristol

Postmark 11th August 1940

My Dear Joan

I arrived back a trifle late as it was 7.00 a.m. when I walked in but I squared it alright. I hope you got back to Elsie's ok after our marvellous 4 days. I had a shock when I asked the Corporal when my 24 hours was due, he said next Saturday. I will try and change with someone as it is rather awkward getting back on Sundays.

Did you have a stern word with your sister Brenda for borrowing your best dance shoes? Don't worry, if she has spoilt them, I will get you some more but lock them up!! The boys always ask me how Joan is when I get back and tell me to hurry up and get married. God Bless you and keep you.

Your loving husband (to be) Tom xxx

T Orton
c/o Mrs Betteridge
13 Southsea Road
Patchway
Bristol

UNDATED

Darling

Thanks so much for your letter received this morning. I shall be having my 24 on Tuesday, so will see you between 7.30 p.m. and 8 p.m.

So ... Joan is getting married! I am going to save every halfpenny I get and as you can see, I am even using both sides of the paper! If I put as much as I can away each week, it will not be long until our big day. I have decided not to even go to the pictures or even drink, so if I send you so much a week, as well as the money Ma is putting away for me, plus the extra tanner a day we are going to get, we shall be quids in!

Some of our chaps are going up for that trade test next week, taking them in alphabetical order going up to 'N' so I am the next on the list. I shall certainly do my best to pass as that will also mean more pay. I am feeling quite proud of myself as I have been put in charge, temporarily just for tonight though, as the Corporals have had to go away for the night, so they must place a certain amount of confidence in your sweetheart.

All my love Tom xxxxxx

T Orton
c/o 13 Southsea Road
Patchway
Bristol

Postmark 15th August 1940

Darling

I have just got back to camp and they tell me that I missed a bit of fun here Tues night, as there was a good dog fight right over the drome and we fetched two "Jerries" down. I told them that I was with you in your air raid shelter.

Let me know which dates you have your 3 days off as I might be able to fix my next 4 days for those dates. I do hope you do not get fed up with seeing me so often! I will send money for you to save next pay day and you can find out what is best to do with it. Tell your Ma and Pa that I wish to be remembered to them and that I enjoyed the stay.

From your loving husband (to be) Tom xxxxxxxxx

c/o 13 Southsea Road
Patchway
Bristol

Postmark 23rd August 1940

(addressed to c/o Mrs Allen, 149 Cromwell Street, Nechells, B'ham)

My Dear Joan

I received your letter this morning and was quite concerned as the first thing I noticed was the different address but felt relieved after reading. I am so sorry things are so bad up there but perhaps you will get a bit more peace where you are now. There is no doubt about it you certainly were in a dangerous area (Castle Bromwich – not far from the Spitfire factory).

I shall be over on Monday for 48 hours and will call round to see you in Nechells.

<u>All</u> my love Tom xxxxxxx

"THE BIRMINGHAM BLITZ" - *BIRMINGHAM and nearby Coventry were integral to the British War effort producing a vast share of the arms, machinery and military supplies for the allied forces. BIRMINGHAM became the most heavily bombed city outside of London with the loss of more than 2,200 citizens (men, women and children) from over* ***75 air-raids.*** *The worst of these raids were carried out between* ***August 1940*** *and* ***May 1941*** *which included 5,000+ high explosive bombs, over 45 parachute land mines and numerous incendiaries being dropped on the city. By the time war broke out, around* ***82,000 Anderson and Morrison air-raid shelters*** *had been built.*

On 25th August 1940 *Birmingham city centre was bombed, destroying the market hall where the Bull Ring now stands.*

"THE SPITFIRE AERODROME FACTORY - Castle Bromwich, Birmingham" was the *most well-known of all the wartime aircraft manufacturers where reportedly approximately 1,200 Spitfires were built. The Castle Bromwich Aerodrome Factory was located very close to Joan's family home, hence Tom's concern described in his letters to her. Joan was subjected to the ritual of emerging from the air raid shelter in the morning to survey the destruction from the raids during the night. The wearing of tin hats and carrying gas masks was an all too familiar sight. During the Blitz there was no guarantee as to whether the bombs would hit their target and no part of the City of Birmingham was safe.*

Letters from Tom to Joan:

c/o 13 Southsea Road
Patchway
Bristol

Postmark 29th August 1940

(addressed to 69 Chipperfield Road, Castle Bromwich, B'ham)

My Dear Joan

I do hope you had a quieter night last night and that you were able to get some sleep. He was over here doing his stuff as usual but he lost pretty well before daylight came. Are you at work today? I expect you are working while I am writing this letter. I don't know how people are going to cope with all this, I think the best thing to do is to go straight to bed after tea and then doze in the old shelter. Still, things can't always be like this my love. I feel proper dull when I get back here after being with you at home. The sun is as hot as fire and there is plenty of work making a roadway.

Keep your chin up and keep smiling. Cheerio for a bit.

From your loving Husband (to be) Tom x

c/o 13 Southsea Road
Patchway
Bristol

Postmark 4th September 1940

My Darling

I do hope you did not lose too much sleep last night. I went to bed about 12.30 and heard one or two eggs drop over your way. I felt a proper cad to think that I had left you. I arrived in Sutton about 11.15 p.m. after walking the whole of the way. I was rather lucky getting a lift back to camp this time as I came in a large car at about 70 m.p.h and what do you think I was in camp 5 minutes early.

Ma says there is a house soon to become empty by the Odeon Picture house (Sutton). I have asked her to see your Ma and Pa about it. Anyway, if she cannot get over, mention it to your Ma and Pa and they may go over and see about it. I am sure you would all feel a lot safer in Sutton and you would be closer to me when I come home. But it is up to your Ma and Pa of course.

The wireless is just playing "I've got my eyes on you" and the time signal has just gone for 5 o'clock. Good bye and God Bless you.

From your loving Husband (to be) Tom xxxx

T Orton
c/o 13 Southsea Road
Patchway
Bristol

UNDATED

My Dear Joan

I received your most welcome letter this morning. It sounds as though you have been having a lively time up in old Brum, according to the wireless. He has been pretty busy down here too but we take no linseed poultice.

Well, my sweet, I am keeping my word, I have not moved out of the camp at all since I was over to see you last. The lads tell me I must be in a bad way when I refuse to go down to the local for a drink! Roll on Monday when we can be together.

From your loving Husband (to be) xxxxxxxxx

TOM RETURNS FROM LIVERPOOL:

Postmark 5th September 1940 **NO ADDRESS!**

My Dear Joan

I do hope you are alright as I have heard that you have been going through the mill.

I returned from my journey to Liverpool today dinner and have to start off again tomorrow, Sunday. I do wish I could hear from you but if I give you this address and you write to here, I might be at some other place by the time it arrives. Anyway Darling, keep your chin up and keep smiling that is the only thing to do. I will get over to see you at the very first opportunity. This is a job and half compared to my previous job and one thing that sticks in my craw is that it has spoilt our communication. Never mind my Dear, I am still hoping that we shall be able to carry out our intentions at Christmas.

I must close now as I am standby driver tonight, worst luck, so I will let you know my permanent address as soon as I can, then I hope to hear from you if only to hear that you are alright.

I am Yours for always Tom xxxxx

p.s. Remember me to your Ma and Pop.

WOLVERHAMPTON – ON WAY TO LIVERPOOL DOCKS

Postmark 12th September 1940 ***NO ADDRESS!***

My Darling Joan

I have been so very worried about having to wait so long for your letter. I was surprised to hear that you did not get mine till Friday as I posted it as soon as I returned! At this moment I am in Wolverhampton on my way the other side of Liverpool but shall be back in Bristol in a couple of days. I have been transferred to the Motor Transport, so don't be surprised if I call round sometime during one of my journeys. I will do my very best anyway.

I went in front of the Squadron Leader yesterday about that new reclassification and I have to go on a course in a week or two, so hopefully I shall soon be in the money. I had a 10 shilling postal to send you last week but when I did not receive a letter, I thought the best thing to do was to hang on to it until I come home in case it did not find you. Goodbye and God Bless you my Dear.

From your ever lovingTom xxxxxxxxxx

p.s. Don't write back until I write to you again as I have got a different address. Excuse scribble

A.C.I. T Orton 849112
935 Sqdn M.T. Room 4
R.A.F. Pucklechurch
Bristol

Postmark 23rd September 1940

Darling

I arrived back in good time last night but could not write straight back as promised, as I clicked for a job as soon as I got in. I am still attached here, as far as I know, so you can write to this address.

I enjoyed my 48 hrs, every minute of it, and very much looking forward to the next one which won't be long. I suppose you will be moving into your new house sometime this week. If you do, don't forget to let me have your new address. I hear from one of our drivers who drove through early in the morning that you had a raid last night. Hoping to hear from you very soon.

From your Loving Husband (to be) Tom xxxxxx

"NEWS BULLETIN" ... 25th September 1940 - RAF FILTON – "BRISTOL 'BLITZ"

"The airfield was attacked just before mid-day today by 57 Heinkel 111 bombers with a Messerschmitt Bf 110 fighter escort. The Luftwaffe raid was primarily aimed at the Bristol Aeroplane Company's works on the south side of the airfield. One air raid shelter on the airfield received a direct hit, 5 others were seriously damaged. Over 200 people killed".

Letters from Tom to Joan:

A.C.I. T Orton 849112
M.T. Section Room 4
R.A.F. Pucklechurch
Bristol

Postmark 27th September 1940

My Darling

Thanks for your letter received yesterday. (The letters do seem to be getting through quicker these days). Ma has written to say she will carry on putting all the money in the bank each week for me, which is very good of her and if I send you as much as I can every pay day, I think we shall be able to manage it alright Christmas.

I expect you have now moved house, which will be a bit safer for you and your family. I do hope you are not being bothered too much by the air-raids. Jerry has been pretty busy down here this last day or two. The place is strewn with wrecked "unker smitts" and we have all got a souvenir apiece.

I am feeling the benefit of the pullover you knitted me as it gets very cold here but I expect it is the same up there. The lads say it is very nice especially the pattern, I say it is very very nice darling.

Tell your pop I hope he will be able to put the shed up alright and that I did not knock it to pieces too much, I am very good at breaking things up! God Bless you and keep you.

Yours for Always Tom xxxxxxxxx

UNDATED

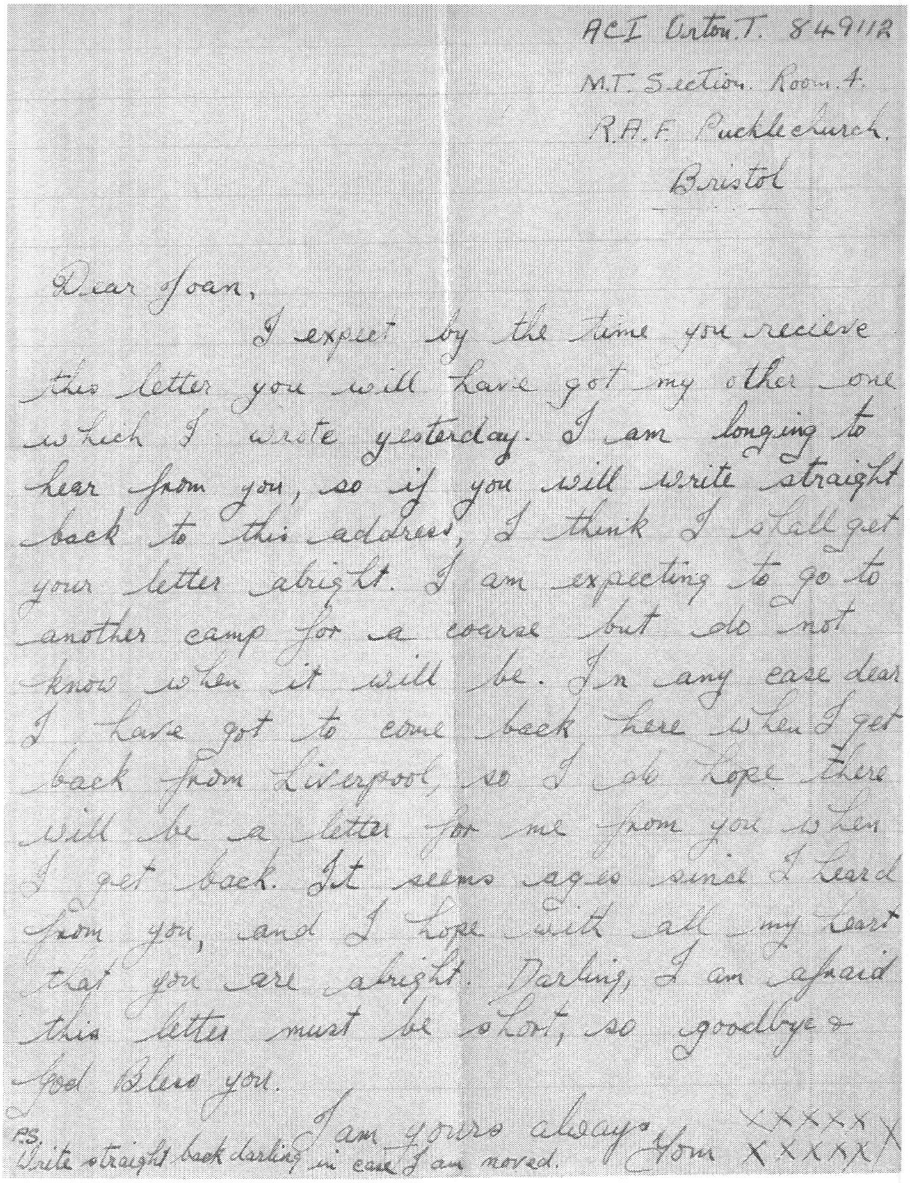

AC1 Orton.T. 849112
M.T. Section Room.4.
R.A.F. Pucklechurch.
Bristol

Dear Joan,

I expect by the time you recieve this letter you will have got my other one which I wrote yesterday. I am longing to hear from you, so if you will write straight back to this address, I think I shall get your letter alright. I am expecting to go to another camp for a course but do not know when it will be. In any case dear I have got to come back here when I get back from Liverpool, so I do hope there will be a letter for me from you when I get back. It seems ages since I heard from you, and I hope with all my heart that you are alright. Darling, I am afraid this letter must be short, so goodbye & God Bless you.

I am yours always.
Tom XXXXXX
XXXXX

P.S.
Write straight back darling in case I am moved.

A.C.I. T. Orton 849112
M.T. Section Room 3
R.A.F. Pucklechurch
Bristol

UNDATED

Darling

I received your letter alright and am sorry I could not write earlier as I have been on the road again. I hope you are settled in your new house and have a quieter time. Fancy the old scrap and reclaim being hit but still they could have done worse. I asked the sergeant about a trip up to Brum and he says I can bring the first wagon that has to come up and I hope to stop overnight if I can work it. Tomorrow is the big day, pay day, so I will send some more clocks for you to save in my next letter.

I went to Gloucester yesterday, if it had been a few miles further on, I could have dropped in to see you. Have you been over to Sutton lately? I am sure Ma would welcome you one of the Sundays. I must go down to the P.O. with all the camp mail now and I will make sure l put this one in first! If I don't get some time off to see you soon, I shall desert (ahem!). Goodbye my love.

Your Loving Sweetheart Tom xxx

p.s. Don't forget to put Room 3 on your reply. I have moved.

WRITTEN WHILST IN LONDON

A.C.I. T. Orton 849112
M.T. Section Room 3
R.A.F. Pucklechurch
Bristol

Postmark 8th October 1940

Darling

I am writing this from London. I arrived Sunday evening so I hope your letter will be waiting for me when I get back to Bristol either tomorrow or the next day. Are still looking forward to Christmas like me darling? I enclose ten bob hoping it reaches you alright. I have also got an RAF brooch for you but I am sorry it is not like the one you had before, it is just the wings and crest. I will bring it next time I come over, about time too (says you!). Remember me to your Ma and Pa.

From your Ever Loving Tom xxxx

RAF The Warren – CARDINGTON

849112 A.C.I. T Orton
Hut 546. 4 Sqdn. 3 Wing
R.A.F. The Warren, Cardington
Beds

Postmark 25th October 1940

My Darling

At last I am able to give you an address so that I can hear from you. I hope you are keeping well and not having too many sleepless nights. I arrived by train last night but could not write as it was after lights out. I might get a long weekend off soon so I will put my skates on to come and see you, although I am here for 5 weeks working from 7.30 a.m. to 8 p.m. so it could be a bit of a bind. But still I will keep smiling as Christmas will soon be here. Write soon as I am anxious to hear from you.

From Your Loving Husband (to be) Tom xxxxx

849112 A.C.I. T Orton
Hut 546. 4 Sqdn.
R.A.F. The Warren,
Cardington, Beds

Postmark 29th October 1940

My Darling

I received your letter today. Of course it is alright with me about the bed, the money is for anything you think we may need. I am so sorry to hear about the A.R.s (air raids), you have certainly been going through the mill. I can have a weekend off but not sure whether it will be next weekend or the one after that, anyway I will let you know. We are allowed from 4.30 p.m. Sat to 12 p.m. Sunday - I think they are a bit skinny with it. We don't get a minute to ourselves as it is, and when we do, we are supposed to be swotting, but that won't stop me from coming over to see you my love.

From Your Loving Husband (to be) Tom xxxxxx

849112 A.C.I. T Orton
M.T.M. Section. 4 Sqdn.
Hut 546. The Warren
Cardington
Beds

Postmark 2nd November 1940

Darling

We should still be on parade but we have been dismissed due to pouring rain. I have completed my first phase of the course, which leaves another 3 phases and 1week for the exam. The group before us finished their exam on Friday and they are to complete their final week in no other place than Birmingham and I believe we shall do the same in our 6th week. They will be based at a firm to do with motors, somewhere in Nechells of all places. We have to be here for Church Parade this Sunday. I am sorry I could not let you know earlier.

Christmas isn't so far off now so you will soon be all mine and when this "B" War is over and done with we will be together always. I enclose half a bar for you and will send more if I pass this examl.

This place is a proper bind, there is more red tape here than there is in a Draper's shop! Every time the sirens go, we have to get up in the middle of the night and take cover but it is only right, as we sleep right by the Airship Hangars and they are a good target. They have not been hit yet but they have been uncomfortably close! God Bless you, I will think of you when I am at Church in the morning.

From Your Loving Husband (to be) Tom xxxx

849112 A.C.I. T Orton
Hut 546
No. 4 Sqdn.
The Warren
Cardington, Beds

Postmark 6th November 1940

Darling

I received your letter and I am so glad to hear you are alright as hearing all those planes going over towards Birmingham, I thought you would be in for a rough time. I was a little more relieved when I heard it was Coventry, although I suppose he came over your way.

I think I may be coming over there for a week, as they are sending another party tomorrow who have finished their exam. I thought it would be 3 weeks but it is only 2 weeks. I am going to drop a line to Ma to see if she has heard from Len. Goodbye and God Bless.

From Your Ever Loving Tom xxxxx

849112 A.C.I. T Orton
Hut 546. No. 4 Sqdn.
R.A.F. The Warren, Cardington
Beds

Postmark 11th November 1940

Darling

I received your letter today and was sorry to hear that you had to wait so long for my letter. I wrote straight back but I have to post them in the camp and think they must be delayed sometimes. Anyway, Darling you are the first one I write to, so you will always get a letter even if it is a bit late.

It is very good of your mother to pay half towards the organ. Give her my thanks.

I am so sorry to hear you have been having another rough time, I get so worried when I hear it has been hard hit in the Midlands. But keep your chin up my darling, it will not last much longer. As for me going abroad, I have not heard anything about going and I certainly shall not push myself, ***especially as we shall soon be married****. I do not think there is anything to worry about. Anyway the last thing I would want to do would be to go abroad, as you say it is bad enough just being this distance away from each other! There is some talk about the Birmingham week being cancelled but I shall have the weekend with you before I go back. I will put in for 7 or 10 days when I return.*

It touched me when you said you had been crying and I could certainly have drained a few at the time but we have got to be brave and keep our chins up, just as your Ma and Pa said.

I shall be glad to get away from here, as I have not had my clothes off for a week! It sure is tough for that friend of yours, but I think her boy will get his leave eventually.

I have written to Ma but not had a letter back yet. I hope to get one tomorrow, so I will let you know what brother Len says. I will bring a couple of pals when we get married, if I can, as all my old pals have been called up. Goodbye for a bit and God Bless you and keep you.

From your Ever Loving Husband (to be) Tom xxxxx

Give my love to your Ma and Pa

HEADLINE NEWS in Birmingham ... 19th November 1940 - *On the night of Tuesday, 19th November 1940 – "Devastating air-raid on BSA, Small Arms Factory, Armoury Road, Small Heath, Birmingham. The BSA factory was one of the main targets for the German Luftwaffe. A low flying aircraft dropped 2 bombs which destroyed the southern end of the BSA building killing 53 workers.*

RAF WINTERBOURNE HOUSE – Winterbourne, Nr. Bristol

849112 A.C.I. T Orton R.A.F.
935 Sqdn. Winterbourne House
Winterbourne, Near Bristol

Postmark 5th December 1940

My Darling

I have put in for 48 from Fri to Sunday night so will see you some time Fri night. They gave us a proper doing last night again but the place I am at now is a little way out so it isn't too bad. Well sweetheart, it will be so good to be with you again at the weekend.

All my love Tom xxxxx

849112 A.C.I. T Orton
R.A.F. Winterbourne House
Winterbourne, Nr Bristol

Postmark 17th December 1940

My Dear Joan

Was I glad to get your letter this morning! I have been so worried not hearing from you that I was going to phone the Dunlop this morning, or send a telegram, anyway I do not care now I have heard from you. Yes! my leave is in the bag but as you say the days do seem to be going slow. I am the first one to get a Christmas card in our room, it is very nice of you. So sorry to hear you have been having such a rough time but keep your chin up my precious, things will come out alright in the finish. I expect the raids are keeping your Pa very busy and he is not getting much time to himself. I had a letter from Gran yesterday saying that she is looking forward to our big day. Goodbye for a bit and God Bless.

From Your Ever Loving Husband (to be) Tom xxxx

849112 A.C.I. T Orton
R.A.F. Winterbourne House
Winterbourne
Nr Bristol

Postmark December 1940

My Darling Joan

On my way here I put the banns in, so that's another bit done towards our big day.

I did so much enjoy the weekend, every minute of it, and I am so looking forward to Jan 4th, it sure will be the biggest and best day of our lives. When this War is over and everything is normal, we will be the happiest couple and I am sure we shall enjoy our married life. I do hope you are having a quiet night and that you get plenty of rest. I do so worry about you being so close to the city and wish you could get a bit further away.

I will bring the certificate for the banns with me on the Thursday I come home to hand to the Vicar, save posting it. I must get brother Len's address by writing to Ma now.

From your Loving Husband (to be) Tom xxxxx

849112 A.C.I. T Orton
R.A.F. Winterbourne House
Winterbourne, Nr Bristol

Postmark December 1940

My Darling Joan

I received your letter this morning also the Christmas card from your Ma and Pa. I have them all on the wall over my bed.

I do hope you have not had many sleepless nights. I'm feeling in the pink, counting the days, but don't they go slow? I didn't go to the Church to hear the banns being read out as they say you should not, although I would have liked to have heard our names. I was represented by some of our lads who go every Sunday. They said it was a pleasure hearing them read out.

Yes darling, it is best to keep the parcel for me. Gran's address is Mrs B Ellis, 33 Victoria Road, Sutton Coldfield. I should send it, I'm sure she won't mind it being a bit late.

I have had the day off today to go into Bristol for your ring and ain't it a beauty the best for you my sweet always. It is identical to your mother's. Roll on the 4th Jan. and I will be with you once again darling for a whole week. I'd better rise and shine now and get myself spick and span for room inspection. Goodbye for a little bit my loved one and God Bless you.

From your Ever Loving Tom xxxxxx

p.s. See you in ten days – 240 hours, - 14400 mins.

849112 A.C.I. T Orton
R.A.F. Winterbourne House
Winterbourne, Nr Bristol

Postmark December 1940

Dear Joan

I wrote to you as soon as I got back last week but have not heard from you. I have been wondering what has happened, whether you have had to leave as I know you had it pretty bad up there during the week. I do hope you are all right and that you go over to Sutton to stay. I have waited patiently every day but still no letter comes. Please write straight back if you get this letter. My 7 days are up on orders so my leave is o.k. and the banns were read out here last Sun:

From your Ever Loving Tom xxxxx

CHRISTMAS 1940

849112 A.C.I. T Orton
R.A.F. Winterbourne House
Winterbourne, Nr Bristol

Postmark December 1940

My Darling

I received your most welcome letter this morning. I have been up to the Rectory to get the certificate so everything is cleared up now at this end. I am glad to hear that you have had a bit of peace for 2 or 3 nights, things have been very quiet here too. We had a bit of a do on Christmas day with a barrel of beer and plenty of Goose and mince pies but I shall enjoy next week much better when I am with you. I will come straight to your house off the train on Thursday but can't say exactly what time, may be around tea time. Goodbye for 3 days – 72 hours – 4320 minutes, it won't be long now. Cheerio.

From your Ever Loving Tom xxxxx

849112 A.C.I. T Orton
R.A.F. Winterbourne House
Winterbourne, Nr Bristol

Postmark December 1940

My Darling Joan

I am so happy to hear you are looking forward to our big day, the same as I am. It is a proper bind having to wait for our letters as they are delayed so much in the post. I am glad you were able to fix up about the flowers and as you say, it was quite reasonable. I sure got a bit panicky when I did not get a letter from you for over a week and was so relieved when I did hear from you. You do not know how much I look forward to reading your letters and I keep on getting your photo out of my wallet to look at you.

From your Ever Loving Tom xxx

p.s. The same from me to your Ma and Pa. Me, forget the ring?!

Letter from Tom's brother Fred (posted in Gibralta)

C'pl F Orton
28 Company, R.A.M.C.
Military Hospital
Gibraltar

9th January 1941

Dear Tom & Joan

Hey you two!! come down to earth for a few minutes and remember Frederick – isolated on a windy piece of rock – a chap who has almost forgotten what wedding cake tastes like and civilisation. Now Tom, you drop that Nickers grin and help. Joan, parcel a tasty portion, not forgetting of course, what you promised me ages ago – a photograph. Well, putting aside all frivolity – congratulations to you both and the very best of luck. I thought up to a short while ago that yours truly would be the first one of the family to meet his doom but I have been "pipped at the post" and apparently when I leave this place I shall be fully qualified to wear a little pillbox cap and shall be commonly known as 'Pensioner Orton'.

Sorry Joan, I have forgotten to introduce myself – Frederick the Prodigal – my good points I have written under the stamp on the envelope, when you have a week to spare Tom will relate all the bad ones. We have never met so far but if my luck holds out I hope to see you at your silver wedding. I have hopes at the back of my mind of course that leave may come my way so that Ethel and I may get married.

Well Tom, how are they treating you? It is ages now since I heard from you and I might add that very little has happened here since I last wrote to you. Ray and I had a fairly decent time together last time he was here but unfortunately I could not get off for very long as we were fairly busy here. He does not like Gib but I comforted him by saying "neither does anyone else". Since he left which is now about eight or nine weeks ago, ***I have gone through two stages of promotion – Lance Corporal and now Corporal.*** *The "ackers" are gradually increasing.*

Well I must close for now but do not forget to drop me a line – both of you – I suggest air mail as the safest and quickest means.

Cheerio and all the best
Fred

TOM & JOAN married 4 January 1941 in Birmingham

From left to right ... Ena Allen (Joan's cousin), Len Orton (Tom's brother), Tom & Joan, Thomas Frederick Mills (Joan's father), Marjorie Mills (Joan's sister)

Tom's letters to Joan: (Married 9 days)

849112 A.C.I. T Orton
R.A.F. Winterbourne House
Winterbourne, Nr Bristol

Postmark 13th January 1941

My Dear Wife

I hope you got home alright last night. I arrived here about 11.30 pm luckily having got a lift from the town. Well Darling I think its proper tough having to come back to this dump after having such a marvellous leave, although I did get a bit of a reception from the lads when I came in last night. They all sat up in bed and cheered when I walked into the room and they wish us all the very best. I felt terrible when the train drew out and I know by the look on your face that you felt the same. But still my precious we will make up for it when this lot is over. When I woke up this a.m. and found that I was here, I felt so rotten, I did not have any breakfast.

I have been out on the motorbike this morning to a breakdown which gave me an appetite so I have just had a good dinner. Honestly darling last week was the best time of my life, I shall never forget it as long as I live. The lads say they are looking forward to meeting my wife, of course only on the photos. I went into the orderly room and gave them all the particulars, so it won't be long before you get the allowance - I shall see to that. I suppose this time tomorrow you will be at the Fort (Dunlop).

Tell your ma that I enjoyed the cobs very much on the train. Goodbye for a bit and God Bless you. We will soon be together again. Remember me to your Ma and Pa and thank them for the good time we had.

Your Ever Loving Husband Tom xxxx

849112 A.C.I. T Orton
R.A.F. Winterbourne House
Winterbourne, Nr Bristol

Postmark 13th January 1941

My Dear Joan

It was a fairly fast train last night arriving in Bristol about 7 pm. I caught a bus and got here about 7.45 pm. I do hope you got home safely via Nechells dear, it was strange waking up this morning and finding myself here sleeping alone. I had a letter from Fred on my return, which I have enclosed for you to read.

Well my precious the 48s are still going strong so I will be seeing you in another fortnight. I will send you the clocks tomorrow when the post office is open and I will mention that they would not change the money order at Bordesley Green P.O. I will send the other to Sladefield Road P.O.

From Your Ever Loving Husband Tom xxx

Tom's brother, Corporal Fred Orton, based in Military Hospital, Gibralta.

Letter to Tom from Brother Fred:

Corporal F Orton 7264089
No: 28 Company, R.A.M.C.
Military Hospital
Gibraltar

14th January 1941

Dear Mono (nickname for Tom by his brothers)

Thanks for your very interesting letter which reached me today. I'm sorry too Tom, that I could not be present at your wedding on the 4th but as you say, we will certainly all have a re-union some day and I hope that day will soon come. I did write rather a mad letter to you but it so happens that I was in rather a mood for frivolity so I decided to "let myself go".

A letter from brother Ray also arrived today, he is very well and all I know is that at present he is "East" which of course is vague. He has not heard from anyone since leaving here about 8 or 9 weeks ago but is rather reconciled by the fact that he is expecting to see me shortly. He has a damn fine pal on board – a fellow from "Brummagem". All I know is that he is called Pat, anyway, the 3 of us had a fairly decent night out before they had to leave.

My letters have dropped off lately as I have been hellishly busy but everything and everyone has eased off a little and I am finding time to answer all the letters received during the last couple of months. Mother sent me a slice off Xmas cake and Oh Boy!! Did I enjoy it.

Well Mono I'm afraid that is all I can muster for the time being but I am looking forward to a letter from you and the wife. I am a little late but – happy New Year to you both.

All the best Your Loving Brother Fred

Letters from Tom to Joan:

849112 A.C.I. T Orton
R.A.F. Winterbourne House
Winterbourne, Nr Bristol

UNDATED *Monday*

My Darling

I have just wired you a green one to help tide you over until your pay comes through and expect it will be waiting for you when you come in from work.

I have spoken to a chap who has his wife staying down here, they live out and draw ration money. He only pays 14/- a week for 2 rooms and I think it would be very nice if we could do the same, perhaps you will think about it and let me know. I could easily find a place as a Birmingham woman who keeps a shop here says she would help me. It is very nice here and they do not know what a siren is. We will have to see about it quickly as people are beginning to evacuate from Bristol and there may not be any places left if we leave it too long. I am just going to write to Ma & your sister Brenda.

Your Ever Loving Husband Tom xxxxxxx

Remember me to Ma & Pa and give them my love.

849112 A.C.I. T Orton
R.A.F. Winterbourne House
Winterbourne, Nr Bristol
Wednesday

UNDATED

My Darling Joan

I shall be leaving here on Saturday morning for West Bromwich for the week's course I should have had when I left Cardington. I will call at your house when I get into Birmingham, it will be so good to see you again, I was cheered to death when the sergeant came and told me about it. When I get there, I will find out if I can sleep out as I can easily travel to and fro. God Bless you.

From your Ever Loving Husband Tom xxxx

849112 A.C.I. T Orton
R.A.F. Winterbourne House
Winterbourne, Nr
Bristol

Monday

My Dear Wife

I could not send your money today as there appears to be a problem with the pay sheet this week but I have an interview with the accounts officer tomorrow. I wrote to brothers Fred and Ray last night to say we will send them a photo when they are done.

I have found since my return that I am 3 brushes short. 2 blacking brushes and 1 clothes brush (Airman for the use of) so I think they may be in that lost case. If you or your mother are in town any time, could you give the Lost Property Office another visit as they may have found it since your mother last called. Goodbye for a bit my precious and God Bless you.

From Your Ever Loving Husband Tom xxxxxxxx

849112 A.C.I. T Orton
R.A.F. Winterbourne House
Winterbourne, Nr Bristol

Postmark Dated 31 January 1941

My Darling Wife

Thanks for your letter received this morning. I had another letter from brother Fred and I have enclosed same. He wants us to write to him, so if you have time will you drop him a line? I have not heard from brother Len but I will write and ask Ma for his new address. I also wrote to brother Ray about Christmas time and not had a reply, perhaps there is a letter on the way.

I am afraid this is rather a short letter but it is nearly lights out. You will have to tell Fred he has had it about the wedding cake! God Bless you.

Your Ever Loving Husband Tom xxxx

849112 A.C.I. T Orton
R.A.F. Winterbourne House
Winterbourne, Nr Bristol

Friday night

My Dear Joan

Here I am again breaking the record writing every day. The lads have just asked me what I keep finding to write about.

I did manage to get my gas bag back ok and leave it to me about getting home, I should get home to see you if I have to do shank's pony.

I will have a mow round to see if I can get your bootees as soon as I can darling and I will post the marriage lines to you with your pay book. Sorry I cannot let you know definitely which day I shall be over yet but I think I can manage to get the weekend. I suppose this time tomorrow you and your ma & pa will be in Sutton, I wish I could be with you. Remember me to them and tell your ma my mouth was watering when you mentioned the soup she was dishing up. I'll bet it went down a treat.

From Your Ever Loving Husband xxxxxx

849112 A.C.I. T Orton
R.A.F. Winterbourne House
Winterbourne, Nr Bristol

Monday night

My Dear Wife

I am on guard 2 on & 4 off parading by the main gate with rifle & fixed bayonet, what a bind! I am on duty all night until 8 in the morning, then I get the day off tomorrow. How are you my duck? I expect you may be sitting in the kitchen knitting with the wireless on. The sergeant told me today that I may have to go up to Pucklechurch on Wednesday as there is so much work to be done. I will let you know so that you can write direct to me there. One thing is for sure, it will make the next 3 weeks go quicker having a change of quarters.

Your Ever Loving Husband Tom xx

849112 A.C.I. T Orton
R.A.F. Winterbourne House
Winterbourne, Nr Bristol

UNDATED

My Darling Wife

I have just arrived back at "hush hush" house and it is about 7 o'clock. I am pleased to say it was a fast train and I slept all the way dreaming of you.

I hope you managed to get a cage for Peter the budgerigar and that you arrived home safe. Tell your Ma I enjoyed the cakes and I am just about to sample some of the lemon curd she gave me. Remember me to them both and give them my love. God Bless you and keep you.

Your Ever Loving Husband Tom xx

RAF PUCKLECHURCH, Bristol

849112. A.C.I. T. Orton
Hut 3. MTM. RAF
Pucklechurch, Bristol

Wednesday

My Darling Wife

Just to let you know my new address. I arrived this afternoon and should be here for a week or more. I have not had a letter from you up till now but received your Valentine this morning. Thanks so much it is very nice. I am so sorry I was unable to send you a Valentine but I could not get one at Winterbourne being only a one-eyed little village. I hope you don't mind. Cheerio for a bit.

Your Loving Husband Tom xxx

849112. A.C.I. T. Orton
Room 15. M.T. R.A.F.
Pucklechurch, Bristol

Friday

My Darling Joan

I was so glad to hear that you were able to get a cage for the budgie. So he won't talk "eh", I expect it is being in a strange place, don't worry, he will talk when he has been with you a while. I was pleased to hear the announcement of our wedding was in the old Gazette and you will get the photos next week, it is about time! I went to the pictures last night at the N.A.A.F.I. on the camp, Errol Flyn was in "The Perfect Specimen" which I saw a few years ago in Colwyn Bay. I hope you have a good time at Sutton.

I have been moved into another hut so please put the number ***(15)****. There is a dance on at the N.A.A.F.I. tonight but I have told the lads I will be busy writing to my dear wife and do some button sewing. God Bless you and roll on the next 48.*

Your Loving Husband Tom xxxx

849112. A.C.I. T. Orton
M.T.R.S. Room 15. R.A.F.
Pucklechurch, Bristol

Tuesday

My Darling Wife

I received the photos this morning, they are lovely and are now on the door of my locker.

What do you think of this for another surprise ... the old case turned up this morning at the guardroom and everything is intact. I do not know who has been so good as to send it.

I have not set foot outside of this camp since I arrived last Wed: week, believe it or not. I think I shall come up by road on Friday if I can get away early enough. Will you ask your Ma if she can get the cement etc for the air-raid shelter as I could do it on Saturday.

I am off to the stores now to see if I can return all the new items that I had replaced in my kit and hopefully they will refund the 9 bob. Cheerio till Friday night. God Bless you.

Tom xxxxxxx

849112. A.C.I. T. Orton
M.T.R.S. Room 15. R.A.F.
Pucklechurch, Bristol

Postmark Dated 21 February 1941

My Darling Wife

Thank you so much for the parcel and 2 letters received this morning. The contents came in very handy as I was just waiting for tomorrow (Friday) pay day. Will you thank Ma for the things she put in and tell her that I shall enjoy the sardines on toast for tonight's supper.

I did receive your letter addressed to Hut 3, I always look forward to receiving them. I worry when the chap comes round with the mail and there is no letter from my dear wife; my face drops a mile.

From Your Ever Loving Husband Tom xxx

Letters from Tom to Joan - RAF WEST KIRBY, Cheshire

849112. A.C.I. T. Orton
M.T.M. No 4 Wing No. P.D.C.
R.A.F. West Kirby
Cheshire

Postmark Dated 12 March 1941

My Darling Wife

I arrived here this morning, after spending the night on Liverpool station, as there was no means of getting here until the early hours of this morning. It is about 12 to 15 miles from Liverpool, Birmingham side. I sent a telegram from Bristol station and hope you got it ok.

I was worried about you getting home safely on Monday. It is such a bind having to be parted like this but I am hoping I may be able to get some more leave from here. I have not been told anything more as yet, all they seem to do here is fall in on Parade twice a day and fall out again after the flight sergeant has mumbled a few words of Bull: perhaps I shall be able to tell you more tomorrow.

I do not think there is anything else to say, especially about this dump anyway. Take care of yourself and God Bless you. There is one thing, it will be easier to get to you from here if only I can.

Your Ever Loving Husband Tom xxx

Will you put M.T.M. in big letters on the top corner of the envelope.

849112. A.C.I. T. Orton MTM
Hut D.3. No 4 Wing No 1 P.D.C.
R.A.F. West Kirby
Cheshire

Postmark Dated 14th March 1941

My Darling Wife

I am sorry to say I have not learnt anything further yet. I have enquired as to whether I can get some leave but they will not give me a definite answer - I will keep on to them. We are proper browned off here but they say it is not as bad as Wilmslow so I guess I have come to the better one of the two. I had the sardines for my supper last night and they were grand, they tasted a lot better than the butchers broth (soup) being dished out at the cookhouse! I do wish I could find out definitely what is happening but they simply will not tell us anything. I will keep writing to you my love and will do my best to get over to see you even if it is only for 48. Give my love to Ma & Pa.

Tom xxxxxx

p.s. How's Peter?

849112. A.C.I. T. Orton MTM
Hut D.11. No 4 Wing P.D.C.
R.A.F. West Kirby
Cheshire

Saturday

My Dear Wife

I have enclosed a little present for you, it is not much as I can't get anything round here right in the wilds as usual. I am still persevering for some leave and I do hope I shall succeed as I long to see you again before I go. No matter where I go, you will always be in my thoughts and dreams. Let us put our trust in God that I may soon be back with you as I will not be satisfied until that day comes and I am sure it will not be long coming. Goodbye for a bit and God Bless you, I pray for you every night.

Your Ever Loving Husband Tom xx

849112. A.C.I. T. Orton MTM
Hut D.11. No 4 Wing P.D.C.
R.A.F. West Kirby
Cheshire

Monday

My Dear Wife

I am afraid I have had it, as they say, there is no more leave!! Our kit goes on Wed: morning so I suppose it will be Wed: or Thurs when I go to the boat. I have been issued with tropical kit so it is somewhere in the East.

My address will be Number, Rank, Name, U.T.V.O. H.Q. R.A.F. c/o A.P.P. 520. I will write to you every day when I get to my destination. There are no clues in the address as to where it will be!

I have not received a letter from you up until now but a lot of mail has just come in so will go up as soon as it is sorted. I hope you are keeping well and that I may soon be back. We must certainly make the best of things as I certainly did not expect this to happen! Anyhow, I am looking forward to bringing you a parrot ahem!

They certainly got fed up of me asking for leave but they eventually told me this afternoon that it was out of the question!

Give my love to your Ma & Pa and please take care of yourself. Cheerio my loved one and God Bless you.

From Your Ever Loving Husband Tom xxxxxx

P.S. Don't lose the Address dear I.T.AL.Y

Telegrams from Tom to Joan: ... Leading up to the boarding of "SS Duchess of York" (Liverpool Docks)

Dated 6th March 1941

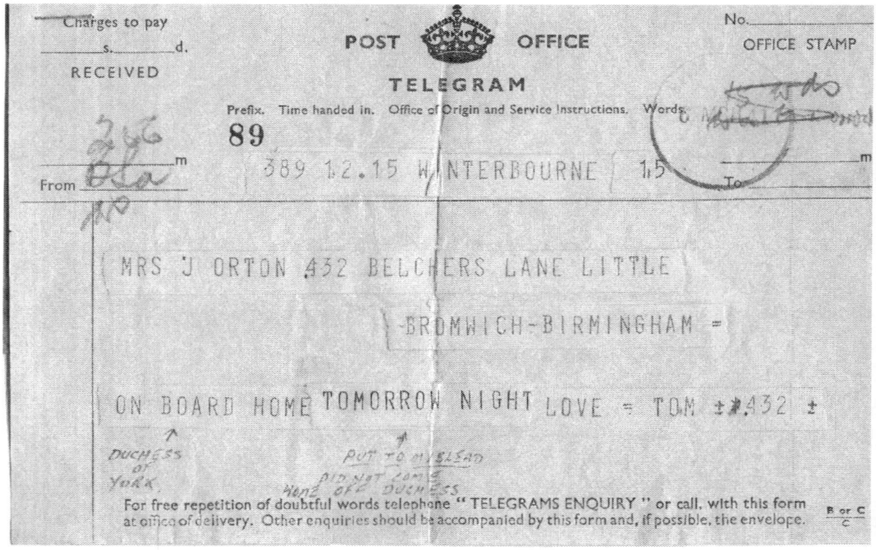

Charges to pay ____ s. ____ d.
RECEIVED

POST OFFICE
TELEGRAM

No. ____
OFFICE STAMP

Prefix. Time handed in. Office of Origin and Service Instructions. Words.
89
389 12.15 WINTERBOURNE 15

From ____ m
To ____ m

MRS J ORTON 432 BELCHERS LANE LITTLE
BROMWICH-BIRMINGHAM =

ON BOARD HOME TOMORROW NIGHT LOVE = TOM ±432 ±

DUCHESS OF YORK
PUT TO MISLEAD
DID NOT COME HOME OFF DUCHESS

For free repetition of doubtful words telephone "TELEGRAMS ENQUIRY" or call, with this form at office of delivery. Other enquiries should be accompanied by this form and, if possible, the envelope.

B or C

Pencilled note by Tom at foot of telegram : "Put to mislead. Did not come home off Duchess"

Dated 11th March 1941

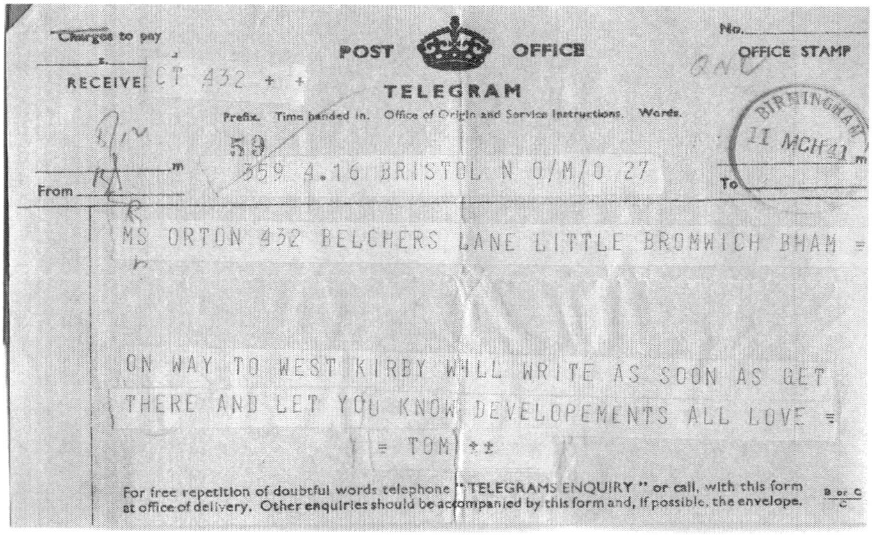

Charges to pay ____ s. ____ d.
RECEIVED CT 432 + +

POST OFFICE
TELEGRAM

No. ____
OFFICE STAMP
BIRMINGHAM 11 MCH 41

Prefix. Time handed in. Office of Origin and Service Instructions. Words.
59
359 4.16 BRISTOL N 0/M/0 27

From ____ m
To ____ m

MS ORTON 432 BELCHERS LANE LITTLE BROMWICH BHAM =

ON WAY TO WEST KIRBY WILL WRITE AS SOON AS GET
THERE AND LET YOU KNOW DEVELOPEMENTS ALL LOVE =
= TOM ++

For free repetition of doubtful words telephone "TELEGRAMS ENQUIRY" or call, with this form at office of delivery. Other enquiries should be accompanied by this form and, if possible, the envelope.

B or C

Letters from Tom to Joan - RAF WEST KIRBY, Cheshire

849112. A.C.I. T. Orton
M.T.M. No 4 Wing No. P.D.C.
R.A.F. West Kirby
Cheshire

Postmark Dated 12 March 1941

My Darling Wife

I arrived here this morning after spending the night on Liverpool station, as there was no means of getting here until the early hours of this morning. It is about 12 to 15 miles from Liverpool, Birmingham side. I sent a telegram from Bristol station and hope you got it ok as I was worried about you getting home safely on Monday. It is such a bind having to be parted like this but I am hoping to get some more leave from here. I have not been told anything more as yet, all they seem to do here is fall in on Parade twice a day and fall out again after the flight sergeant has mumbled a few words of Bull: perhaps I shall be able to tell you more tomorrow.

I do not think there is anything else to say, especially about this dump anyway. Take care of yourself and God Bless you. There is one thing, it will be easier to get to you from here if only I can.

Your <u>Ever</u> Loving Husband Tom xxx

Will you put M.T.M. in large letters on the top corner of the envelope.

849112. A.C.I. T. Orton MTM
Hut D.3. No 4 Wing No 1 P.D.C.
R.A.F. West Kirby
Cheshire

Postmark Dated 14th March 1941

My Darling Wife

I am sorry to say I have not learnt anything further yet. I have enquired as to whether I can get some leave but they will not give me a definite answer! We are proper browned off here but they say it is not as bad as Wilmslow so it appears I have come to the better one of the two. I had the sardines for my supper last night and they were grand, they tasted a lot better than the butcher's broth (soup) that they were dishing out at the cookhouse! I do wish I could find out definitely what is happening but they simply will not tell us anything. I will keep writing to you my love and will do my best to get over to see you even if it is only for 48. Give my love to Ma & Pa.

Tom xxxxxx

p.s. How's Peter?

849112. A.C.I. T. Orton MTM
Hut D.11. No 4 Wing P.D.C.
R.A.F. West Kirby
Cheshire

Saturday

My Dear Wife

I have enclosed a little present for you, it is not much as I can't get anything round here right in the wilds as usual. I am still persevering for some leave and I do hope I shall succeed as I long to see you again before I go. I love you and no matter where I go, you will always be in my thoughts and dreams. Let us put our trust in God that I may soon be back with you as I will not be satisfied until that day comes and I am sure it will not be long coming. Goodbye for a bit and God Bless you, I pray for you every night.

Your Ever Loving Husband Tom xx

849112. A.C.I. T. Orton MTM
Hut D.11. No 4 Wing P.D.C.
R.A.F. West Kirby
Cheshire

Monday

My Dear Wife

I am afraid I have had it - there is no more leave!! Our kit goes on Wed: morning so I suppose it will be Wed: or Thurs when I go to the boat. I have been issued with tropical kit so it is somewhere in the East.

My address will be Number, Rank, Name, U.T.V.O. H.Q. R.A.F. c/o A.P.P. 520. I will write to you every day when I get to my destination but there are no clues in the address as to where it will be!

I have not received a letter from you up until now but a lot of mail has just come in.

I hope you are keeping well and that I may soon be back. We must certainly make the best of things as I certainly did not expect this to happen! Anyhow, I am looking forward to bringing you a parrot ahem!

They certainly got fed up of me asking for leave but they eventually told me this afternoon that it was out of the question; they could have said that in the first place!

Give my love to your Ma & Pa and please take care of yourself. Cheerio my loved one and God Bless you.

From Your Ever Loving Husband Tom xxxxxx

P.S. Don't lose the Address dear I.T.AL.Y

NO ADDRESS!

849112. A.C.I. T. Orton
(NO ADDRESS)

Postmark Dated 20 March 1941

My Dear Wife

I shall be on the boat tomorrow, Thursday, at Liverpool, so my precious I am having to let you know by post as we have been confined to camp for 4 days and there was no chance of sending a wire. I expect the idea is that no one should spill the beans to anyone outside! If I get a chance to send a line or a letter from the boat or any port, I will let you know how things are but will not be able to put any address.

I feel so relieved that you have decided to go to Sutton in case of emergency. Ma says she would put you and your Ma & Pa up any time, although I wish you were there for good as it is a lot safer.

*Yes, you have met **Frank Barwell**, the day we were waiting for the bus at Sutton in the rain. I introduced you to him and his girl, he was in civvies.*

I am so sorry we are unable to see each other again before I go but I am confined to camp. Never mind my dear, I will soon be back with you and when I get out of this RAF I will not even join a Christmas club! We will never part again once we have settled down, and as you say, we pray it will not be long. Anyway darling, I am convinced that it will not be.

It sure hurts to be parted. The saying "absence makes the heart grow fonder", why I could not be any fonder of you than I am and I will always be the same my darling always. I must close now as I have a lot to do for the morning. We were up again all last night parading for the last instructions and bags of Bull so I will say Goodbye for a bit and God Bless you as I know he will for me. Give my regards to Ma & Pa.

Your Ever Loving Husband Tom xxxxxxx

Letter from Tom's Brother Fred to Joan:

No 28 Company
Military Hospital
Gibraltar

24th March 1941

Dear Joan.

Thanks so much for the letter, very glad indeed to hear from you, you see we are not exactly strangers now as I have received the group photograph from Mother and at present it is holding up a letter rack in the office, just in front of my head as I sit down. Yes, I must admit I miss those familiar faces and look forward to seeing them again for a short while.

You two certainly look happy and I am glad you are both settling down, I suppose you will sure miss brother Tom (Mono) whilst he is away but I do not think he will be away very long, according to the present pace of the War at any rate.

By the way Frederick is having his photograph taken next week so one will eventually be sent to Mr & Mrs T.W.H. that is of course providing I do not have to pay the studio too much for the inevitable cracked camera.

Well thanks again for the letter and I shall certainly look forward to another from you before long, so for the present.

Cheerio
Your loving Brother-in-Law Fred xxxxx

Chapter 3

ABOARD SS DUCHESS OF YORK - Destination Unknown ... Tom's Story Begins

A grey day in March 1941 .... we embark on to the Duchess of York *(later to be nicknamed the "Dipping Duchess")* at Liverpool docks. The ship must have been converted into a troopship some time ago looking at her appearance! It's packed with troops, mainly Army personnel, Navy and Marines.

(I later learn a little more about the **"SS Duchess of York"**. She was a 20,021 ton ocean liner launched in September 1928 and re-commissioned by the British Admiralty as a troop ship in 1940. The original name was intended to be **"SS Duchess of Cornwall"**. The ship unfortunately did not survive the War. She was crippled by a German air attack on 11 July 1943 and sunk the next day by the Royal Navy.)

I am one of approximately 400 RAF personnel. This is only my second voyage by sea; the first being only from Dover to Ostend, an experience I will never forget as I am not a very good sailor! We are not sure of our destination; a clue perhaps is in the tropical kit issued to us. All aboard, gangway up, we leave our native land with the thoughts and memories of the severe bombing by the German Air Force which had recently taken place in Coventry, Birmingham and Bristol. Bristol was my last tour of duty, which has left me with very bitter thoughts, as their targets were not only the aircraft works but also the small compact City of Bristol itself which was well away from the aircraft industrial area.

On leaving the Mersey and sailing north, it seems the convoy doubles in the number of troopships as we rendezvous with many others from the Clyde. It is not long before I begin to feel queasy, especially down on the mess deck (which is to be our home for a longer period of time than anticipated). I find it not so bad on the top deck so I've brought most of my things, including my personal kit, and decide to sleep in the saloon aft of the ship.

The sea is pretty rough and I have been seasick for the first hours of the fourth and fifth days, eating nothing and being excused daily routine parades. I am, of course, being kept well informed and up-to-date by my comrades; noting particularly the large number of other troopships from the Clyde. The convoy I think must be one of the largest to leave Britain up until this time. I am sure there must be about 40 vessels, including the Naval vessel escort.

(I have since managed to find out the names of a number of the other ships: ***"Duchess of Athol", "Empress of Canada", "Strathedan", "Viceroy of India", "Orion", "Orcades", "Oceanic", "Stirling Castle", "Athlone Castle", "Majestic", "Andes", "Voltaire", "Johan van Oldenbarnavelt", "Orantes", "Louise Pasteur" and of course the "Duchess of York")***

Still aboard the Duchess of York, I am desperate to keep in touch with my wife Joan as I am so worried about her living and working in a dangerous part of the City of Birmingham in the Blitz. I am pleased we are allowed to write to our loved ones but **all letters must be censored**.

(According to records, approximately 55,500 British military personnel were sent out to the Far East in 1941/42 and captured by the Japanese.)

SS Duchess of York

Letters from Tom to Joan - ABOARD SS DUCHESS OF YORK

(Aboard Ship)
849112 A.C.I. T Orton
U.T.V.O. H.Q. R.A.F.
c/o A.P.O. 520

1st April 1941

My Dear Wife

I am writing this aboard ship about half way to my destination. I am sorry I cannot put where it is until we arrive. I shall post this letter at the first port we call at, so darling, I do hope you will get it pretty quick. I hope you are keeping well and hope to be back with you pretty soon. I may get a letter from you when I get to my station.

How is Peter the budgie getting on? I suppose Bill (black cocker spaniel) is beginning to get used to him by now and that when I come home, he will be able to talk pretty well.

I cannot tell you much as our letters are censored but it is only right at a time like this, otherwise I could write a couple of dozen pages. We should reach the first calling place in a couple of days. The first couple or three days at sea were a bit of a bind but I am quite a good sailor now. I felt so queasy that I did not eat for 3 days after we left, although there was plenty of the best of everything. This time last week I began to pick up and now I am fighting fit so the voyage is doing me the world of good but there is only one thing missing darling, that is you. We shall be changing into tropical clothes any time now, so you can tell what the weather is like ... phew! All I do all day is sit on deck basking in the sunshine and we do our p.t. first thing in the morning when it is nice and cool. There is no doubt about it, it is a lovely trip and I think we should have a trip like this for our second honeymoon. What did you say? When was the first?

I cannot write anything else for a while but you can expect a nice long letter in a couple of weeks. Cheerio for a bit my dear and God Bless you.

From Your Ever Loving Husband Tom - With tons of kisses

849112 A.C.I. T Orton
U.T.V.O. H.Q. R.A.F.
c/o A.P.O. 520

4th April 1941

My Darling Wife

I do hope you are managing to keep out of harm's way during the Blitz. I heard news that Brum has been hit hard again and I hope with all my heart that you have been staying in Sutton.

I hope you got my letter posted at the last port. I am posting this at the next port so I am only about half the distance that I have got to go, worst luck. We crossed the equator the other day and had to go through the usual ceremony of being shaved and having a good ducking. The weather is still very hot and we cannot leave our tops off for a second or we should be down with sun stroke.

I do not think I shall be away for a very long time my precious, I will soon be back with you, never to leave you again. This letter will be posted in 2 – 3 days and I do hope you have written to the address I gave you, then I shall have a letter waiting for me when I get there, wherever it is! I hope your Ma and Pa are keeping well, tell them not to forget the old saying "chin up and head down" and tell them I wish them all the very, very best. I do so hope to be with you all again very soon.

At the last port the natives came all round the boat selling things and I have bought some nice gifts for you. Guess what I could have bought? A monkey! If I had been on my way back, I would have bought one, only a wee one of course! I will close now as I cannot put much in my letters until I reach my destination. God Bless you and keep you my precious.

From Your Ever Loving Husband Tom - with tons of kisses

Tom's story continues ...

Our course takes us into the Atlantic Ocean, by-passing the Azores towards the West coast our first port of call. We dock here for a short time along with other ships, I think for taking on supplies. The main attraction here is the fascination of the "Boat Boys" and their antics in trying to negotiate the highest prices for their bananas, mangos, pineapples etc. It seems strange to see some of the boys wearing bowler hats, top hats, even dickie bows! Their boats are laden with fresh tropical fruit; such a treat for us as most of this type of fruit back home is only available in cans! The boys are most trusting; they just throw up their ropes with loaded baskets and ask us what we want to buy and shout the prices, a great opportunity to buy fresh tropical fruit, although the food on the "Duchess" is quite good.

Our ship leaves **Freetown** with the rest of the convoy, heading South. All personnel are enjoying the warmth of the tropical sunshine and of course a calmer sea. I do notice that the larger naval escort ships have now left us. This may be due to the fact that we are not out of range of German Luftwaffe, although the convoy of ships are still "zig-zagging" desperately trying to avoid lurking U boats.

There is plenty of entertainment on the deck of the Duchess including boxing, wrestling etc between the three branches of the HM Services. The main conversation is always speculation about where we are we bound for? We can only assume it is somewhere East as everyone has been issued with a tropical kit!

During the nights, I lie thinking about my life at home, my parents and family in Sutton Coldfield and of course my beautiful new wife Joan. As we only married in January, just two months prior to sailing, it was a terrible wrench leaving her. I can't help but worry about them all having to endure German air raids taking place nearly every night in the Birmingham area; their safety is constantly on my mind.

We reach **Cape Town** but only about half of the convoy make for the harbour; the rest carry on round to Durban. As soon as the ship has anchored, we are told that we are to be allowed shore leave but only in certain numbers. I suppose this is to be expected as the number of personnel aboard ship must run into many thousands.

I am attached to the "Mess Deck", and we have now been called to go ashore. We're all "spruced up" ready and anxious to get away from the "Duchess" as it has been roughly one month since we boarded her.

On reaching the shore we are briefed by the Military Police, advising us, in no uncertain terms, where and what parts are out of bounds to us. On leaving the dock gates we are amazed to see hundreds of "Europeans" in cars waiting to welcome us and offering to take us in either ones, pairs or threes, according to the size of the car, for a tour of sightseeing. They even welcome us into their homes with a promise that they will get us back to the docks in time tonight, as scheduled.

Letter from Tom to Joan - CAPETOWN

Capetown 17th April

Postmark Dated 22nd April 1941

My Darling Wife

I hope you have received the letters posted from the boat. At present I am in port and have just got on shore.

I hope with all my heart you are keeping well and that you are over at Sutton or somewhere out of the Blitz's, as it makes me wonder not being able to hear from you.

I shall be here for 2 or 3 days and then our journey will continue but I cannot tell you where yet as it may get me into hot water! I shall continue to write at every possible opportunity and do hope that you receive my letters in good time. I am in good health and feeling as fit as a fiddle but there is only one thing that I cannot get used to, that is being away from you and I am longing for the day you will be in my arms again.

Well my precious this is a short letter but I am sure you will understand, as this is against orders writing home in port. Goodbye, God Bless and keep you safe.

Fom Your Ever Loving Husband Tom - Tons of kisses

Remember me to Ma & Pa

My address will be the same and hope to hear from you as soon as I get to my destination.

Tom's story continues ...

I have palled up with a Manchester chap, **Nobby Clarke**, a member of the MTB section of the RAF. Our extremely kind and friendly hosts take us for a spin half way up **Table Mountain** where we stand and take in the amazingly spectacular view looking down on to the city and harbour ... a beautiful and breathtaking sight. Towards evening, Nobby and I are taken to their house where we have an interesting chat about things back home in England, our family and life in general and, of course, 'The War'. One thing is for sure, we can't talk about our destination as we have no idea of this at all, which I guess is to our advantage for security reasons. A delicious evening meal is served and I am unable to resist the temptation of mentioning the incredible difference between the 'rations' back in England and here. Naturally our hosts are very sorry to hear about this.

It's time for us to return to the "Duchess" and our hosts kindly drive us back to the docks. We bid our hosts of Cape Town a reluctant farewell and thank them sincerely for the kind and generous hospitality bestowed upon us. Boarding the "Duchess" in good time, we certainly don't want any supper and turn in for the night.

After our most enjoyable visit to Cape Town, the ships move out and join up with the rest of the convoy, sailing North up the **Indian Ocean**. During this part of the voyage, we have only experienced one German submarine scare which thankfully came to nothing as most of our Naval escorts have now left us.

Letter from Tom to Joan:

849112 A.C.I. T Orton
U.T.V.O. H.Q. R.A.F.
c/o A.P.O. 520

25th April 1941

My Darling Wife

I have not reached my destination as yet but I expect I shall be there by the time you get this letter. I miss you so much and do hope I shall be back very soon. I am so sorry I still cannot tell you my destination but I shall will write and let you know where I am as soon as I arrive.

This is a very long trip, much longer than I thought it would be but I will write at every opportunity so you should get a steady stream of letters. I am worried that I have not heard from you for such a long time but I know there will be a letter for me when I get to my station, so roll on this "B" boat, as I am so anxious to hear from you. It is 5 weeks yesterday since we set sail and it seems like 5 years being away from you dear.

How is Peter? Does he talk yet? I expect he will be talking quite well when I come home.

What I am longing to hear in the first letter I get from you is that you are staying in Sutton or somewhere safe. I know I said this in my last letter but it is always on my mind.

I am going to write to brother Fred in Gibraltar and expect he will still be writing to Ma and Ray also. I hope your Ma and Pa are alright, I wish them all the very best also your sisters. (Marjorie and Brenda).

I expect you are beginning to have some nice weather in dear old England by now. I hope it is not as hot as it is here, it sure is enough to cook anybody, although I am getting used to it now. There is one thing I shall never get used to and that is being away from my dear wife. So as soon as this lot is over, I shall be on the first boat back to be with you for always. God Bless & Keep you.

Your Ever Loving Husband Tom - with tons of kisses

Tom's story continues ...

On our approach towards the **North of the Indian Ocean** most of the convoy turn North West, leaving about four ships bound for, I guess, Bombay. The "Duchess" is one of them.

Dropping anchor in **Bombay (now Mumbai)** harbour, we are allowed shore-leave for one day. There is definitely something fascinating about Bombay, to me anyway. There are not so many Europeans, except for military personnel. Our stay is short but certainly appreciated; a welcome rest from the continual sailing and fairly monotonous routine of being aboard the "Duchess" for such a long period of time.

Our next Port of call is **Colombo, Ceylon (now Sri Lanka)**. On our arrival we are given an extremely moving reception by a coloured pipe band. I have always enjoyed the 'skirl' of the pipes and the sound of the drums and to my mind these are equal to any Scottish band – they have no doubt been taught by the Scots! Sadly, our stay in **Ceylon** is short and sweet and on saying our farewell we discover that our course is to be East. We are not entirely sure but there is a strong rumour that our next port could well be **Singapore**.

Chapter 4

OUR FINAL DESTINATION "SINGAPORE" The Beginning of my diary

14 May 1941 – Keppel harbour, Singapore – the "Duchess" sails into the harbour ... she touches in like a feather! At last, we have reached the end of our long voyage and orders are given to prepare for disembarkation. Each of our Ports of call have been very colourful compared with the greyness of the month of March back in "blighty" but Singapore has to be the most colourful of all.

We have been aboard the "Duchess" for two whole months.

Thursday, 15 May 1941 – I am posted to 151 MU (Maintenance Unit) and I am now on my way to **Seletar Aerodrome**, the largest on the island.

(Seletar Airfield - RAF station in Singapore, later became the target of carpet bombing by the Japanese "navy" bombers when they carried out the first air raid on Singapore. At the time of the Japanese invasion of Malaya and Singapore, Seletar housed the RAF's 205 Squadron along with ***151 Maintenance Unit****. The runway built in Seletar during the Japanese occupation continues to be used today.)*

On our arrival at the aerodrome, we are assembled into the "palatious" camp cinema and given a warm welcome by the Station Padre but we are also asked to take heed of a few words of advice about visiting the city during our off-duty periods. He tells us about it being a "gay city", with plenty of gay entertainment, but warns us of the danger of the vice girls, of which there are many nationalities. He also warns us against the perils of VD, the number of cases of which is becoming quite high amongst the service personnel!

We are shown to our billets, which to me look like blocks of flats with open-air verandahs. I'm delighted to learn that Nobby Clarke, my old pal from the "Duchess", myself and two others are to be billeted in a house in married quarters, which have been vacant for some time.

ALL LETTERS CONTINUE TO BE "CENSORED"

Letter from Tom to Joan – RAF SELETAR – Singapore

849112 A.C.I. T Orton
R.A.F. Station, Seletar
Singapore S.S.

15th May 1941

My Darling Wife

I have arrived at last and relieved that I am finally able to give my address. As far as I know I am to be stationed here but do hope I shall soon be back with you again. I am so longing to hear from you my precious. I can write to you as often as I like but the letters must not be too long. I will write regularly and hope you have received my other letters as I wrote as many as I could during transit.

This place is very nice, we have all kinds of sports, football, swimming, tennis and pictures, in fact everything you can think of all on the camp. I am living in the married quarters and some of the airmen that have been here since before the War have their wives and families with them, lucky devils. They are quite modern houses with gardens at the front and back, with lovely flowers and palm trees, darling they are simply marvellous. I only wish you were here. It rains pretty well every day, which makes everything look green, I mean the grass and trees, not me!! On the whole it is not bad weather as there is more sunshine than rain. The town itself is very nice as far as I could see whilst on the bus to the camp. As usual we are well away from it. It appeared to me like an American town such as you see on the pictures although the people are mainly natives and Chinese. According to the papers here things are beginning to look better, what with Jerry leaders coming to the old country among other things.

How are your Ma and Pa & sisters? Give them my regards. I suppose by now you are getting into the summer and nice weather and hopefully you will be having a holiday.

We get paid in dollars and cents, which takes some getting used to, I'll say. I have written to Ma and Pa, Gran and brothers Ray, Fred.

Goodbye for a bit and God Bless you and keep you. Looking forward to the days when I shall be with you again forever which I do not think will be long.

From Your Ever Loving Husband Tom - With tons of love And kisses

By the way, do not forget to Write to this address and scrap the old one.

Tom's story continues from notes in his diary:

Friday, 16th May 1941 – I've decided to make a few diary notes in a small book periodically (I manage to conceal this diary under the waterproof lining of my RAF cap, which is later to be nicknamed "the cheesecutter" by my comrades)

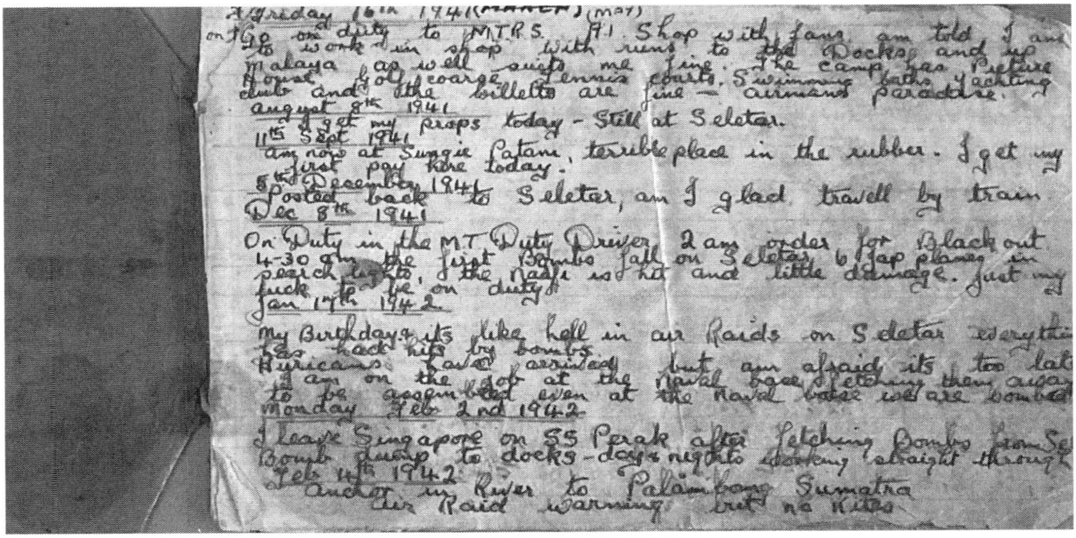
Friday 16th 1941 (May)
on I go on duty to M.T.R.S. A1 Shop with fans am told I am to work in shop with runs to the Docks and up Malaya as well suits me fine. The camp has Picture House, Golf course, Tennis courts, Swimming baths, Yachting club and the billets are fine – airmans paradise.
August 8th 1941
I get my props today – Still at Seletar.
11th Sept 1941
am now at Sungie Patani, terrible place in the rubber. I get my first pay here today.
5th December 1941
Posted back to Seletar, am I glad travell by train
Dec 8th 1941
On Duty in the M.T. Duty Driver 2 am order for Black out 4-30 am the first Bombs fall on Seletar 6 Jap planes in search lights, the Naafi is hit and little damage. Just my luck to be on duty.
Jan 17th 1942
My Birthday & its like hell in air Raids on Seletar
Hurricans have arrived but am afraid its too late
to be assembled even at the Naval base we are bombed
Monday Feb 2nd 1942
I leave Singapore on SS Perak after fetching Bombs from Seletar
docks – days & nights working straight through
Feb 14th 1942
Anchor in River to Palambang Sumatra
Air Raid warning but no Kites

Reporting for duty at **MTRS Seletar, Flight Lieutenant Burnett** is in charge of the section, also a Warrant Officer and **Corporal Nicholls**. In our section we have **AC Bert Melluish,** a Welsh chap, another AC and myself, together with a few members of the STC (Special Technical Corps) comprising Malays, Chinese and a couple of Indians. **Bert Melluish** and myself soon become pals. Part of our duties and responsibilities as MTM's (Motor Transport Mechanics) is to ferry new motor vehicles, of all types, from the docks to Seletar where they are checked over both mechanically and otherwise. We then deliver them to the 'Command Reserve', which is a dispersal point right towards the top of **Bukit Timah Hill on the road to the Causeway.** I am told this is the highest natural peak in Singapore.

During our off-duty hours there are plenty of recreational activities, e.g. swimming, yachting, golf and many other pastimes, so there is really no need to go down to the city. We also have the opportunity to watch some good films at the Station Cinema. I have decided to take lessons in the Malay language *(little do I realise at this point in time how these lessons will be to my advantage in the days which lie ahead of me).*

We are allowed to send short telegrams to our loved ones back home.

Cable from Tom to Joan – Dated 25th May 1941

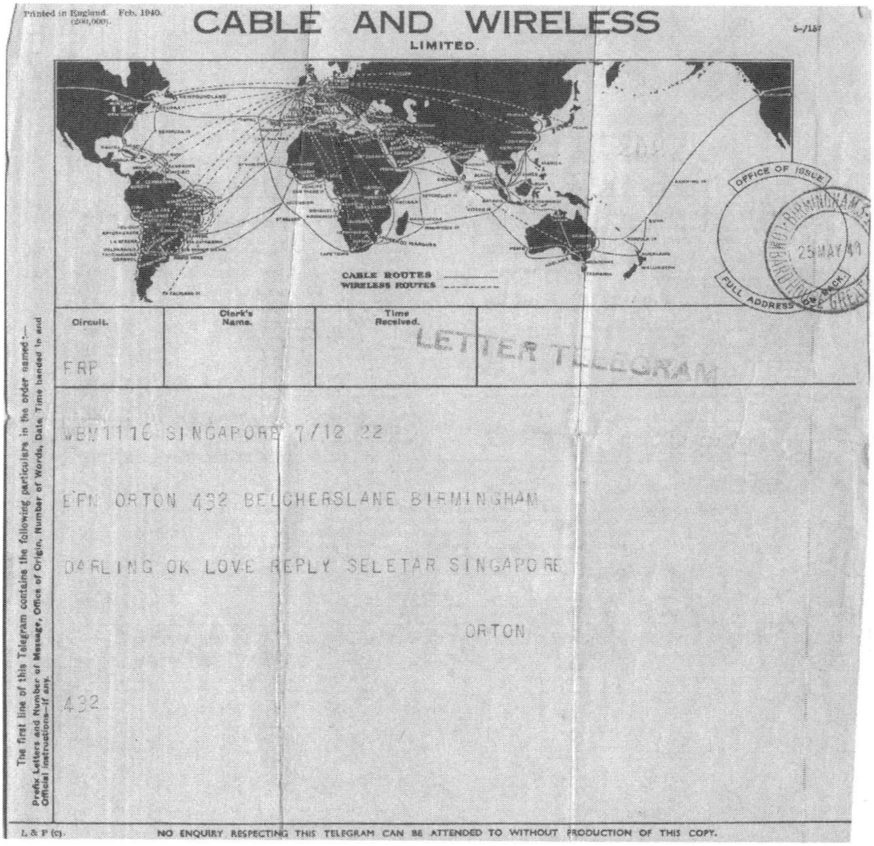

Printed in England. Feb. 1940. (200,000).

CABLE AND WIRELESS
LIMITED.

CABLE ROUTES
WIRELESS ROUTES

OFFICE OF ISSUE
BIRMINGHAM
25 MAY 41
FULL ADDRESS ON BACK

The first line of this Telegram contains the following particulars in the order named:— Prefix Letters and Number of Message, Office of Origin, Number of Words, Date, Time handed in and Official Instructions—if any.

Circuit.	Clerk's Name.	Time Received.
ERP		

LETTER TELEGRAM

WBM1116 SINGAPORE 7/12 22

EFM ORTON 432 BELCHERSLANE BIRMINGHAM

DARLING OK LOVE REPLY SELETAR SINGAPORE

ORTON

432

L & P (c).

NO ENQUIRY RESPECTING THIS TELEGRAM CAN BE ATTENDED TO WITHOUT PRODUCTION OF THIS COPY.

Letters from Tom to Joan:

849112 A.C.I. T Orton
A.D.F.E. R.A.F. Station, Seletar
Singapore S.S.

25th May 1941

My Darling Wife

I received your cable and the first letter yesterday and was so glad to hear from you. Although I received the cable a couple of days after I had sent one to you, I was very much relieved after hearing the news about the Blitz in Birmingham again. You say in your letter that it was a shock for you to hear that we may not see each other for months, perhaps years, and that you hope I would think of you sometimes. Let me tell you my precious, you are never out of my mind, no matter what I am doing, or where I am and I am trusting I shall not be away from you for too long. I believe the married airmen come home from here before the single blokes so that I am thankful for.

I have not heard from anyone at home yet, yours is the only letter so far. Anyway, I have written to them all and given them the address. I do hope you are keeping well. Remember me to your Ma, Pa and everyone at home. I will send you some photos at the first opportunity. I often look at those you gave me, wishing, always wishing, that I was with you again but never mind Darling, we must keep our peckers up, as it will all be made up to us and we shall soon be together again.

I go to the pictures or swimming pool in the camp quite often and the time goes pretty quick, as the days are shorter here in this part of the world. Please do write often as there isn't anything I like better than to read your letters. Goodbye for a bit my precious and God Bless you and keep you.

From Your Ever Loving Husband Tom With tons of kisses.

Tom – Seletar 1941

849112 A.C.I. T Orton
R.A.F Seletar
Singapore S.S.

1st June 1941

My Darling Wife

I enclose a photo and hope at the same time that I may get a letter from you soon, as I have only received the one so far and I am longing to know how you are getting on. Do not look at my uniform on the photo, as it is new and they are generally a bit too big before they have been washed. I had some taken with a small camera the other day and will send them in my next letter. The lads just called me out to have some more snaps taken, including a few with the Malay Boys that do our cleaning, boots, buttons etc, so I will let you have bags of snaps in the near future.

The weather is very hot here, apparently it is the same all the year round as there are no seasons, such as we get in England, but when it rains it simply pours and that is the only time it cools off a bit. I do not go out much as there is bags of recreation on the camp, including the pictures showing a fresh picture every 2 days, so I am putting plenty of time in at the picture house.

I am hoping and wishing that I may soon be back with you, never to leave you again. Cheerio for a bit my loved one and keep the old chin up.

From Your Ever Loving Husband Tom xxx

849112 A.C.I. T Orton
R.A.F Seletar
Singapore S.S.

9th June 1941

My Darling Wife

I have been here a month now and am sorry to say Darling that up until now I have only received your one letter and cable, I do wish I could get some word from you pretty soon.

It has poured with rain pretty well all day today and talk about thunder and lightning, it sure beats any storm I've ever seen before. I have enclosed some more photos for you. We get pretty well of time on our hands, so we have plenty of time for taking snaps.

I went to Mohamadan's wedding yesterday, he is an Indian chap in the service and works in the same place as me so of course he invited us all. At the reception there were all nationalities, Malayans, Chinese, Indians ... quite a mixture. Our W.O. was also there. Everything was similar to a European Wedding reception but of course the Wedding ceremony itself was quite different. We all sat down to the table and drinks were served, real scotch whisky into the bargain with bags of ice. We also had Malayan beer. The only thing I did not like was the Chop Suey they served so I had bread and cheese sandwiches! This was the first time I have had anything intoxicating to drink, as they say it is not good for you in this climate.

The photos are taken at the back of our billet, as you can see, they are quite nice houses but Darling, I only wish you were here everything would be perfect then. It is such a big blow for us both with me being posted out here after being married for such a short time but I am sure it will not be for long. I went to the pictures on Saturday to see Anna Neagle in a picture called "Irene", it was quite a good film. I find that going to the pictures helps to forget one is so far away from home.

I was also going to send your letters by airmail but it says on orders that it is being suspended for a short time. They say the mail would not be any quicker as it only goes by air for some of the distance and then by sea for the rest. Will you write as often as you can, just to read your letters makes it easier as being away from you for so long is pretty tough, as I am sure it is for you darling. Roll on the day when we shall be together again for always. Cheerio for a bit and God Bless you.

From Your Ever Loving Husband Tom With tons of Xs

849112 A.C.I. T Orton
R.A.F Seletar
Singapore S.S.

13th June 1941

My Darling Wife

I received 2 letters from you today and I am so glad to hear from you. They were posted on April 23rd & 24th, that is nearly 2 months but I do not care how long it takes my precious as long as I hear from you.

I will send a cable next payday to let you know I have received 3 letters from you so far, so you will receive the news long before you get this letter, as it only takes 5 or 6 days for it to come through. I had a letter from Ma and 2 from Gran a couple of days ago and I was beginning to wonder whatever had become of your's. I am so relieved. I sent you some letters a couple of days ago with some photos I had taken. Darling, would you send me some of yourself with your next letter, I should like to have some recent ones of you.

You mentioned going over to Sutton at the weekend, I do hope you had a good time. I am sorry to hear you were caught in Erdington when the sirens went and I bet you felt a bit nervy. Never mind my precious it will soon be all over and as you say, keep the old chin up. How are your Ma and Pa? I will drop them a line when I have finished this one. The weather here is 'B' warm and I am sweating cobs. The most one can do is go to the pictures (on the camp) and we have a different film every two nights. It costs 25 cents, that's about seven pence in English money. I am hoping to get my props soon which should be through by now I am thinking.

I have not heard from Ray or Fred (Tom's brothers) *yet but I expect I shall be getting some word from them soon. I have written twice. I am glad you have got a cage for Peter, a blue one too. I am glad you liked the scarf I sent, it would have been blue but that is the only colour they had got at that time. I will send you some more photos as soon as I can and don't forget mine will you darling.*

If I am going to write to your Ma & Pa, I must close now before lights out. Cheerio for a bit and God Bless you. I shall soon be with you again.

From Your Ever Loving Husband Tom With tons of kisses.

Please excuse envelope as it is the only sort I can get.

Letter from Tom to Joan's Parents

849112 A.C.I. T Orton
R.A.F Seletar
Singapore S.S.

13th June 1941

Dear Ma & Pa

I have just written a letter to Joan, so I thought I would write you a few lines. I trust you are both keeping well and are having the benefit of the summer which I suppose, by the time you get this letter, will be at its best. The weather is very hot here and it is the same all the year round as there no seasons such as we get in good old England. I used to shiver some times in the cold weather but I should sure like to see a bit of snow right now! I will sure be glad to get back to Joan and settle down. It must have been such a shock for her, just being married and now being parted. It certainly was a shock to me but I am glad we got married and I know I have got the best wife in the world. I often think of the good times we had at 432 (Belchers Lane) – one gets plenty of time to think here! I have received 3 letters so far from Joan and I am sending a cable to her next week.

I have heard from everyone at home except my brothers Ray & Fred but I am hoping to get a couple of letters soon as I have written twice to them. Remember me to Marjorie and Brenda? (Joan's sisters). Roll on my return and here's wishing you both the very best.

From Your Ever Loving Son in Law Tom

Letter from Tom to Joan:

No. 5

849112 A.C.I. T Orton
R.A.F Seletar
Singapore S.S.

27th June 1941

My Darling Wife

I received 2 letters from you today dated 15th & 16th April. I am so glad to hear you are alright after your ordeal in the blitz on the Wednesday and that you went over to Sutton.

I am sorry I did not remember our 12 month anniversary of our first date. I am afraid I am not very good at remembering dates but my precious, I always think of the days when we shall be together again. I often think of the good times we had and miss you now all the time I am away from you.

I am glad to hear Sheila is getting on well and don't suppose I shall recognise her when I come home. I had a letter from brother Fred today, which he posted to Bristol and it followed me all the way here! He says he received a letter from you and Ma with a photo of our wedding group. Was he pleased with it? He sure was!

You say in your letter about the 10/- gift from the Elmsdale Club. It certainly is real good of them, I sure will write and thank them. I wrote to Alf Lewis *at the club last and wished to be remembered to everyone. I think you should put it in the bank as it would cost too much to send all the way here. Yes my dear you must have a grey coat if you want one but you know me I sure go for blue. Anyway, I don't mind what colour it is as long as it is not red!*

I had a letter from Gran the other day and it tickled me to death to read that she had taught the bird to say "Bugger Hitler"; she is a comic! Remember me to everyone and sure I am keeping my chin up like you honey. Goodbye for a bit and God Bless and keep you.

Your Ever Loving Husband Tom With tons of kisses & love

I have had 5 letters from you since arriving

p.s. I am numbering letters from now on so that you can tell if there are any lost xxxx

Cable from Tom to Joan dated 27th June 1941 – Malaya

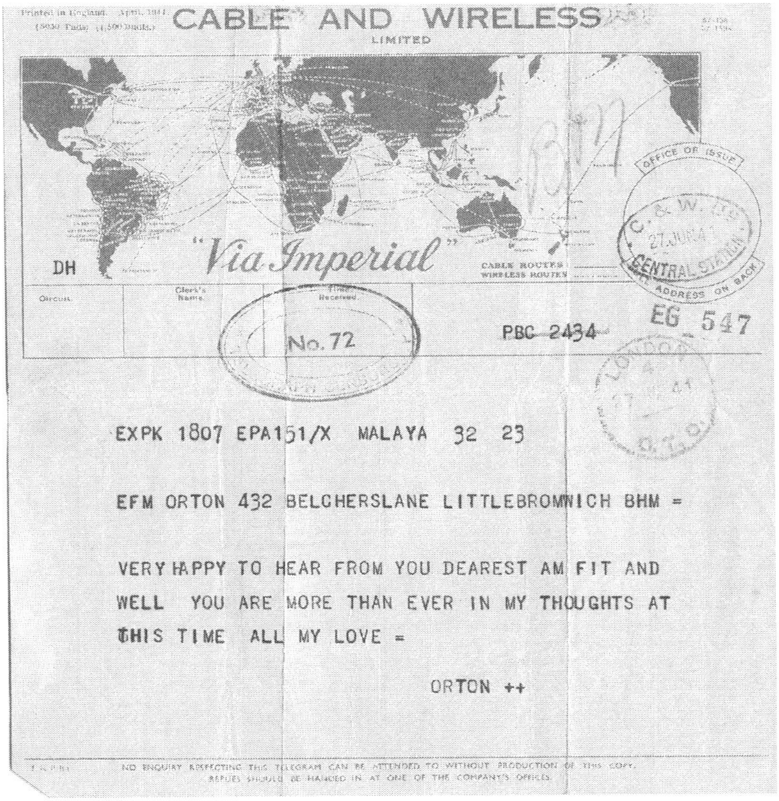
Printed in England. April 1941

CABLE AND WIRELESS LIMITED

"Via Imperial"

CABLE ROUTES
WIRELESS ROUTES

DH

OFFICE OF ISSUE
C. & W. Ltd
27 JUN 41
CENTRAL STATION
ADDRESS ON BACK

Circuit.	Clerk's Name.	Time Received.
		No. 72

PBC 2434

EG 547

LONDON
27 JU 41

EXPK 1807 EPA151/X MALAYA 32 23

EFM ORTON 432 BELCHERSLANE LITTLEBROMWICH BHM =

VERY HAPPY TO HEAR FROM YOU DEAREST AM FIT AND
WELL YOU ARE MORE THAN EVER IN MY THOUGHTS AT
THIS TIME ALL MY LOVE =

ORTON ++

NO ENQUIRY RESPECTING THIS TELEGRAM CAN BE ATTENDED TO WITHOUT PRODUCTION OF THIS COPY.
REPLIES SHOULD BE HANDED IN AT ONE OF THE COMPANY'S OFFICES.

No. 6

849112 A.C.I. T Orton
R.A.F Seletar
Singapore S.S.

29th June 1941

My Darling Wife

I am feeling quite pleased at getting so many letters from you. I received your air mail letter only yesterday, so you see darling air mail does not get them through any quicker.

Fancy Gran telling you off about bucking yourself up but still it is only her way darling. Of course I shall come back to you my precious, you leave it to me! Anyway, my time is up in another 18 months or just over, so it is not long.

So you have met Ethel, brother Fred's future wife. I have never seen her myself, only a photo of her but Fred seems quite keen. I shall have to tell him off about putting kisses on the bottom of the letter when he writes to my wife. I feel quite jealous!!!

I have written and thanked the Elmsdale Club for the 15/-, it is very decent of them. By the way Darling, you say you are having the ring done for me, have you got the size alright?

I still regularly go to the pictures and play snooker, so tell Alf Lewis at the Club that I am keeping my hand in at the game with plenty of practice! I am going to the pictures tonight to see Ronald Coleman in "The Light that failed" or something. I went to the Dental Officer yesterday, and have to go again Monday week, Your Birthday. I am sorry I can't send you a birthday present as there is so much duty to pay on things from here but there sure are some lovely things I could send if it was not so far. Anyway, I will send you a cable on Monday, in good time for the 7th.

I have seen the Officer of our section to discuss my application for an interview about my props. He said if they do not come through within the next month, he would do something about it as it is high time I had them. A number of chaps sailed for home recently after finishing their time out here. That will be the time Darling when I come home to you. One thing to be thankful for, the married airmen get the privilege of coming home first. I think it is 12 months sooner.

Remember me to your Ma & Pa and everyone at home. God Bless my precious and keep you.

From Your Ever Loving Husband With tons of kisses Tom

p.s. By the way, there is a new way to send cables. If you ask at the Post Office they will give you a selection of sentences to pick from which are all numbered. What we can do here is send 3 numbers representing any 3 sentences we choose, they are then coded when they reach the other end and it only costs a dollar from here.

No. 7

849112 A.C.I. T Orton
R.A.F Seletar
Singapore S.S.

2nd July 1941

My Darling Wife

I am duty fitter tonight on standby, so I have got plenty of time to write you a nice long letter, that is, if I am not called out. Well dearest how are you? Pretty browned off I suppose, I know I am being so far away from you. It is pretty tough but I try to make the best of it and I know I can count on you. I always try to think of the day we shall be together again, what a day Darling and I am quite confident it will not be all that long, never to leave you again.

I went to the pictures last night to see "Till we meet again" with Merle Oberon and George Brent and it was real good.

I sent your cable off yesterday which you should receive in time for your birthday on Monday. It must be about dinner time now in England, I have just had my tea, (dinner we call it here) and it is dark, it always gets dark around 7 p.m. all the year round. I suppose it is light now until about 10.30 in the home country.

I have been here exactly 7 weeks today and I don't think it seems like 7 months since we got married, does it to you darling? By the time you get this letter it will be about 9 to 10 months. I expect you will soon receive the letters that I sent as soon as I arrived here as it takes a couple of months for them to get through. I do write pretty often, so then I know that you will get at least one if not more by every boat that comes in.

In another month I shall be due 7 days leave, not quite so enjoyable as the leave I had in England, when I could come home to be with you darling. We have the opportunity to go up into Malaya and spend our leave at a big house run especially for the RAF. It is a bit like the Dunlop's place at Rhos on Sea. It only costs $20 and a dollar is worth 2/4d so it is quite reasonable and everything is found. There is plenty of sport, such as fishing, hunting and swimming. I think if I go, hunting will be more in my line but it will be a bit different to the old rabbiting days we used to have at Xmas time, as there is plenty of jungle. I can see myself bringing you back some tiger or leopard skins for rugs in our new home "ahem"!

How is our little Peter getting on? I expect he will be able to talk quite well when I see him, does he still do his exercises up and down the perch? How are your Ma & Pa and your sisters? Remember me to them all and wish them all the best. Cheerio for a bit and God Bless you my loved one.

From Your Ever Loving Husband Tom xxxxxxx

Letter from Tom to Joan:

No. 8

849112 A.C.I. T Orton
R.A.F Seletar
Singapore S.S.

6th July 1941

My Darling Wife

I have sent a parcel which you should receive about the same time as this letter. You may have to pay a small amount of duty on it as it is a pair of satin pyjamas but I hope it is not too much.

Are you hearing from me pretty regularly as I am writing often? I read in the paper today that some of the mail posted here in March has been lost but I have received letters dated April so I do not think any of your letters are missing.

I hope you are all well at home. I am in good nick but shall feel a lot better when I am on the way home to you my precious. I have not heard from brothers Ray or Fred as yet but hope to get a couple of letters soon. Will you let me know if you get the parcel ok. Cheerio for a bit and God Bless you.

Your Ever Loving Husband Tom xxxxxx

Cable from Tom to Joan Dated 8th July 1941

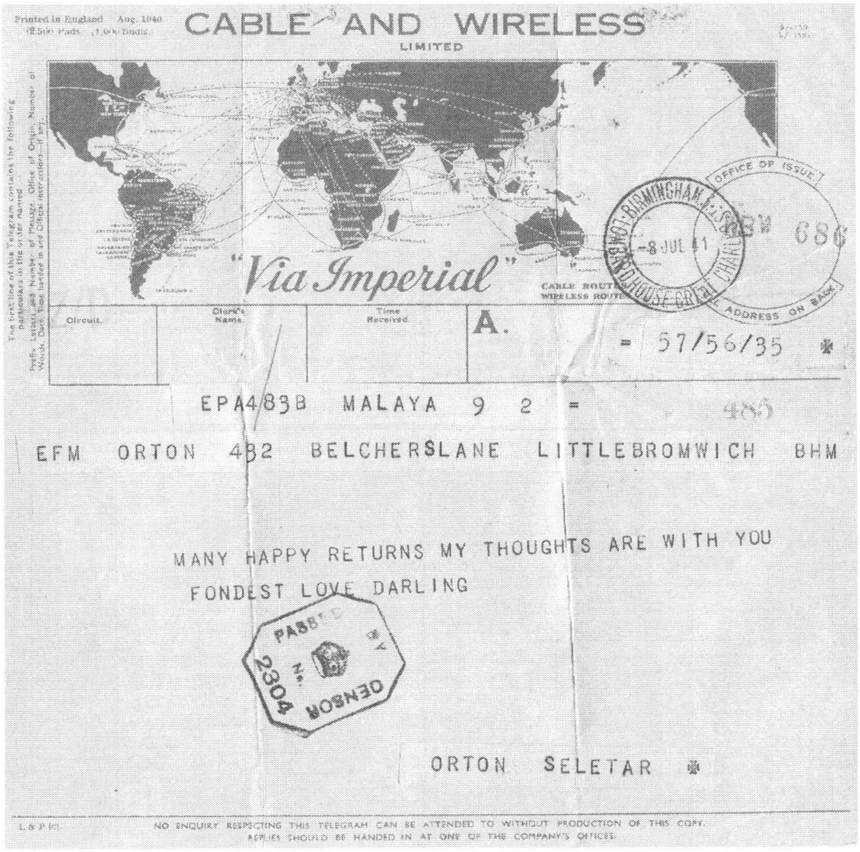
Printed in England Aug. 1940.

CABLE AND WIRELESS
LIMITED

"Via Imperial"

BIRMINGHAM
-8 JUL 41

OFFICE OF ISSUE

ADDRESS ON BACK

Circuit. | Clerk's Name. | Time Received. | A.

= 57/56/35

EPA483B MALAYA 9 2 =

EFM ORTON 482 BELCHERSLANE LITTLEBROMWICH BHM

MANY HAPPY RETURNS MY THOUGHTS ARE WITH YOU
FONDEST LOVE DARLING

PASSED BY CENSOR No. 2304

ORTON SELETAR

NO ENQUIRY RESPECTING THIS TELEGRAM CAN BE ATTENDED TO WITHOUT PRODUCTION OF THIS COPY.
REPLIES SHOULD BE HANDED IN AT ONE OF THE COMPANY'S OFFICES.

Seletar RAF Camp – 151 M.U. Singapore 1941

Tom front row on right | Tom on right at back

Letters from Tom to Joan:

No. 9

849112 A.C.I. T Orton
R.A.F Seletar
Singapore S.S.

17th July 1941

My Darling Wife

I am pleased to say that I have received 2 letters from you today dated 29th April and 3rd May with Ray's letter enclosed. You do not know how different it makes me feel when your letters are handed to me and I am so relieved to hear that you have been over to Sutton to stay.

Fancy brother Len shaking at the knees over asking Gladys' father if he could get married. You ask about living at Sutton with Len and Gladys, I'll leave it with you, as I know that you will be doing the best thing whatever you do darling. I expect your mother is a bit cut up about the idea but I myself would feel much better if you were living in Sutton as I am sure it is much safer. I do worry so much when I hear on the wireless or in the paper that the Midlands have had it! I am always living for that day when we are together again and feel confident that we don't have to wait much longer my dear. Fancy our kid saying in his letter that it was about time he heard from me, I wrote 2 letters in January at Bristol and I have written at least half a dozen times since I left England.

I was sorry to hear about Peter snuffing it. Maybe I could bring a parrot home when I come, there sure are some lovely coloured ones here.

I enclose some more photos - one taken with the Indian boys who clean our shoes and buttons and make our beds. We sure get looked after well don't we? The other one is with the chap from Birmingham, who is my snooker partner – he is in the swimming outfit in the bottom left hand corner. By the way I am red hot at snooker now, having so much practice! It is the only thing one can do at night besides go to the camp pictures and I sure put plenty of time in there. I went the other night to see Merle Oberon and it struck me that she reminded me of you. You are certainly a lot like her, my mates back me up with your photo, they say you are the image of her.

I am looking forward to getting some letters from you direct to here. You know not UTVO. I suppose they will be here anytime now as I have been here 2 months and a week and it takes 2 months for them to get here. I have sent you 4 cables, did you get them all? I hope you did, especially the one for your birthday.

From Your Ever Loving Husband Tom xxxxx

No. 10

849112 A.C.I. T Orton
R.A.F Seletar
Singapore S.S.

24th July 1941

My Darling Wife

I have just received your letter dated 9/5 and your cable. It has been about a week since I had your last 2 letters. I have sent you 4 cables. It seems that you have been very busy getting things for our home, I sure am very lucky darling to have a wife like you.

What do you think has happened today? I have been recommended for my props at last, so it won't be long before I am L.A.C. What do you say ... it's high time I became a Corporal! Well you know me my sweet, I never push myself and hope to be back with you by the time I get my 2.

I have decided to send you a cable each month as it only takes under a week as far as I know. If you do move to Sutton, please send a cable, so that I shall know where to write to. I should like to hear how brother Len got on in his interview with Gladys' father and hope they will soon be married.

I have not been out of camp for a few months, except up to a little village not far from here. The town does not appeal to me very much, so I buy all I want from the kampong (village).

From your Every Loving Husband Tom xxxxx

p.s. Thank you for the card, I have put it with my Valentine xxx

NEWS BACK HOME IN BLIGHTY:

27th July 1941 – *A Lone German aircraft falls in an attempt to bomb Solihull gasworks.*

28th July 1941 – *Air-raid from 1.43 a.m. to 3.39 a.m. on the west and south sides of Birmingham City. 263 fires are reported.*

Letter from Tom to Joan:

No. 11

849112 A.C.I. T Orton
R.A.F Seletar
Singapore S.S.

30th July 1941

My Dear Wife

Your letter dated 20/4 was a bit late as I had already received one from you posted in May. I also received 2 letters from Gran posted in April.

It certainly was a stiff price you had to pay for the ring, you say I am worth it, believe me, I will always live up to those words. It was very good of Mrs Henley (Coles Lane, Sutton Coldfield) *presenting the towels to you.*

You say we should get gloriously drunk the day I come home - I think after a couple, I will be on my head as I have not had alcohol for 2 months! I do not like the beastly stuff out here, anyway, it is not good for you in this climate. "Oh" for that wonderful day when we will be together again will come quicker than we think.

I have had my photo taken for my driving licence and enclose one that is over buckshee. How do you like your husband in working attire? It is only to identify my fissogg when I go up country. Please excuse scribble as the writing table is full, I got there last, so I have had to write this on my knee. All my Love.

Your Ever Loving Husband Tom xxxxxxx

NEWS BACK HOME IN BLIGHTY:

31st July 1941 – *Air-raid on Birmingham City Centre. 41 fires reported.*

3rd August 1941 – *Air-raid alert 2.57 a.m. to 3.28 a.m. and again 1.54 p.m. to 2.13 p.m.*

Cable from Tom to Joan - Dated 7th August 1941

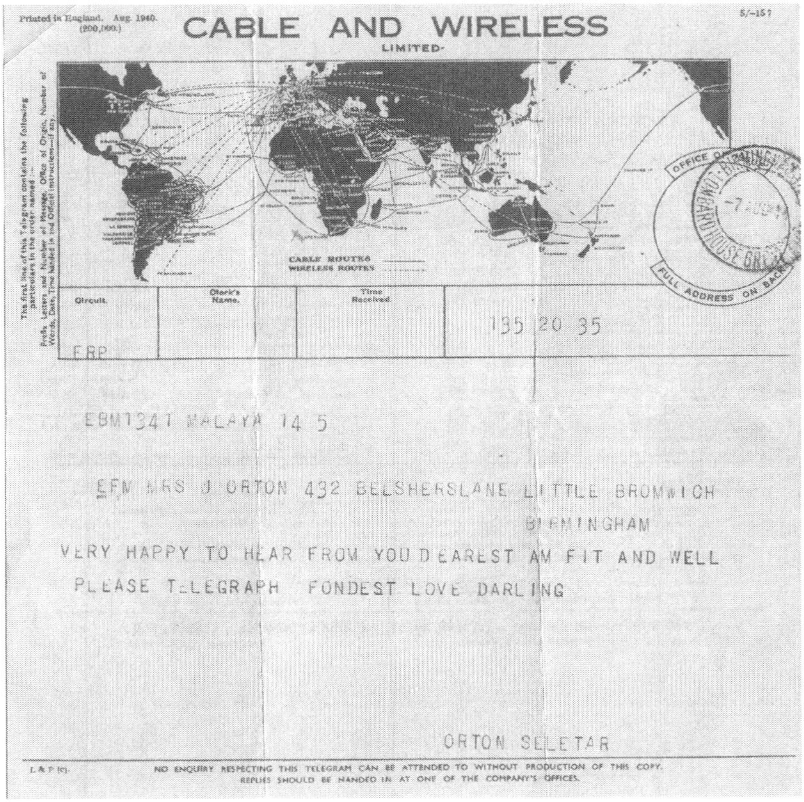
Printed in England. Aug. 1940. (200,000.)

CABLE AND WIRELESS LIMITED

The first line of this Telegram contains the following particulars in the order named:— Prefix Letters and Number of Message, Office of Origin, Number of Words, Date, Time handed in and Official instructions—if any.

CABLE ROUTES
WIRELESS ROUTES

Circuit.	Clerk's Name.	Time Received.	
FRP			135 20 35

EBM1341 MALAYA 14 5

EFM MRS J ORTON 432 BELSHERSLANE LITTLE BROMWICH
BIRMINGHAM

VERY HAPPY TO HEAR FROM YOU DEAREST AM FIT AND WELL
PLEASE TELEGRAPH FONDEST LOVE DARLING

ORTON SELETAR

NO ENQUIRY RESPECTING THIS TELEGRAM CAN BE ATTENDED TO WITHOUT PRODUCTION OF THIS COPY.
REPLIES SHOULD BE HANDED IN AT ONE OF THE COMPANY'S OFFICES.

NEWS BACK HOME IN BLIGHTY

8th August 1941 – *Air-raid alert 11.59 pm - 1.25 am*

Letter from Tom to Joan:

No.12

849112 A.C.I. T Orton
R.A.F Seletar
Singapore S.S.

10th August 1941

My Dear Wife

I hope you received my cable sent at the beginning of this week. I have sent you 5 cables altogether. Did you find out at the Post Office about the new method I mentioned. You can send 3 numbers, each number represents a sentence and there are a whole lot of numbers to pick from.

I am so browned off us being apart like this. There are not many nights pass without me dreaming of you. The worst part about it is when I wake! I do realise how you must be feeling too but the only thing to do is to keep smiling and praying for the day when we are together again.

I found out that one of my school friends has been here for two & a half years, he lived in Victoria Road (Sutton Coldfield) *opposite Gran,* **Alan Guest** *is his name. Will you mention it to Gran, she will know him, I am sure. I haven't heard from Ma lately but suppose I shall receive a pile of letters altogether. The only letter I had off the last boat that came in was from Gran. Was I disappointed not having one from my dear wife but still I mustn't grumble as I have done very well with letters from you so far. I suppose Len will be married by now, he sure is lucky not being separated like you and I. We will have it made up to us very soon I'm sure. There are quite a lot of Birmingham chaps here, from Ladywood, Court Lane, Erdington, Kings Heath, Walmley and the chap from Sutton that I mentioned. There is also another chap from my school here but I have not come across him yet.*

I shall soon have 7 days leave and might go up to Malaya for a few days. I may even come across a couple of chaps I worked with at Fort Dunlop who came out here and now have a big plantation somewhere.

I'm always hoping and praying that I may soon be with you again.

Your Ever Loving Husband Tom xxxxxxx
I.T.A.L.Y. Darling

NEWS BACK HOME IN BLIGHTY

12th August 1941 – Birmingham *Air-raid alert 1.51 a.m. to 2.06 a.m.*

Letter from Tom to Joan:

No. 13

849112 A.C.I. T Orton
R.A.F Seletar
Singapore S.S.

15th August 1941

My Darling Wife

I received your letter today posted lst June and I am so glad to hear that you got my first cable. I am pleased that you are keeping safe and staying in Sutton away from the city.

So Len and Gladys are married, I wrote them a letter a couple or three days ago. You say you wish we could have our wedding day over again, well the day I return to you will be just as good, we sure will celebrate my precious.

I received a letter from your sister Brenda today saying she was in Manchester. She asked for a photo of just you and I as you had only sent her one of the wedding group. If you have got one to spare, will you send her one darling.

I have not had any leave as yet but I am not worrying about leave while I am here as I used to when I was able to come home to you my dear. I did so look forward to those days when I could be with you in 3 or 4 hours but we shall soon be together again my loved one, for good too.

Did Len and Gladys take Gran's house in Victoria Road and are you living with them by now? God Bless you my dear and cheerio for a short time.

Your Ever Loving Husband Tom xxx

No 14

849112 A.C.I. T Orton
R.A.F Seletar
Singapore S.S.

18th August 1941

My Darling Wife

I was so glad to get your cable today. I only wrote to you a couple of days ago so I expect you will get 2 letters at the same time. It certainly is good to think that I can cable you and get an answer within a fortnight darling. According to the cable it was sent from Weston Super Mare and I am thinking perhaps you have had your holiday. I do hope you had a good rest. I am sure the change will have done you good, that is if I am right. I have received letters from Ma & brother Ray. Ray's letter had been to Bristol, West Kirby and all over the place! I only wrote to both of them the other day, so I have got to write to them again now. By the way Ray wished to be remembered to "the wife", so I am to convey his best respects to you. Goodbye for a bit and God Bless you.

Your Ever Loving Husband Tom xxxx

Tom & Gran prior to W.W.II

No. 15

849112 L.A.C. T Orton
R.A.F Seletar
Singapore S.S.

25th August 1941

My Darling Wife

I received your letter today posted 5/6/41 and your cable sent from Clevedon, near Weston Super Mare so I suppose you are still on holiday at this moment. I do hope you are having a nice time. **(Joan was in fact in a convalescent home!)**

It certainly is very sweet of you to get blue blankets darling, always thinking of my favourite colour.

Fancy writing to me at 3 am in the morning, I do hope the air raid did not last much longer and you were able to get to bed after writing my letter. I miss you terribly too but I am sure it will not be for much longer in my estimation. You can see from the above that I've been promoted to L.A.C. since I last wrote to you. I received a letter from Gran saying you were all busy getting ready for brother Len's wedding, I hope it went off ok. Goodbye for a bit and God Bless you.

Your Ever loving Husband xxxxx

No. 16

849112 L.A.C. T Orton
R.A.F Seletar
Singapore S.S.

29th August 1941

My Darling Wife

I hope you are receiving my letters alright. I will send a cable in the morning as it is just a month since the last one. I am on standby for posting and expect it will be somewhere in Malaya. In any case Darling your letters will find me and I shall let you know my new address as soon as I get to my new station. That is, of course, if I do move, it is not definite as yet! I received my L.A.C's pay today, it sure has made a difference and I shall be getting my good conduct stripe at the beginning of next year, which will mean another 3/6d a week.

I suppose brother Len and Gladys are enjoying married life. Are you staying with them in Sutton, as you said you might do? I saw by your cable that you used the number system, a good idea don't you think? It will be very near Christmas when you get this letter and I am struggling to imagine what cold weather is like these days. I sure would like to see a good snowstorm, as it has been as hot as ever here today.

I am on my own at the moment as nearly all of the lads go down the town. Most are single and they pull my leg because I do not go out much, although I did go to the pictures last night to see Bing Crosby and Dorothy Lamour in "The Road to Singapore". Whenever we get a bit browned off we say "Well roll on the boat" wishing we were on it back to "Blighty". God Bless you Darling.

Your Ever LovingHusband Tom xxxx

Chapter 5

ON THE MOVE TO SUNGAI PETANI, Kedah, Malaysia ... Tom's last letter to Joan 1 December 1941

SUNGAI PETANI *is in the district of Kedah in Malaysia. It is Kedah's largest city which lies South of Thailand, East of Singapore and North of Kuala Lumpur. Kedah was the first part of Malaya to be invaded by Japan.* ***Penang Island*** *lies south of Sungai Petani.*

Tom's Story continues ...

Early September 1941 – Bert Melluish and myself are posted up country to *Sungai Petani, which is a fairly new drome in the middle of the rubber plantations just north of Penang. (*Sungai Petani translates to "Farmer's River" – an area with a huge concentration of paddy fields and farmers).

There are two squadrons of aircraft, one consists of obsolete old Blenheims, the other a squadron of Buffalos. The latter belongs to the Royal Australian Air Force. Our duties are mainly driving and repair work and I notice the billets are constructed of wood with atap roofing. We manage to spend an evening on the Penang Island which is quite a pleasant place, crossing over and back by ferry.

Telegram from Tom to Joan Dated 4th September:

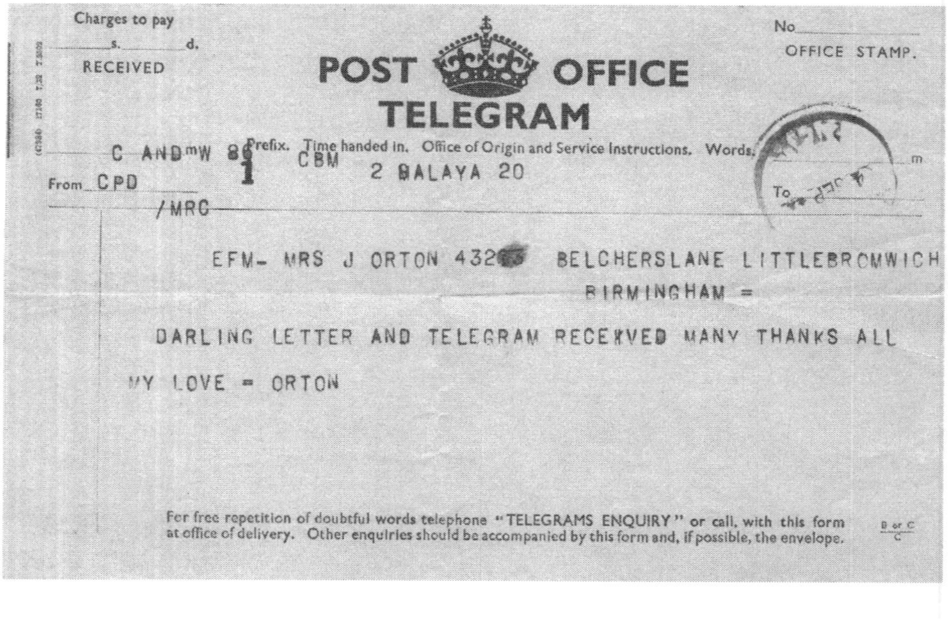

Charges to pay
s. d.
RECEIVED

No.
OFFICE STAMP.

POST OFFICE
TELEGRAM

C ANDmW 8 Prefix. Time handed in. Office of Origin and Service Instructions. Words.
1 CBM 2 BALAYA 20 m
From CPD
/MRC
To

EFM- MRS J ORTON 432[illegible] BELCHERSLANE LITTLEBROMWICH
BIRMINGHAM =
DARLING LETTER AND TELEGRAM RECEKVED MANY THANKS ALL
MY LOVE = ORTON

For free repetition of doubtful words telephone "TELEGRAMS ENQUIRY" or call, with this form at office of delivery. Other enquiries should be accompanied by this form and, if possible, the envelope.

B or C
C

Letters from Tom to Joan:

No. 17

849112 L.A.C. T. Orton
R.A.F Sungai Petani.
Kedah
Malaya

5th September 1941

My Darling Wife

I received your letter dated 18th June the day I left Seletar. This place is about 600 miles from Singapore and I brought a lorry all the way by road taking nearly 3 days. I am only attached to this station so I may be going back to Seletar after a short time. I hope so anyway as this place is right in the wilds.

I do hope you are well. You say in your letter that you are lonely, I am the same myself but we must keep our chins up and be patient. I really do not think it will last much longer and I pray that I shall soon be back with you my loved one.

I hope you received my cable and will you thank Ma for the photo? Sheila certainly does look well and that goes for Ma & Tony. I have not received the parcel yet and I am wondering if you got the one I sent to you a couple of months ago. I was very lucky to get your letter minutes before I left, which certainly helped me start my journey in higher spirits.

You say you had to register for Government work, I do hope you don't have to work away from home.

I suppose it will be Christmas time when you get this letter, so I will wish you a very happy Christmas, although I shall be cabling you before then. It seems strange having to wish my wife a Happy Christmas in September whilst sitting here writing, sweating cobbs right in the jungle. I had put in for 7 days leave before I was sent here so I suppose I have had it now! I must get back to duty now. God Bless and may I be back with you soon. Remember me to all.

Your Ever loving Husband Tom xxxxxx

No. 18

849112 L.A.C. T. Orton
R.A.F. Sungai Petani
Kedah
Malaya

8th September 1941

My Darling Wife

I am still at the same station as you can see by the address but I don't know for how long. It is pouring with rain here, in fact it has rained ever since I arrived but it certainly cools the place down a lot. The worst thing about the joint are the mosquitoes; there's bags of 'em and as you know they like me.

I am going to write to Ma, Gran, brothers Ray and Fred so I will be busy tonight but there is not much more you can do here except read, and I get fed up with that. Anyway my precious I never get fed up of writing to you. When I feel browned off, I always look at our photos and think of the day when I return home to you, never to leave you again.

I am getting pretty good money and will have a bit saved up for when I come home. Let's hope that this will be the only Christmas I shall be away from you. Goodbye for the present and God Bless you and keep you.

Your Ever Loving Husband Tom xxxxxx

No. 18 (again!!)

849112 L.A.C. Orton
R.A.F. Sungai Petani
Kedah
Malaya

14th September 1941

My Darling Wife

I am still at the same place and daresay I shall be here indefinitely by all accounts but I should get your mail ok if you address it here. I have not heard from you since I arrived but I expect there are some letters on the way up from Seletar for me.

How are things at home? I do hope you are not working too hard and I shall be glad when I am home you will not have to work at all. I certainly think things are looking up and that I shall be home with you again soon. I expect you are wondering why I do not tell you much in my letters about this part of the world but we cannot put much as all letters are censored before they leave the camp, which of course is only right under the circumstances. Things were a bit tense in this part but may have eased off a little, anyway I suppose you get most of the gen on the wireless and in the papers.

Your parcel has not arrived yet so I think it may have got lost. Although things are pretty plentiful here, I don't like to think that you have wasted your money. I am still wondering if you got the pyjama suit I sent you and if you did, I do hope the duty was not much on it.

I will close by wishing you a very happy Christmas that is if you get this letter soon enough. God Bless you my loved one.

Your Ever Loving Husband Tom xxxxxx
I.T.A.L.Y. xxxxxxx

No. 19

849112 L.A.C. Orton
R.A.F. Sungai Petani
Kedah
Malaya

19th September 1941

My Darling Wife

I received your letter today dated 25th June. I hope your foot will soon get better but please don't worry about work and not being able to save, you being safe and well is more important to me.

My time will be up in just over 12 months and I will be on my way home, if not before if the War finishes. Married men are always given the preference of getting home first. Do not worry I shall be one of the first to jump on the first available boat home to you when it is over. I miss you terribly stuck out here right in the wilds but I shall always be patient for that day when I come back to you.

I went to the pictures in Penang as transport was arranged for us so I thought I might as well go as we have no pictures here on the camp like Seletar. We travelled about 25 miles and the picture was not up to much, it was a nice house though. I was starving half way through the film and freezing cold as it was air conditioned so I was glad to come out, it was like a refrigerator.

I received a letter from your sister Brenda and I replied to the address she put so I suppose she got it alright.

Well darling "lakas" and get that foot better, but don't for heaven's sake worry about your work. I had a letter from Gran today saying that you often go and see her and that you are ideal! Goodbye for the present my dear and God Bless and keep you. Remember me to your Ma & Pa.

Your Ever Loving Husband Tom xxxx

p.s. Your parcel has not turned up yet, has mine?

No. 20

849112 L.A.C. Orton
R.A.F. Sungai Petani
Kedah
Malaya

20th September 1941

My Darling Wife

Thank you for the parcel received today. It is so sweet of you to think of me like this. All of the items are in perfect condition. I have just sampled the chocolate and now enjoying a real English Players. We can get Woodbines and Players here but I do not think they are as good.

So, you are a Godmother, well I am sure Ma is very grateful to you and your pop.

I should imagine it is pretty tough with all the rationing etc but let's hope it does not last much longer darling. I miss you terribly and always pray that we shall be together again very soon.

Please thank your Ma & Pa for the chocolate, cigs and butterscotch. I was surprised to see that all the items had kept so well in the heat, maybe they kept them in a fridge.

I will send a cable next week. I know you will be patient until the day I return and please do not think it will be too long as I am sure our prayers will be answered. God Bless.

From Your Ever Loving Husband Tom xxxxxx
I.T.A.L.Y.

No. 21

849112 L.A.C. Orton
R.A.F. Sungai Petani
Kedah
Malaya

30th September 1941

My Darling Wife

I sent your cable last Thursday and I have just written to Ma as I have not heard from home lately.

I have 7 days leave in 2 weeks but still living on camp. I may go into town for a few things and have a look round the country; a change from the routine for a bit. It is pouring with rain as usual but it is cool when it rains so I don't mind, except that it drives the mossies into the billet, and they are pests.

I thought about writing to the Elmsdale Club to wish them compliments for Christmas but I don't think I will in case it isn't still open on account of all the chaps being called up. If I am wrong, will you wish them all the best for me? I do hope this is the only Christmas I shall be away from you but I shall be patient until I am with you again and I know you will my dear. Will you remember me to your Ma and Pa, and wish them well.

There is a chap here who was at Castle Bromwich for a good while, he says he wishes he was there now - I told him he isn't by himself, although things seem to be brightening up a bit and I am confident I shall be with you again before long.

I haven't heard from brothers Ray and Fred yet but still living in hope of some news one of these days. I told them in my last letters I hope to race them home when the time comes. You bet I will!

I hope you are having quiet nights if you have returned back home again, as you said you might in your last letter. According to the news, you are not being troubled lately. I am always looking at our photos on my locker and thinking of you always. God Bless you and keep you, keep that lovely chin up my precious.

Your Ever Loving Husband Tom

Ray

Fred

Len

(THREE OF TOM'S BROTHERS)

Telegram from Tom to Joan dated October 1941

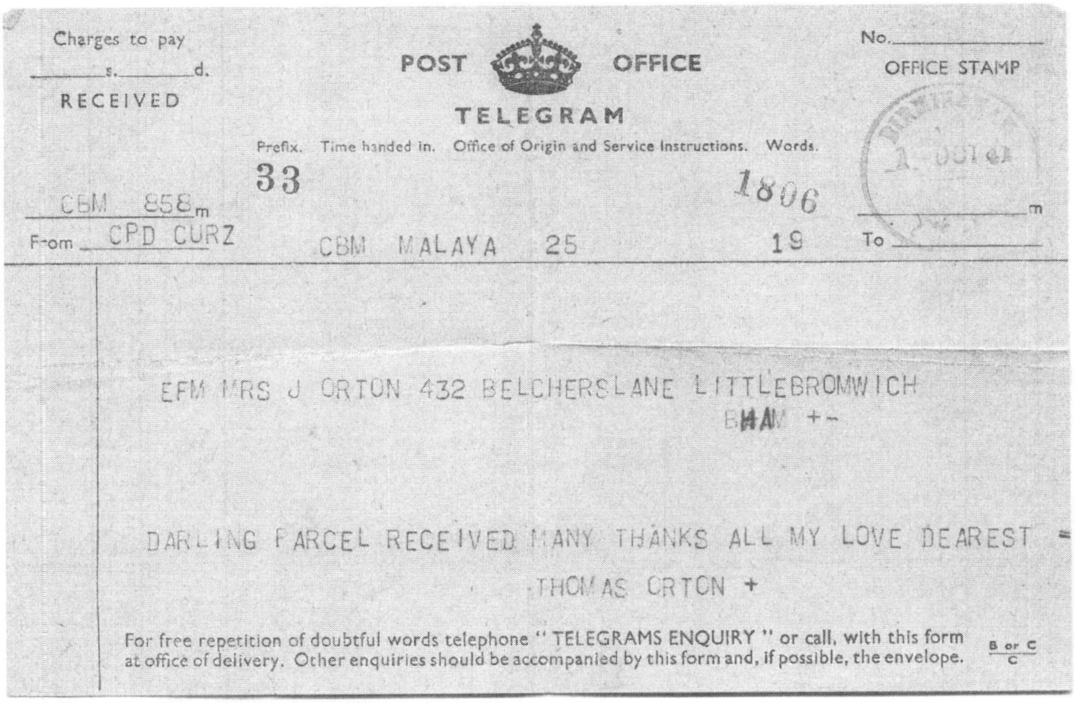
Charges to pay
s. d.
RECEIVED

POST OFFICE
TELEGRAM

No.
OFFICE STAMP

Prefix. Time handed in. Office of Origin and Service Instructions. Words.

33

CBM 858m
From CPD CURZ

1806

CBM MALAYA 25 19

To

EFM MRS J ORTON 432 BELCHERSLANE LITTLEBROMWICH
BHAM +-

DARLING PARCEL RECEIVED MANY THANKS ALL MY LOVE DEAREST =
THOMAS ORTON +

For free repetition of doubtful words telephone "TELEGRAMS ENQUIRY" or call, with this form at office of delivery. Other enquiries should be accompanied by this form and, if possible, the envelope.

B or C
C

No. 22

849112 L.A.C. Orton
R.A.F. Sungai Petani
Kedah
Malaya

3rd October 1941

My Darling Wife

I received 3 letters from you today posted lst, 5th and 19th July and I was surprised to hear that you had not had any of my letters for a long while. I wrote to you as soon as I arrived at Seletar and it was the first thing I did, as I am always thinking of you. You say in one of your letters that you hope I will be the same when I return, I know that my love for you will never change never!

I will write to the Elmsdale Club as soon as I have finished this letter and thank them for their kindness. I am glad to hear your air raid shelter is finished at last, but Darling please go to Sutton if the raids start again, although I hope for your sake that they never will.

One of the letters had stamps on costing 1/3d and was posted pretty near the same time as the others costing 1½d so there is no point in sending them by air as they are no quicker. I can imagine it must be a bit of a "B" having to queue for 3 hrs for a ½lb of tomatoes, things must be tough!

I certainly am glad if you had that holiday but as I said in my last letter from Seletar, maybe you changed your mind about Rhyl as one of your cables was marked Weston. I sent you a photo yesterday which I am afraid it isn't up to much. One of the lads was trying to make me laugh and it may come across as being rather cynical, as I do miss you terribly.

Your Ever Loving Husband Tom xxxxxx

Letters from Joan to Tom – "RETURN TO SENDER on Air Ministry Instructions"

432 Belchers Lane
Little Bromwich
B'ham

15th October 1941

My Darling

I received 3 letters from you 3 weeks ago and a cable a fortnight ago but not a word since! I am being patient though and keeping my chin up, as I hope you are too. I have not been to your house in Sutton for 3 weeks and honestly I know your mom will be very upset and probably shout!

I am going down to the Singer in the morning on the Coventry Road for a job. I have not been to work for nearly 6 months, so I think it is about time I started again, don't you? Darling you won't have a home to come to, one of our own I mean, if I don't hurry and save up.

Auntie May has given me her canary, he's a beauty and sings lovely, I do hope he doesn't strangle himself like our little Peter did! Auntie May's little girl Jean is staying with us and she insists on writing to you, so I enclose a note from her, mind you she is only 4 years old. She is always asking me about when you are coming home. I have bought a coat darling, it is grey with big patch pockets. Please let me know what the first parcel was like when you receive it. I bet the eatables were no good were they. I have sent you another parcel with cigs and a tin of toffees but it is a problem to know what to send you so please write and let me know, don't forget.

I went to the pictures last night to see "Convicted Woman", it was quite a good picture. I will close now as I am too upset to write anymore - they are playing "I'll think of you" on the wireless. Cheerio Darling, God Bless you and a speedy and safe return.

From Your Ever Loving And Lonely Wife Joan xxxxx

432 Belchers Lane
Little Bromwich
B'ham

22nd October 1941

My Darling

I received a letter from you yesterday 21/10 dated 1/8/41, it contained a small photograph. Oh darling you have gone thin, you don't look the same, I suppose it could be the heat. Have you received my photograph yet?

I bought a cake tray and some bread pudding tins yesterday, so at least I shall be able to make you some bread pudding. Did you enjoy your 7 days? I only wish I could have spent them with you. Cousin Jean is standing by the side of me asking who am I writing to. She says "what writing to Uncle Tom again". Mom and Dad send their love and mom says she hopes she will be seeing you soon and so do I darling, I pray for you every night and my thoughts are with you all the time. Have you had a letter from sister Brenda yet? Each time she writes, she always asks about you. Jean says "give Uncle Tom a big kiss for me Joan", so here you are dear xx (she has drawn them herself). God Bless you and keep you safe.

From Your Ever Loving Wife Joan xxxxx

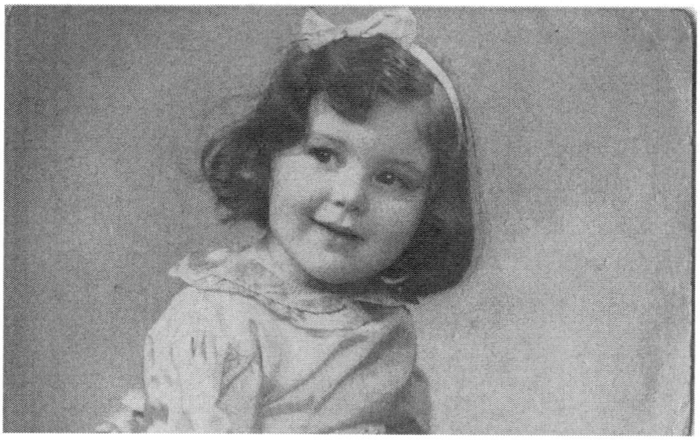

Joan's Cousin Jean

Letter from Tom to Joan:

849112 L.A.C. Orton
R.A.F. Sungai Petani
Kedah
Malaya

22nd October 1941

My Darling Wife

I do hope that you are feeling better and I wish to God that I could get a letter from you saying that you are my dear. I will send another cable at the weekend asking for a reply from you, as I haven't had a word from you since your letter dated July 16th stating you were going into a convalescent home and I do so worry about you. I had a letter from Gran today posted on August 5th saying everyone enjoyed themselves at Len's wedding.

The Padre was speaking to some of the chaps on the drome today telling them that the term of service out here was 2 years for married men and 3 years for single men, so even if this lot does not end within the next 12 months, I shall be coming home soon, as I will have already done 12 months by the time you get this letter. I do think it stands a good chance that the War will be over soon and I shall be home before then.

Things are pretty well the same here although sometimes the news is pretty tense on account of the Japs but then it eases off again, in any case if they do start anything they will have a shock to see what they are up against. The papers today say that they will think twice before starting anything as they know the odds are against them. I am still longing to receive a letter to say that you are well again. God Bless you.

Your Ever Loving Husband Tom xxxx

Cable from Tom to Joan dated 27th October 1941

Printed in England. Aug. 1940.
(200,000.)

5/-157

CABLE AND WIRELESS
LIMITED

The first line of this Telegram contains the following particulars in the order named:—
Prefix Letters and Number of Message, Office of Origin, Number of Words, Date, Time handed in and Official instructions—if any.

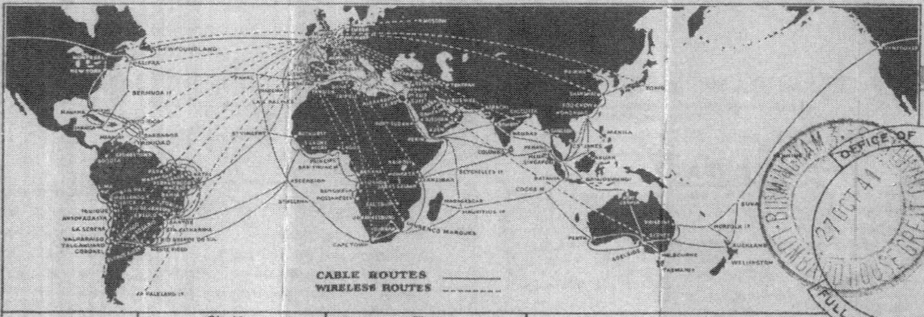

OFFICE OF ISSUE
27 OCT 41
FULL ADDRESS ON BACK

Circuit.	Clerk's Name.	Time Received.	
	30 76 32		

CGM
HB ~~EBM350/BG~~ MALAYA 13 25

EFM MRS J ORTON 432 BELCHERSLANE LITTLEBROMWICH BHAM

DARLING PLEASE TELEGRAPH THAT YOU ARE WELL
ALL MY LOVE DEAREST

THOMAS ORTON

L. & P. (c).

NO ENQUIRY RESPECTING THIS TELEGRAM CAN BE ATTENDED TO WITHOUT PRODUCTION OF THIS COPY.
REPLIES SHOULD BE HANDED IN AT ONE OF THE COMPANY'S OFFICES.

Letters from Joan to Tom – "RETURN TO SENDER on Air Ministry Instructions"

432 Belchers Lane
Little Bromwich
B'ham

28th October 1941

My Darling

I have received 2 letters and a cable from you today, the dates on them are 18th and 26th July, it just shows how they mess the letters about as I had a letter from you last week dated lst August. I don't mind though as long as I keep hearing from you. In the one letter received this morning there were 3 photographs, oh my duck you have gone thin!

The reason I have not sent you a cable for some time is because I have not been able to afford it. You see I have not been to work since 14/7/41 and it is now 28/10/41 but I am starting at the Hercules in the morning, the hours are 7.30 a.m. till 6 p.m. and 2 o'clock on Saturday. The wages are £2.10s to start, plus a bonus after a while, so that isn't too bad at all is it? I promise that as soon as I do start to get paid, I will send a cable every other week as I can't have you worrying like this. All the time I have been at home I have had to spend your money each week, or my allowance shall I say. I have to give to mom £1, 2/4d insurance and then there's the bed money, so you can guess how much I had left but It isn't fair for me to moan like this to you, so I will pack it up! You have told me in one or two of your letters about your props. I expect you have had them by now and Darling, I must congratulate you, I am so proud of my husband. God Bless you always.

I went to the River Cole last Sunday to take the dog a run. Do you remember Morden Road? It did bring back pleasant and happy memories. I could picture you all the time I was there. Cheerio for a bit. God Bless you and keep you safe. I'm thinking of you always.

From your Ever Loving Wife Joan xxx

Air Mail Postcard dated 30th October 1941 from Joan to Tom "RETURNED by Air Ministry"

432 Belchers Lane
Little Bromwich
B'ham

29th October 1941

My Dear Tom

I have received another letter from you today 29/10. To think I have had 3 letters and a cable in one week isn't it lovely. Darling I want to wish you a Merry Christmas and I trust to God it will be the last Christmas we have to spend apart. The weather here is terribly cold, it is cold enough for snow. I hope you are still fit and well and still keeping your old chin up as I am trying to do. I do not have much more to say as I only sent you a 5 page letter yesterday telling you all the news. Go and see the picture "Bitter Sweet" if it comes to your place it is worth seeing. God Bless you

Your Loving Wife Joan xxxxxx

Air Mail Postcard from Joan's parents to Tom dated 30th October 1941 – "RETURNED by Air Ministry"

BY AIR MAIL
PAR AVION
POST CARD
AIR MAIL
POSTAGE REVENUE 3D
RETURN TO SENDER ON AIR MINISTRY INSTRUCTIONS
847412 A.C.1 T. Orton
R.A.F. ....SIG. OF C.O.
Seletar
Singapore
S.S.

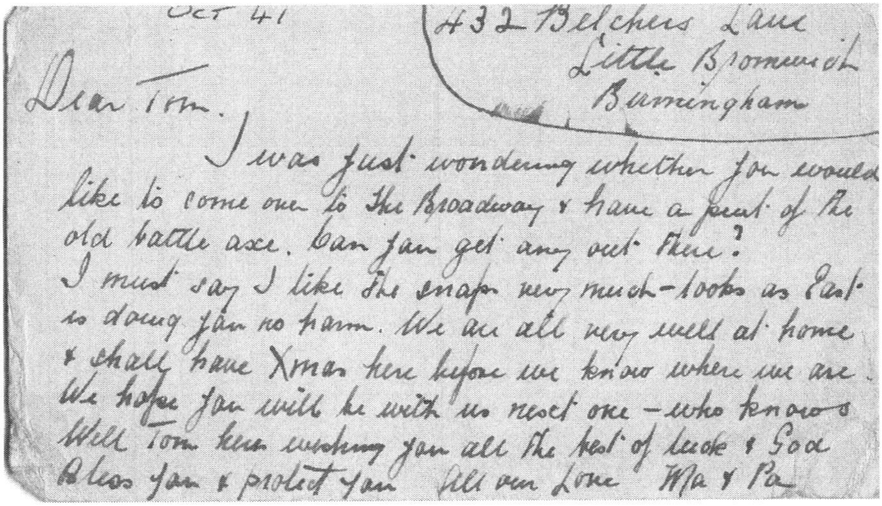

Oct 41
432 Belchers Lane
Little Bromwich
Birmingham

Dear Tom.

I was just wondering whether you would like to come over to The Broadway & have a pint of the old battle axe. Can you get any out there?
I must say I like the snap very much – looks as East is doing you no harm. We are all very well at home & shall have Xmas here before we know where we are.
We hope you will be with us next one – who knows.
Well Tom here wishing you all the best of luck & God Bless you & protect you All our Love Ma & Pa

Letters from Joan to Tom – "RETURN TO SENDER on Air Ministry Instructions"

Mom says will you pop over and bath the dog for her.

432 Belchers Lane
Little Bromwich
B'ham

30th October 1941

My Darling

I hope you have received the cable I sent this morning at the Beaufort Post Office. I bet you are wondering what I was doing up by the Beaufort in the morning. Well, they let me down at the Hercules. Anyway, I went down to Parkinson Stove Co. in Stechford this morning to see if they had any suitable jobs and I really thought my luck was out again as they only want girls that can do nights. I can't do nights as I tremble somewhat terribly when the sirens go. Well, I have definitely got a job at Parkinsons as a Checking Clerk. The man that interviewed me said "of course you have to have your head screwed on" and "it is a very good job if you can tackle it". The hours are 7.30 a.m. - 6 o'clock and 12.30 p.m. on Saturday, the pay is £2.10 plus paid overtime which I will try and do. I don't think we shall be apart for much longer, do you dear. God Bless you and keep you safe.

From your Ever Loving Wife Joan xxxx

432 Belchers Lane
Little Bromwich
B'ham

8th November 1941

My Darling Tom

Oh my duck, I have just had a shock! I found the poor little bird stiff at the bottom of the cage. I don't know, really my luck is out with birds. I can't seem to keep them 5 minutes and I shan't have another one until you come home.

I received a letter from sister Brenda the other day, my goodness she is thrilled because she has received a letter from you. I have counted my letters from you, there are 108 and 16 telegrams, so darling you must love me. You say in you never go out, I think you should go out and enjoy yourself, but do no harm.

I have completed my first week at work, it's alright but there's not enough to do, all I have to do all day is walk around the shop, ordering the workers to get on with their work. I am going to your house in Sutton again next weekend. You should see Len and Gladys' wedding photographs, they are lovely. By the way, Gladys is going to have a baby, I only wish I was dear, do you?

The news seems a bit more promising now doesn't it? And it is lovely and quiet here. I have still not received my parcel so guess it has got lost. Cheerio my loved one, God Bless you and keep you safe.

From your Ever Loving Wife Joan xxxx

432 Belchers Lane
Little Bromwich
B'ham

10th November 1941

My Darling

I have come home from work to a lovely surprise ... the pyjamas you sent came this afternoon, oh my aren't they marvellous. I really can't express on paper how thrilled I am with them. I have had to pay 5/9d duty. Oh and I have had a letter as well dated 12/8/41.

I will ask Gran on Saturday when I go to your house about that fellow Alan Guest. By the way, I was in the Broadway last night with mom and Auntie May and there were 3 Air Force fellows standing next to us. One recognised your brooch on my coat and asked whether you were in the Air Force and your name. He said he knew you well. I thought he was pulling my leg at first! He said "Now, next time you write to your husband, ask him if he remembers ***Ron Barrows off old 15 site?"*** *He also said to ask you if you have seen anything of* ***Smythe*** *because no-one in England has heard from him at all. I did tell him that by the time I get an answer back from you, he might be there himself! By the way, his name is Ron Barrows.*

I am saving my beautiful pyjamas for our honeymoon. We are going to have one aren't we? Cheerio my loved one, God Bless and keep you safe.

From Your Ever Loving Wife Joan xxxx

Joan's Auntie May

Joan's Sister Brenda

Letter from Tom To Joan:

849112 L.A.C. Orton
R.A.F. Sungie Petani
Malaya

14th November 1941

My Darling Joan

I was so glad to get your cable and to hear that you are well. I received your letter posted July and you mentioned going into a convalescent home, I am sure the rest will do you good. I am not getting so many letters from you lately which made me a bit uneasy as I do so look forward to your letters. I received a letter from Gran yesterday, posted 27th Aug so I hope some of your letters may roll in soon.

I went on a trip up river today in a motorboat which I reconditioned for one of the officers. There were so many beautiful coloured birds and hundreds of monkeys - I've never seen so many. But for all the interesting things here, I shall not be satisfied until I am back home with you again and I am still praying for that day. The sooner this lot is over the better, which should not be too long and I shall be back with you never to leave you again.

I should soon be getting my G.C. stripe, so I shall be getting another 3d a day. It does not sound much but it all helps as the "old lady" said. Goodbye and God Bless you and keep you.

Your Ever Loving Husband Tom xxxxxxx

Postcard & Letters from Joan to Tom – "RETURNED by the Air Ministry"

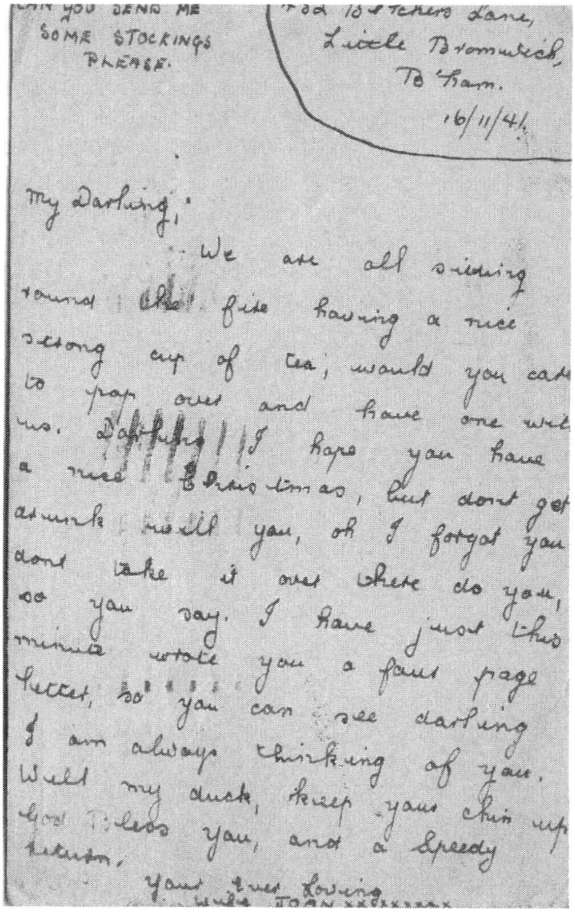

Can you send me
some stockings
please.

733 Butchers Lane,
Little Bromwich,
B'ham.
16/11/41.

My Darling,

We are all sitting round the fire having a nice strong cup of tea; would you care to pop over and have one with us. Darling!!! I hope you have a nice Christmas, but dont get drunk will you, oh I forgot you dont take it over there do you, so you say. I have just this minute wrote you a four page letter, so you can see darling I am always thinking of you. Well my duck, keep your chin up God Bless you, and a speedy return.

Your Ever Loving
Wife JOAN xxxxxxxx

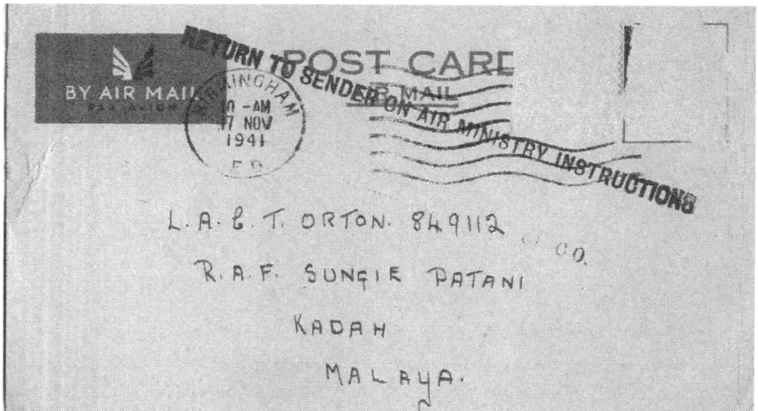

BY AIR MAIL
PAR AVION
POST CARD
RETURN TO SENDER ON AIR MINISTRY INSTRUCTIONS
BIRMINGHAM 10 -AM 17 NOV 1941

L.A.C. T. ORTON. 849112
R.A.F. SUNGIE PATANI
KADAH
MALAYA.

Letter from Joan to Tom:

432 Belchers Lane
Little Bromwich
B'ham

16th November 1941

My Darling Tom

Hello my loved one, are you still keeping your chin up? Just think this time last year we were both very excited, getting ready for our wedding but I expect by the time you get this letter, it will be turned January 4th. I have been looking at my bunch of heather this morning that Gran gave to me at the Church door? It is a bit brown but I shall keep it until you come back to me. Gran was very pleased to see me when I went over to Sutton last weekend. She said "Oh our Joan, I love you as much as my Tom and it is so nice to see you. But Darling she is lovely isn't she?

I am still waiting to see that picture "Road to Singapore", it has not come here yet but I did go to the Kingston last night to see Gordon Harker in "Once a Crook", it was a laugh, although he did swear!

I certainly wouldn't dream of wearing my beautiful pyjamas until you come home and I only hope the moths don't get to them but I think you will be home before the moths get a chance, don't you? Have you received your parcel yet with the cigarettes and toffees in? I tried to buy the blankets but I could not get a pair under 6 guineas, so I will leave them until after the War.

Today reminds me of our wedding day last January 4th, it is so cold! I very often think of that week you spent at West Bromwich being able to see you every night but still I shall soon be seeing you for good. God Bless you and keep you safe.

From Your Ever Loving Wife Joan xxxxxxxx

Letter from Tom to Joan

No. 26

849112 L.A.C. Orton
R.A.F. Sungie Petani
Kedah
Malaya

18th November 1941

My Dear Joan

I received your letter and photo posted Aug 8th, also the cable saying you received the parcel alright. Most importantly, I am so glad to hear that you are well again after a good rest at the convalescent home in Clevedon. You say it may have been due to worrying over me, please do not worry, I am quite well and my only ailment is being away from you. Your photo always reminds me that I have a wife waiting patiently back home and I live for the day when I can be with you again. I have nearly completed 12 months, leaving just over another year to do; that is if the War is still on. If it finishes before, as I pray it may, then it will be sooner. I forgot to number my last letter to you, it was No. 25, so let me know if there are any missing.

I haven't had a reply from Len & Gladys yet or from Ray or Fred. I certainly have put some writing hours in to them and hope to hear from them soon. God Bless you.

Your Ever Loving Husband Tom xxxxxxx

Air Mail Postcard from Joan to Tom dated 24th November 1941 – "RETURNED by the Air Ministry"

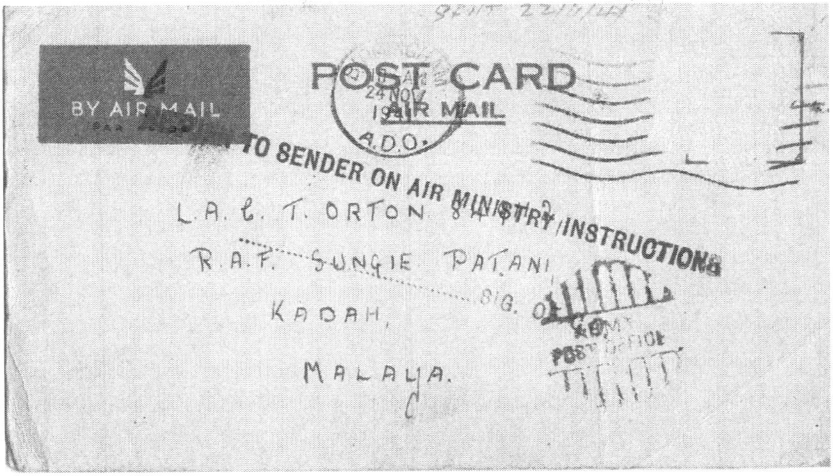
BY AIR MAIL

POST CARD
AIR MAIL

24 NOV 1941
A.D.O.

TO SENDER ON AIR MINISTRY INSTRUCTIONS

L.A.C. T. ORTON
R.A.F. SUNGIE PATANI
KADAH,
MALAYA.

POST OFFICE

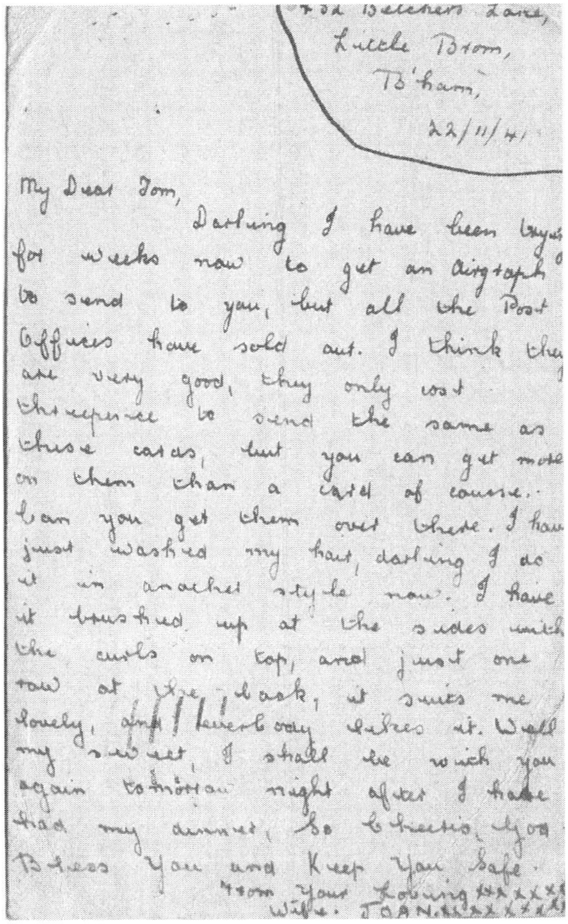
32 Belchers Lane,
Little Brom,
B'ham,
22/11/41

My Dear Tom,

Darling I have been trying for weeks now to get an airgraph to send to you, but all the Post Offices have sold out. I think they are very good, they only cost threepence to send the same as these cards, but you can get more on them than a card of course. Can you get them over there. I have just washed my hair, darling I do it in another style now. I have it brushed up at the sides with the curls on top, and just one row at the back, it suits me lovely, and everybody likes it. Well my sweet, I shall be with you again tomorrow night after I have had my dinner, so cheerio, God Bless You and Keep You Safe.

From Your Loving xxxx
Wife. JOAN. xxxxx

LAST LETTER FROM TOM TO JOAN

This appears to be the last letter to be written by Tom prior to his captivity by the Japanese.

No. 27

849112 L.A.C. Orton
R.A.F. Sungie Petani
KedahMalaya

1st December 1941

My Darling Joan

I have just received your air mail letter posted lst September and am so glad to hear that you are well again. I was a bit puzzled when I got your cable sent from Clevedon especially as your letter said you were thinking of going on holiday, I just forget where, some other seaside place. I did think perhaps you had changed your mind as to where, of course, never dreaming that you were in a convalescent home!

I am glad you got the photos o.k. I will write to the Elmsdale Club again and thank them for the 10/-, it sure is good of them. I received a letter from brother Len today, he says everything is alright and that he's had a letter from brother Ray. I cannot think why I have not heard from him!

I have enclosed another snap for you. Cheerio for the present and God Bless you, my thoughts are with you always.

Your Ever Loving Husband Tom xxxxxx

Remember me to your Ma & Pa & wish them All the very best for me.

NEWS BACK IN BLIGHTY ... 1st December 1941 – *A points rationing scheme in force.*

Applications for cable forms pour into the Post Room at the Far East Section

Letter to Tom from Joan – "RETURN TO SENDER on Air Ministry Instructions"

432 Belchers Lane
Little Bromwich
B'ham

4th December 1941

My Dear Tom

Here I am again, I have sent you about 12 letters since I last heard from you 5 weeks ago. Have you received my cable I sent a fortnight ago and by the way have you had your parcel yet?

Well, 3 weeks today will be Christmas Day and I do hope it will be the last one we have apart. I must tell you that the Elmsdale Club have sent you a £1 this time for your Christmas box. I have sent a letter thanking them but darling you will send them a line won't you? I do think it is thoughtful of them. Fancy that is £2 you have had since you have been abroad and I have put it in the Bank for you. By the way, is there anything you need? Do write and let me know won't you.

I am going to your house in Sutton this weekend from Saturday afternoon until Sunday evening, so that will be a change. I do hope you will excuse this paper, it is the only kind I can put my hands on. You would be surprised how scarce paper is, it is like everything though.

I have bought a lovely picture of an aircraft made out of metal with an oak back and a chrome chain, it cost me 12/6d, but it is worth it, for it's lovely. It will look very nice over our sideboard.

I shall be able to write more when I hear from you, so please hurry up and write. God Bless you and keep you safe.

From Your Ever Loving Wife Joan xxxxx

p.s. Momm & Dad send their love.

NEWS HEADLINES ... 7th December 1941 – *"360 Japanese planes make surprise attack on home base of US Pacific Fleet at Pearl Harbour".*

Air Mail Postcard from Joan's parents to Tom dated 8th December 1941 – "RETURNED by the Air Ministry"

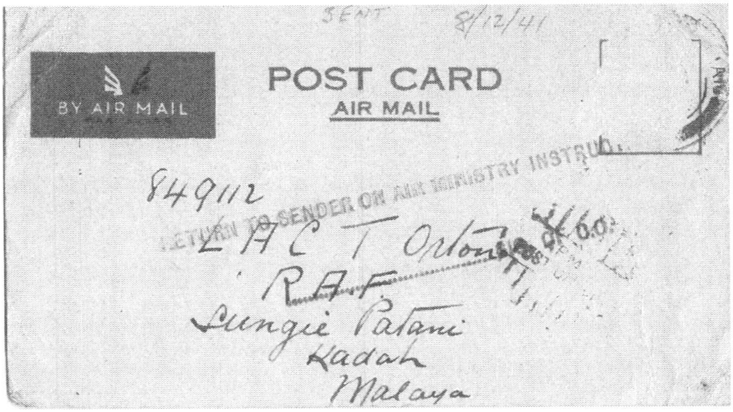
SENT 8/12/41
BY AIR MAIL
POST CARD
AIR MAIL
RETURN TO SENDER ON AIR MINISTRY INSTRU
849112
LAC T Orton
RAF
Sungie Patani
Kadah
Malaya

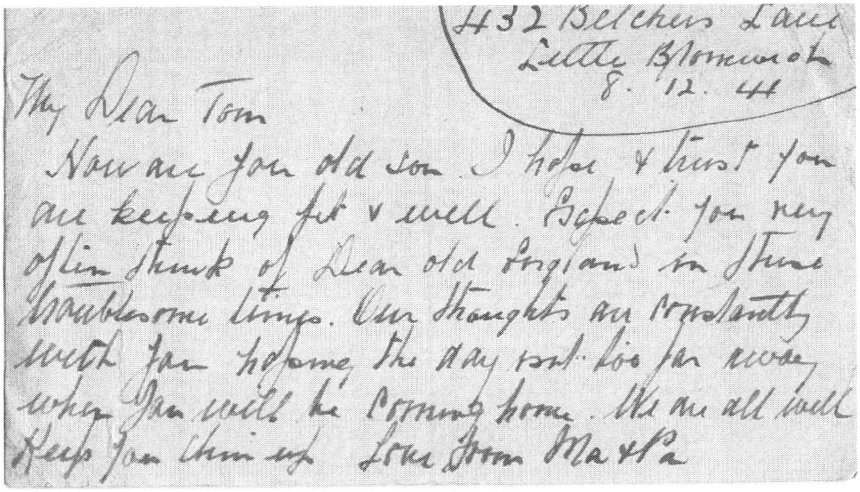
432 Belchers Lane
Little Bromwich
8. 12. 41

My Dear Tom

How are you old son. I hope & trust you are keeping fit & well. Expect you very often think of Dear old England in these troublesome times. Our thoughts are constantly with you hoping the day isn't too far away when you will be coming home. We are all well Keep your chin up Love from Ma & Pa

Chapter 6

BACK AT SELETAR - WORRYING ORDERS & AIR-RAIDS ~ BRITAIN & USA DECLARE WAR ON JAPAN ~

NEWS HEADLINES BACK IN BLIGHTY ... 8th December 1941 – "BRITAIN & USA DECLARE WAR ON JAPAN". *Japanese attack Singapore between 03.30 and 04.00 hrs.*

Tom's story continues ...

8th December 1941 – *(The first Japanese bombs are dropped on Seletar from 6 Japanese planes but there is little damage).*

Back at Seletar, I am duty MT Driver on night duty. We have been given orders from Station Head Quarters that there is to be a complete blackout of the drome. A mobile oxygen unit crew are working in our section and at approximately 03.20 hours I decide to pay them a visit to scrounge a cup of tea. Climbing up the steps on to the Crossley and trailer before entering the compressor, I stand on the platform connected to the trailer and lean back to look up at the clear night sky. I see what I think are 6 Blenheim aircraft flying in formation in the direction of the drome with the searchlights on them sighted around the perimeter. The compressor is very noisy but I manage to shout loud enough to make the Corporal in charge hear me above the din of the compressor and he comes out to have a look. *(I am not long out from blighty and have experienced the air raids prior to leaving – I was stationed at **Filton, Bristol**).* I can definitely hear the anti-aircraft guns open up and the familiar noise of bombs falling even through the noise and vibration of the oxygen plant. Informing the Corporal that bombs have fallen onto the camp, I instinctively jump from the platform to the ground. Taking cover under the vehicle, I feel concussed! The Corporal has not experienced air-raids before as he has been based at Seletar for quite some time. He believes it is night practise ops and does not agree with me that this is for real! In spite of his response, I feel it is my duty to jump into the staff car and race up to Air Head Quarters. On arrival, I find the Sikh armed guard crouching in the storm dyke. The concrete building is splattered with shrapnel (he must have moved in time or he would have been a "stiff"!). I tell the armed guard that these raids are all over and report to the duty officer. I swiftly drive the duty officer around the drome to all the aircraft dispersals and luckily there are no hits on any of them.

The aircraft have been identified as antique Blenheims, Swordfish, Wildebeests and Buffalos, the rest being old Singapore Flying Boats and a couple of Catalinas. The latter are used for routine reconnaissance purposes. We discover that the only hits are the NAAFI and a water main burst. So much for the early hours of December 8th, for at the same time, during these early hours, we hear the news that the **Japanese have raised Sungai Petani (Kedah) and Pearl Harbour.**

Air Mail postcard from Joan to Tom dated 9th December 1941 – "Returned by the Air Ministry"

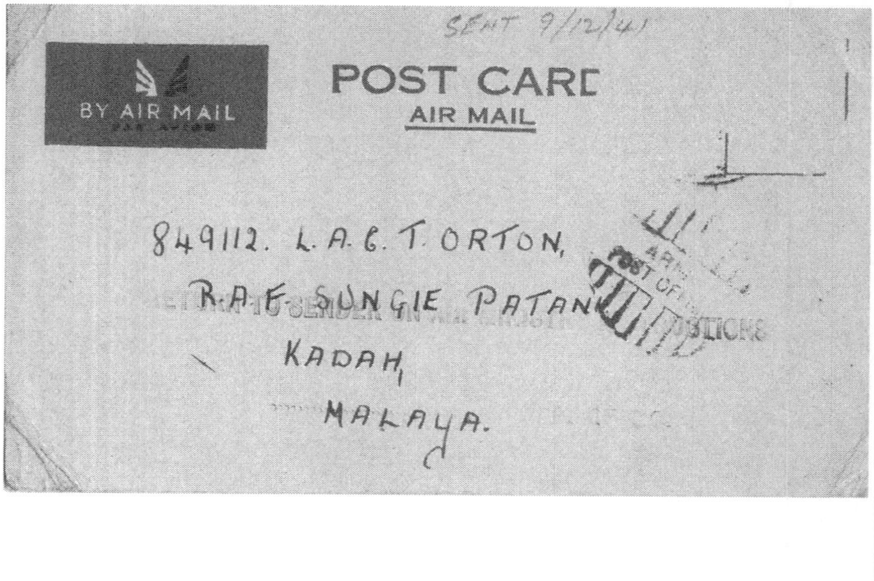

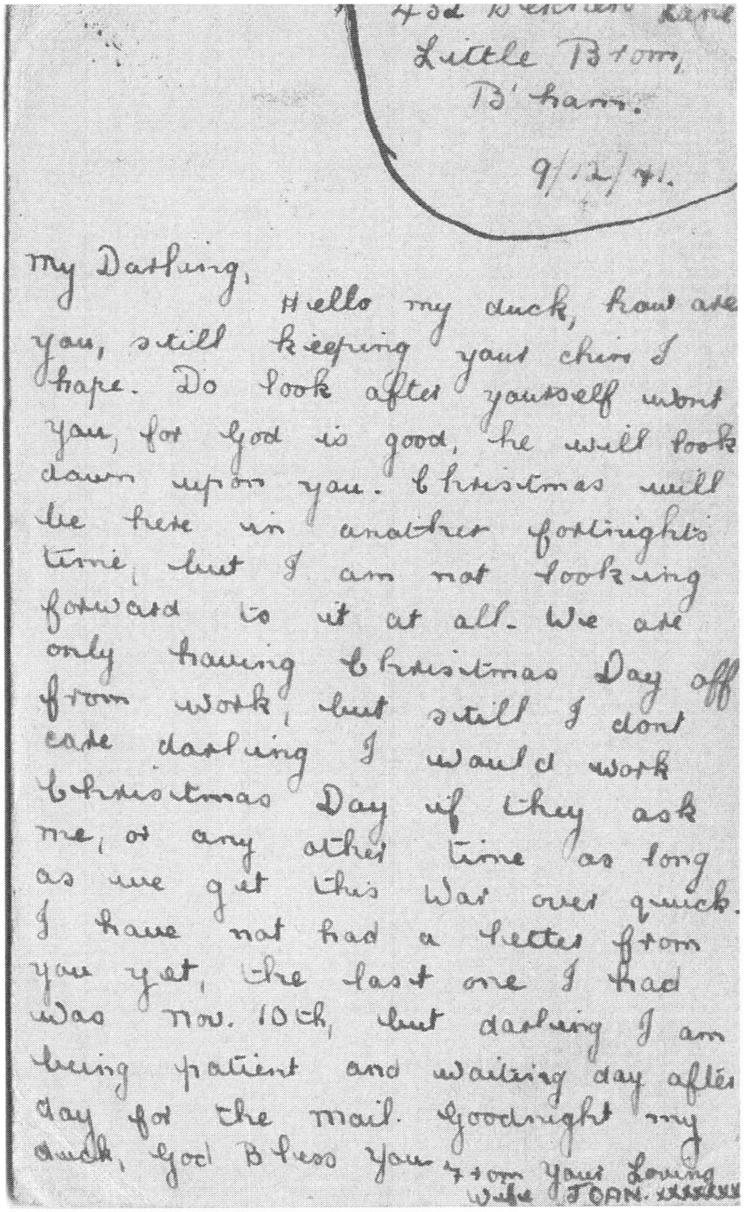

432 Belchers Lane
Little Brom,
B'ham.

9/12/41.

My Darling,

Hello my duck, how are you, still keeping your chin I hope. Do look after yourself won't you, for God is good, he will look down upon you. Christmas will be here in another fortnight's time, but I am not looking forward to it at all. We are only having Christmas Day off from work, but still I don't care darling I would work Christmas Day if they ask me, or any other time as long as we get this War over quick. I have not had a letter from you yet, the last one I had was Nov. 10th, but darling I am being patient and waiting day after day for the mail. Goodnight my duck, God Bless You from your Loving Wife JOAN. xxxxxxx

Letters from Joan to Tom – returned by Air Ministry

432 Belchers Lane
Little Bromwich
B'ham

UNDATED

My Darling Hubby

I have not heard from you for 5 weeks but I hope to soon have a bundle of letters from you, Everyone I have shown my pyjamas to have properly fallen for them and would like to buy them off me, but darling I would not part with them for anything in the world, or even dream of it!

Dolly from the Broadway said "Your husband is a nice looking fellow and he always looks smart. I always remember him asking for beer and telling me there was a big shortage in Bristol". It was so nice to hear her talk about you that way but everybody does - I am so proud of you. Do you remember that water bottle you bought me off Sutton Parade last winter? It is such a comfort to me now. I must close now as it is nearly black out time. God Bless you and Keep you Safe.

From Your Ever Loving Wife Joan xxxxxx

432 Belchers Lane
Little Bromwich
B'ham

14th December 1941

My Darling

Well, here I am again darling still writing and writing, but receiving no letters from you.

I spent the weekend at your house and saw Alf Osborne in the Elmsdale Club. I have put the £1 Christmas Box from the Club into the Bank for you with the other. Please let me know if you need anything, do you need any money? By the way the Elmsdale Club have invited me to their New Years Eve Party, I do so wish you were here so that we could go together. Both families are in the best of health, including your little wife. I went to town last Saturday to try and get some shoes. I was there from 11.15 a.m. until 5.15 p.m. and then I did not get any! Our holiday break at work will be Christmas Day only as we are in Boxing Day for stocktaking.

By the sound of things I shall be in the A.T.S. soon! I do know that if I could come over to you, I would join the W.A.A.F. tomorrow. When they sound that last all clear, how happy we will be and what a day it will be. I am going to write you an Air Mail Card now so cheerio for about 5 minutes as I am about to put some coal on the fire. God Bless you and protect you.

From your Ever Loving Wife Joan xxxx

Air Mail Postcard sent from Joan to Tom dated 14th December 1941 – returned by Air Ministry

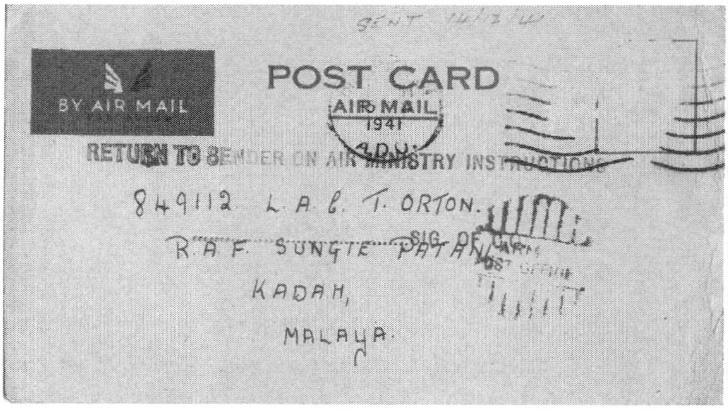

SENT 14/12/41

BY AIR MAIL

POST CARD

AIR MAIL 1941

RETURN TO SENDER ON AIR MINISTRY INSTRUCTIONS

849112 L.A.C. T. ORTON.
R.A.F. SUNGIE PATANI
KADAH,
MALAYA.

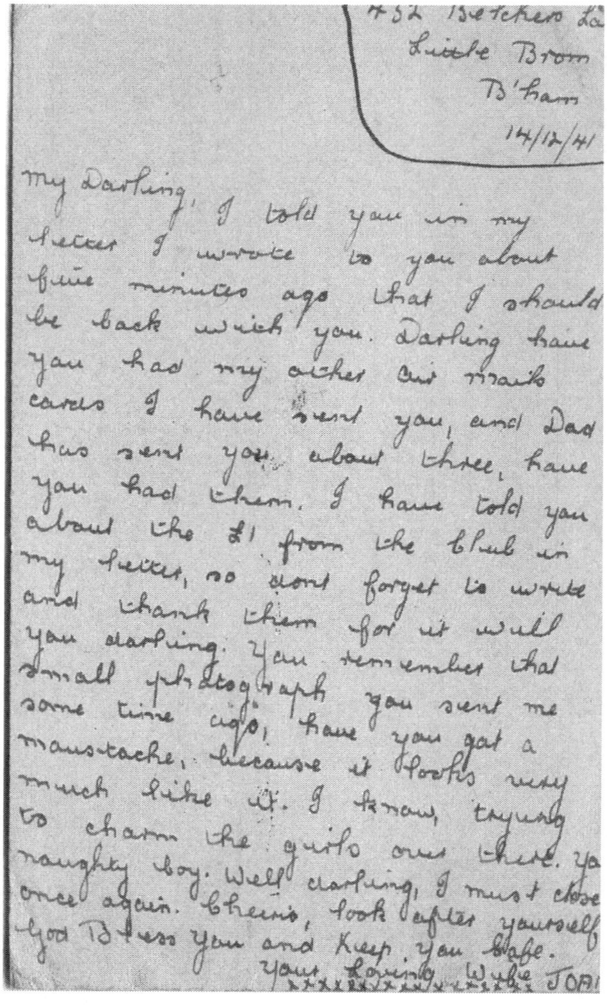

432 Belchers La
Little Brom
B'ham
14/12/41

My Darling,
I told you in my letter I wrote to you about five minutes ago that I should be back with you. Darling have you had my other air mail cards I have sent you, and Dad has sent you about three, have you had them. I have told you about the £1 from the Club in my letter, so dont forget to write and thank them for it will you darling. You remember that small photograph you sent me some time ago, have you got a moustache, because it looks very much like it. I know, trying to charm the girls out there. You naughty boy. Well darling, I must close once again. Cheerio, look after yourself God Bless You and Keep You Safe.
Your Loving Wife JOAN
xxxxxxxxxxxxxxxxxxx

Letter from Tom's brother Fred to Joan

No. 7264089 L/Sgt F Orton
Military Hospital
Gibralta

21st December 1941

Dear Joan

First of all, I must thank you for the card which arrived a short while ago. It is rather a long time since I last wrote you but you will most probably realise that, as so very little of general interest happens here, it is difficult to concoct letters regularly. Of course I am always being told off by Mom and May, so I think I had better start considering a turn over of the page in the new year. A couple of letters arrived here from Tom a fortnight ago in which he said your letters are reaching him o.k.

I hear you are having rather a rough winter at home, well believe me I would prefer to face all the blizzards in creation, rainstorms, snowstorms, hailstorms, lipstorms or any other old storm, to watching (which I must admit are very beautiful and picturesque) the sunsets over Spain. Quite a lot of us are still wearing our khaki drill as it is sometimes a little too warm for service dress, especially when going for a walk. In peace time I am sure you would love to come here for a holiday, it never rains in the summer, plenty of bathing at Catalan Bay, trips into Spain, including La Linea, Algiers etc, then one can take a trip across the water to the north coast of Africa. Tangiers is a very interesting spot with its old market square, mosque ad Sultans Palace. Ask Mother to show you the photographs I sent home, they include snaps of all these places, I'm sure you will be interested. Before I came here, I ridiculed any artist who had painted a background of blue mountains, numerous tinges of gold, yellow and white for the sky but I look upon that man now as a traveller also, because it is to be seen here, it is almost an impossibility to describe it. Unfortunately, having seen nothing but these sights for the last 3 years and not been allowed any further than the Frontier at North Front and certainly not over to Tangier, we are all tired of this station and would willingly change for some remote spot in England, if it were possible. If I do come home within the next 6 months, on leave, which is quite possible, I shall certainly have a lot to tell you all. Well Joan, I must close for now. Please give my love to all, hope you have a jolly good time at Christmas. If we were all with you at the next I assure you it will be 100% better.

Cheerio for now, write soon.
Your Loving B in Law Fred xxxxx

Letter from Joan to Tom – "Returned by the Air Ministry"

432 Belchers Lane
Little Bromwich
B'ham

21st December 1941

My Darling Hubby

Well here I am again, writing you a letter as I promised on my card. I have been so worried these last 7 weeks, not hearing from you but when mom rang me up at work on Friday morning and told me I had 3 letters, why I couldn't get home quick enough. To think it will be 12 months next month we have been married.

I have been studying your letters and your handwriting. Darling you seem so different but of course I expect it is the heat etc. People do pull my leg about you being out there saying things like "Oh your husband is alright, there are plenty of charming women there". Fancy you being frozen in that picture house in "P", I thought it was very hot out there. Cheerio for a bit, keep your chin up, God Bless you and protect you.

From Your Ever Loving Wife Joan xxxx

P.S. Mom & Dad send their love

~ CHRISTMAS 1941 ~

NEWS HEADLINES ... 25th December 1941 – *"Hong Kong Surrenders to Japanese"*

Letters from Joan to Tom – returned by Air Ministry

432 Belchers Lane
Little Bromwich
B'ham

25th December 1941 (Christmas Day)

My Darling

As you can see by the date, it is Christmas Day, and what a Christmas? There's nothing to buy, no presents, no beer, or anything but we mustn't grumble as long as we reach Victory and I have you back again for good.

After 7 weeks, I have received 3 letters from you but they were from September 16, 19 and 23rd. The 2 girls in the office bought me a diary - the one girl, Mrs Stockton, says her husband is in Egypt, she is very fortunate though as she gets 3 or 4 letters every week, isn't she lucky? I am going to your house on Saturday for the weekend. Oh, and mom has bought us some forks as well. I have received a card from Gran "To my dear grand-daughter and my dear Tommy". She thinks the world of you my darling, we are always talking about you. I do wish I could send a cable, but I can't yet, the Post Office say that they can't get them through. I hope and pray to God that you are sitting with us next Christmas. Cheerio, God Bless you and protect you.

From your Ever Loving Wife Joan xxxxxxxx

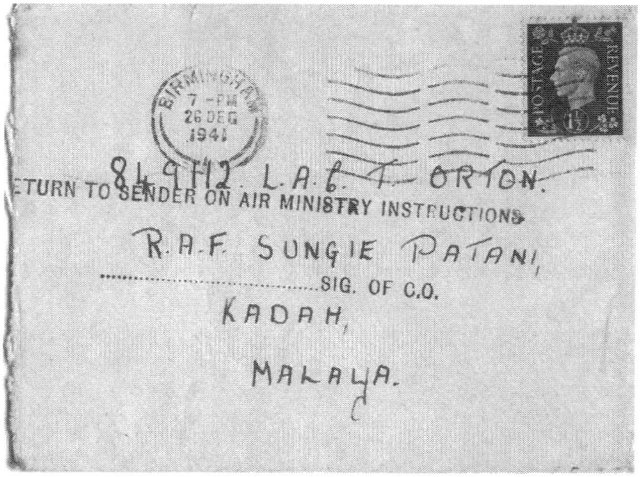

432 Belchers Lane
Little Bromwich
B'ham

29th December 1941

My Darling

I do wish I could hear from you although I know it isn't your fault. Don't forget, but I know you won't my darling, it is our first wedding anniversary next Sunday.

I spent the weekend at your house in Sutton and I went to a Christmas party at the Elmsdale Club with your dad and gran. Alf Lewis gave the women a free gin and pep and the men a free ale. Alf looked quite posh wearing a black coat and striped trousers. You would have smiled at Mr Holloway dressed up as a woman with a painted face and Mr Cooper dressed as a sheik. Alf gave a speech with a special mention to the chaps who were abroad, which made me upset and shed a few tears. Don't forget to write to the Club and thank them for the £1 for Christmas.

Are you hearing from me often as I write to you nearly every night. I am sure our prayers will be answered very soon. God Bless you and protect you.

From Your Ever Loving Wife Joan (waiting patiently) xxxxx

p.s. A girl in the office gave me a lovely BLUE table runner for Christmas.

432 Belchers Lane
Little Bromwich
B'ham

1st January 1942

My Dear Tom

Happy New Year to you darling. I have just said to mom, "To think this time last year we had Tom with us". Do you remember when you took me to town in all that snow and bought me those lovely fur back gloves? I had a letter from you this morning dated 30/9/41 oh and a Christmas card from your brother Fred.

I am going to your house again tomorrow for the weekend, if I am well enough, as I am on the panel again. I don't know, I have only been at this new job for 2 months and have to crock up again. I expect you are thinking to yourself, well I married a poor thing, she is always bad! I think I have been in a draft somewhere, I have bronchial colic. Oh the pain has been awful but don't you get worrying because I shall be alright in another week I hope.

I went to the Hippodrome with mom to see Vera Lynn, she was lovely, they call her the Forces Sweetheart. Do you ever hear her on a Sunday night at 9.20? She sings to the Forces. I nearly forgot to tell you, Gran sent us a New Year's card as well as a Christmas card. You say in your letter you have my photo on your locker. Why, I have got one on the mantelpiece, one in the front room, you remember the one in the silver frame that we bought from Lewis's in Birmingham, and another one in the bedroom. It is so nice to keep looking at you, it doesn't matter which room I go into, you are there. God Bless you (KEEP SMILING).

From Your Ever Loving Wife Joan xxxxx

432 Belchers Lane
Little Bromwich
B'ham

5th January 1942

My Dearest

I have written to Fred thanking him for the Christmas card which was such a surprise as I have been waiting for an answer to my letter I sent to him last March.

I have just returned home from your house after a lovely weekend. Your mom has been very good to me. Yesterday was Sunday and she sent Leslie (Tom's younger brother) *chasing all around the chemists for some Thermogene and she rubbed it into my ribs for about 10 minutes. I think I told you in my last letter that I am on the panel again with bronchial colic but it I shouldn't tell you my troubles all the time.*

Your dad made me laugh on Saturday night, he said "Listen to me my wench ... we'll stay in one of the nights when you come over and you can help me to write to the lads because I am "B" if I can put a letter together". You can guess what the "B" stands for can't you? He is a devil! Oh, and he told me to tell you that John Bennett is getting married on Jan 6th. Goodnight my dear, God Bless you and protect you.

From Your Ever Loving Wife Joan xxxxxxxx

432 Belchers Lane
Little Bromwich
B'ham

8th January 1942

My Dear Tom

I received 2 letters from you this morning dated 3rd and 4th of October, well the one was the photograph. You look so nice with a moustache. How long have you had it? I was wondering is it still ginger? I sent you a cable only an hour ago and expect you will get it a long time before this letter. The G.P.O. have just started to let us send them again, so you will be getting one from me every fortnight. Do try and send me one if you can. I have asked you in one or two of my letters, if you need anything so don't forget to write and tell me. Please don't get worrying over me still being in B'ham, I am quite alright, everything is lovely and quiet.

You seem to be worried over the postmarks on the 2 cables I sent last August. I did write and tell you all about going to a convalescent home for a fortnight at Clevedon. I know the one cable had a Clevedon postmark on it and the other one Weston-Super-Mare. There were 4 girls and myself, we spent a day at Weston, it is only 1/10d from Clevedon and I sent you a cable from there. We had to be in by 8 o'clock. I got friendly with a girl in the home that came from London, she has suffered so badly through the air raids, she has got scars all over her. She has written to me asking me to visit for a weekend, she is married with 2 children. Her husband is also abroad.

I am sorry to hear that you are so browned off but I am sure we shall soon be back together again. Keep your chin up my duck. Cheerio for a bit and God Bless You.

From Your Ever Loving Wife Joan xxxxxxxxxxxx

p.s. Mom & Dad send their love

My thoughts are always with you

432 Belchers Lane
Little Bromwich
B'ham

12th January 1942

My Darling

I had a letter from Fred this morning, it was a surprise because it is the first time I have heard from him since last March, with the exception of the Christmas card of course. He tells me there is a possible chance of him coming home in about 6 months time. I can't wait until the day when you write and tell me you are coming home.

I am still on the old box as the doctor won't sign me off, he said what is the use of going back to work half better.

Your mom rang me last Friday saying she has a parcel for me, I don't know what it is, all she said was that she wants me to have it as soon as possible because I shall feel the benefit of it.

I am so worried not being able to work with no money being saved again! I was at home 6 months before and have only been at this new job 2 months and here I am at home again! You must be fed up with me being bad all the time? I wonder if you can guess how much I have saved, do write and tell me but don't shock me too much. I shall really have to close as my feet are just like two blocks of ice and I must try and get to the fire. God Bless you.

From Your Ever Loving (Wife) Joan xxxxxxxxxxxxxxxx

Mom & Dad send their love

Always thinking of you

Chapter 7

"TOM'S BIRTHDAY" AND THE "JAPANESE BOMBERS"
Seletar, Singapore

The RAF base at Seletar, Singapore became a target of carpet bombing by the Japanese. Tom's 151 Maintenance Unit remained in Seletar until the end of January 1942.

Tom's story continues ...

17th January 1942 – "my 28th birthday". **Singapore is being raided by Japanese bombers daily.** They appear every morning at approximately 00.11 hours. Always seventeen bombers in tight formation dropping the lot in pattern style. The siren has sounded and we do not know whether the target is Seletar, the docks, naval base or any other part of the island, *(but we shall get our share).* The "Navy O's", the name we have nicknamed their fighters, are a light radial engine, carrier based fighter, which are far superior to any aircraft the RAF can put into combat against them. I must say our pilots put up a good show even with the inferior aircraft they have at their disposal.

It soon becomes evident that the Japs have air supremacy over the island and the MT Section is given orders to transport all the stores and equipment to the docks. We are also given orders to clear the ZMU bomb dump. There are hundreds of bombs which require transporting to the docks and we are busy working around the clock. We have been told that these bombs are destined for some place where they can be used against the Japs if aircraft become available. We are promised these aircraft are on the way.

Letters returned to Joan by Air Ministry

432 Belchers Lane
Little Bromwich
B'ham

19th January 1942

My Darling Tom

Have you received my cables? I wish I could hear from you. Your mother has kindly given me a parcel of 2 woollen vests, and 2 pairs of woollen trunks, you know like knickers. I was ever so pleased as they are just what I wanted. I went to the Hippodrome last Tuesday with mom and sister Marjorie to see Evelyn Doll. Have you ever seen her? She was with Sam Brown and Max Bacon. I received a letter from Fred and I have written back telling him off about not writing to you. My sister Brenda has written and asked for your address again so you will be hearing from her. She always asks about you every time she writes to me every fortnight. Cheerio for a bit. God Bless you and keep you safe.

From Your Ever Loving Wife Joan xxxxx

432 Belchers Lane
Little Bromwich
B'ham

20th January 1942

My Darling Tom

I received your letter dated 22nd October and posted 24th. You ask me to write to you, why my sweet I write to you as regular as clockwork and send you cables. I can't understand it at all! Have you received any of my air mail cards? I have sent you about a dozen. Please don't get worrying over me, as I am alright and everybody else in both families. I can quite understand though as I am in the same boat, worrying myself to death over you.

Fancy the married men being allowed home before the single men but I have a feeling I shall see you before the next 12 months are over. It seems as though you have been away from me for 10 years instead of 10 months and when you do come home to me, I won't let you out of my sight.

God Bless you and Keep your chin up.

From Your Ever Loving Wife Joan xxxxxx

Letter from Tom's brother Fred to Joan:

No. 7264089 Sgt F. Orton
Military Hospital
Gibraltar

25th January 1942

Dear Joan

Thanks a million for your very welcome letter. I was very pleased to hear from you and that you are alright. I was surprised that you have not received my letter and photograph which I sent very soon after receiving yours in March last. Just another for Davy Jones I suppose – never mind I have enclosed another – not too good and not too bad considering it was taken by Gibraltar's best photographer. I told him he would make a darn fine pavement artist in London (he was not amused).

There is nothing unusual to report here – we are in the middle of winter (?) with the sun shining slightly outside and it is not cold at all. I think we may call our winter the equivalent to an English spring. In fact all we need to create a small paradise is a little freedom – but is that not practically one hundred per cent of our needs these days? I suppose we have to relinquish that when confined to a Garrison.

Hooray!! The post corporal has just arrived with a letter from Tom, dated 8th September, 4 months ago, not bad. He is well, and tells me all about the mosquitoes as big as butterflies flying around in formation. Gee – some mossies!!! I write very regularly to him these days as we were great pals before I left and I am longing to see him again.

I had a chance for some leave about 3 weeks ago but at the same time they told me I should lose my promotion to full Sergeant if I took it, so I accepted the stripes. My second chance will come round in 5 months time. May and I are definitely going to get married when I do come (scared!!)

Well Joan – if you don't mind me making a suggestion – why not tell me a little about yourself and a photograph would be very acceptable. I have the one of the marriage but would like one to go with those of mother, Ray, Tom, Len etc: I have a big space to cover with photographs here you know. As for myself – well you have probably been told all about me. The black sheep you know. Too fond of the girls (don't tell May that) and of leaving home.

Well Joan, I do not think there is anymore I can write just now.

Cheerio for now & all the best Your Loving Brother in Law Fred xx

Letters from Joan to Tom – Returned by Air Ministry

432 Belchers Lane
Little Bromwich
B'ham

26th January 1942

My Darling Tom

Are you receiving my letters now? Honestly you have got me worried stiff, especially after receiving a letter from you last week saying you had not had a letter from me since July 16th. I can't understand it at all as I write to you every night and sometimes twice.

Gran was telling me that you received a letter from her dated August, well why can't mine come through like that? Oh dear, oh dear I am trying to be a Briton and keep my chin up, I do hope you are too. Have you received my letter telling you about the £1 they gave to me from the Elmsdale Club to send to you for Christmas? Have you received my Christmas card? Mom and Dad sent you one as well, and my cables.

How wonderful to think this time next year we may be both sitting by the fire in our own little home. I do hope so. Mom and Dad send their fondest love and tell you to keep your chin up. My thoughts are always with you ALWAYS. Goodnight my loved one, until tomorrow, God Bless you.

From Your Ever Loving Wife Joan xxxxx

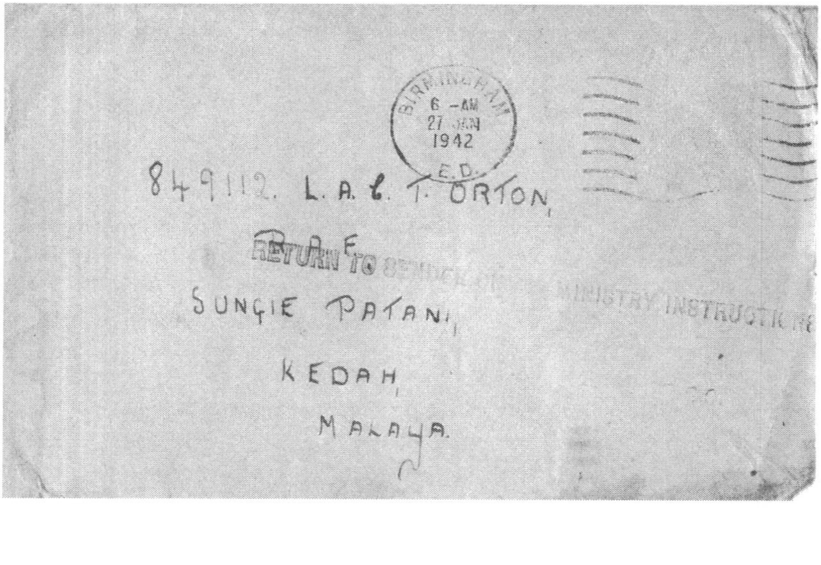

432 Belchers Lane
Little Bromwich
B'ham

27th January 1942

My Darling Tom

I received a letter from you today dated 24/11/41. I wish you would not keep saying write as much as you can because I write every night. I would not neglect you for the world.

By the way, I am 4 letters short, I have received 24 instead of 28 but I expect they will come through in due course. I only wish I had numbered mine now but you can tell by the dates can't you? Won't it be heavenly when we are together again not having to bother keep writing letters? I have been counting your letters this morning and I have got 105, besides the telegrams.

Len and Gladys are going to have a baby due in July, or twins because of Len being a twin.

Please excuse my scribble, only I am writing this on my knee by the fire. Mom and Dad tell you to still keep your chin up and your head down. We will have such a party when you come home, which won't be long. I have written to Fred and told him off about not writing to you. God Bless You.

Your Ever Loving Wife Joan xxxxxxx

Chapter 8

REPAIR & SALVAGE UNIT ABOARD SS PERAK
"Leaving Singapore for Palembang (South Sumatra)"

Sumatra is a large island west of Java Island. Palembang is a port city and the capital of South Sumatra.

Tom's story continues ......

Monday, 2nd February 1942 – We have been working through the day and night for some time now. This morning, I am included in those of the **MT Section of 151 MU** (Maintenance Unit) to parade for orders and the object of this exercise is to form a repair and salvage unit (RSU). **Bert Melluish** and myself are detailed as two MTMs and we are put with Aircraft Fitters, Riggers, Armourers and other personnel. We pack our kit, load it on to transport, then Bert and myself drive to the docks, together with **Flight Lieutenant Burnett** and two Warrant Officers plus NCO's in charge.

Boarding a small coastal vessel the **SS Perak**, it is not long before the familiar sound of the air-raid siren is heard. The Japs are early this morning but the Captain does not hang about. As we leave Keppel Harbour, Singapore we find that we have the company of **Group Captain Walkington** on board, Officer in charge of Seletar. We also discover that the SS Perak is loaded with naval torpedoes which have been taken from the naval base. Due to lack of space in the holds on the ship, the only accommodation available for the unit is up on deck. We are aware that the Jap bombers are over the docks but I think, owing to the fact that the SS Perak is only a small vessel, we are not one of their targets – they are after the larger ships, of which there are a number, including the **Empire Star**, *(which we later learn has been attacked with troops aboard).*

5th February 1942 – we arrive at Palembang, South Sumatra and tie up at the quayside. No orders are given but **Group Captain Walkington** disembarks. Still aboard, nightfall arrives and it looks as though we may spend the night exposed and sleeping on the deck. We notice quite a large ship nearby which I think is named **"Whang Pu"**. The holds on this ship are empty so we are allowed to go aboard and sleep in the holds for the night. It is definitely for the best as we are having a heavy downpour of rain.

Letter from Joan to Tom – returned by the Air Ministry

432 Belchers Lane
Little Bromwich
B'ham

5th February 1942

My Dearest Tom

Have you received my cable sent a fortnight ago and are you getting my mail better now? I only wish I could get a cable from you darling saying you are fit and well, oh it is a worry.

My sister Brenda wrote to me asking if she could borrow your photographs, so I sent her the eight that you have sent to me since you have been away and she has sent them back in order. She says she likes the one where you are standing with your hands on your hips the best, that is my favourite too.

Well my darling, I am lost for words it is awful really to say it, but I can't say any more only I still love you with all my heart, so I will say cheerio for a bit my sweet, God Bless you and keep you safe.

From Your Ever Loving Wife Joan xxxxxxxxxx

p.s. Mom & Dad send their love

Chapter 9

~ "THE FALL OF SINGAPORE" ~ (Surrender of JAVA to the Japs) Invasion of PALEMBANG, Sumatra - Handing over our Arms

NEWS HEADLINES... 6th February 1942 – *The first Japanese air raid on P.1 at Palembang, Sumatra. Shortly after **Amboina** fell to the Japanese many Australians were massacred by the Japanese.*

8th February 1942 – *"23,000 Japanese soldiers attack **Singapore**". A Japanese invasion fleet were sailing towards Palembang, Sumatra (oilfield where oil in this region was most abundant)*

Tom's story continues ...

9th February 1942 – Palembang has its first air raid warning. We are still on the "SS Perak" and we witness the **Japs bomb Aerodrome P.I.** not far away. *(There were 2 Allied airfields in Sumatra. **P.1 (Pangkalan, Benteng, South Sumatra)** and the secret airbase **P.2 in Prabumulih**).*

We are sent to **LAHQ Schwartz Hotel**, Palembang. **Bert** and myself are posted to **Aerodrome P.2**. with the RSU (Repair & Salvage Unit), travelling approximately 70 kilometres south by motor transport.

Aerodrome P.1. is a Dutch drome with a turf runway. Aircraft include a small number of hurricanes which are the remnants of those we unloaded from a large merchantman at the naval base prior to our departure from Singapore. We have been told that these hurricanes are too heavily armed and it is believed that they had originally been destined for the Middle East. There is also talk that the air intake is not suitable, as these are designed specifically for not taking in the sand. There is definitely no sand here!

Letter to Tom (nicknamed "Mono") from Brother Fred – returned undelivered

No. 7264089 Sgt F. Orton
Military Hospital
Gibraltar

10th February 1942

Dear Mono

Many thanks for the letter you wrote on October 22nd, it arrived today. As a lot has happened around your portion of the globe since that letter was written and that my letter, if bearing your address as I know it, would stand little chance of reaching you, I have addressed it c/ o Joan, hoping that she will have heard from you since the evacuation.

You gave me a ticking off for not having written you. Well, you rather surprise me as I was thinking how pleased you would be to receive a reply in answer to those you have written with a few odd ones thrown in. My last one of many was posted on lst January, you have probably received that by now, then I sent a photograph of myself about 4 months ago and one of our Sgt's Mess members & self, 3months ago – have you got those yet?

Yes Mono I am still on the Rock and according to your few words about Singapore being a 2 year station its looks as though you may beat me to it. I may be home for Xmas but that remains to be seen. I have 3 years overseas service in on April 23rd and Gib is still supposed to be a 4 year station so unless they change their minds it looks as though I am doomed for another 12 months or so here. As I mentioned in a letter to you a short while ago, they offered me leave but at the same time pointed out that I should not be promoted to Sgt: as well so I refused the offer and was made up a few days later. It takes 6 months to obtain a more substantive rank, that means if I leave here before that period elapses, I have to revert to Corporal again – so I prefer to wait. But when that 6 months is up Boy will I worry 'em for that leave!!

I have not heard from Ray for some time now – not since he left the Bahrain, still I suppose a letter from him will arrive one day. I have written to him. What do you mean by "the many bombs which have pounded on the Rock?" Why we have almost forgotten what a ruddy bomb looks like – and have not received a present from Jerry since 1940 – that was the time when we gave him more than he bargained for and we are ready to repeat the treatment. I laughed like hell as I watched one "B...." bale out and float gracefully to a watery grave and there's plenty of room in the same place for more of 'em.

By permission of the R.A.F. here, I am taking a flight very soon – it is to be a "test flight" I believe – hope those mechanics have done the job properly!! I ain't aiming to get my feet wet yet awhile.

I am going to get a ring made in Spain on which will be a photograph of yourself, actually it will be reproduced in miniature from that photograph of you in uniform, and I shall send it to your wife. I have one of May and have sent her one of myself. If I can get one of Joan (I have asked her) I will get one made for you and keep it until you return. I would not risk sending it to you, it may go the same way as I believe my letters to you have gone (to Davy Jones' locker). Well Mono I guess that is all for now except – I am as fit as a fiddle.

Cheerio   Your Loving Brother Fred

Letters to Tom from Joan – returned undelivered

432 Belchers Lane
Little Bromwich
B'ham

10th February 1942

My Darling

I received a letter from you this morning dated 14/11/41, airmail, and the one I had a fortnight ago was dated 24/11/41, so it just proves how they get mixed up on the way. The one I had this morning smells ever so fusty! I am still waiting patiently to hear of some recent news from you.

I have just said to mother, "I will go and have my photograph taken tomorrow" to send to you, so you can start looking out for one from me. I shall have it taken in my new coat and then you can see whether you like it. To think in another month's time, it will be 12 months since I last saw you, if you remember you went back off leave on 10/3/41, it's such a long while.

Your mother rang me last night and mentioned your friend Alan Guest, who you were with. His mother received a cable from him recently and I am really envious. I keep on to you about sending me a cable but I know you would definitely send me one if you could.

By the way, I am sending your dad a Valentine card for a laugh. I hope he doesn't find out who has sent it because I have written (from your lover), he is lovely though isn't he?

I had to smile, when I read your letter about the monkeys, whatever you do, don't bring one home with you! I don't mind a bird, or a camel, but not a monkey, you can see one when you look at me!

Keep your fingers crossed darling and hurry up home to me, as I am fed up of being a grass widow and sleeping on my own. I don't know what I would have done if you had not bought me that water bottle, oh it is a comfort. Keep your chin up, God Bless You and protect you.

From Your Ever Loving Wife Joan xxxxxx

p.s. Mom & Dad send their love.

432 Belchers Lane
Little Bromwich
B'ham

12th February 1942

My Darling Tom

Here is the photograph I promised you. I have never seen so many people having their photographs taken, I had to wait an hour and a quarter, and now it is a failure. Just look at my legs, like drum sticks aren't they and my bony knees and the photographer didn't even give me time to put my coat straight or anything.

I do so wish I could send you a parcel, don't think I am neglecting you but they have stopped us sending them. I very often look at the things in your drawer and and clean your shoes and slippers for you. I did notice on one of your slippers that there are still Bill's teeth marks where he went for you that day when you teased him, do you remember?

Have you heard from sister Brenda yet? Everything is still lovely and quiet here, thank goodness. God Bless You and keep you safe.

From Your Ever Loving Wife Joan xxxx

NEWS HEADLINES ... 14th February – *8.00 a.m. Palembang air raid wardens warned of big Japanese attack.*

Tom's story continues ...

14th February 1942 – What aircraft we have available are operating against the **Jap convoys attacking Sumatra.** All available Blenheims (British light bombers designed and built by the Bristol Aeroplane Company) are being used around the clock with very little fighter support to stem off the Jap invasion. Rumour is that they have taken **Aerodrome P.1.** by means of waves of paratroops and the main road from Palembang is being manned with British artillery. I am driving taking supplies of rations from the drome up to the British artillery as they are not getting any whatsoever. We find out that the Japs have not as yet located **Aerodrome P.2.** owing to the fact that the Dutch have done such a good job of camouflaging it so well and there is no visibility of any building from the air.

Our unit is now billeted and we are sleeping rough in an old rice barn at the nearby village of **Lambak (North Sumatra)**. We hear another rumour that the Jap paratroops have been wiped out.

NEW HEADLINES ... 15th February 1942 – *"THE FALL OF SINGAPORE" (Britain's Key Naval Base).*

Tom's story continues ...

SALVAGING THREE CRASHED BLENHEIMS, DITCHING WEAPONS, TRAIN TO OOSTHAVEN, SUMATRA (Island West of Java)

15th February 1942 – Three Blenheims have crashed on the drome upon their return from operating against the invasion convoy during the night. Needless to say, there is plenty of work for our R.S.U. (Repair & Salvage Unit) party. Word comes through that the Japs have got a foothold in at Palembang, Sumatra. Orders are given for all personnel to pack and stand by to be on the move. I am on the list as a driver to transport personnel to a railway station, five or six kilometres south. The orders for our party are given "All equipment and unserviceable aircraft are to be destroyed" which are carried out by other members of our party as I am responsible for transporting the rest to the railway station where they will be taken south for **Oosthaven, Sumatra.** Having made quite a number of trips back and forth to the railway station, I have now cleared the drome of all personnel and other members of our unit have more or less blasted everything up on the drome. A necessary preventative measure against the Japanese which has been done most methodically. It is now my responsibility to transport the final remaining members of our party, which takes two trips. Some ride on the roof of the old wagon, which now has an inside rear tyre flat from overloading.

Arriving at the railway station with the last load, the station master informs us that the last available engine has been used. Bad news for us as it appears that we are stranded! Thankfully not for long though as a line of goods vans have been spotted sitting in the railway siding. Our Officers in charge suggest we unload all the contents onto the side of the track in case the station master is correct in saying that if there is any possible chance of getting an engine back to the junction, he would make sure it happens. We proceed to empty the vans containing cases of tea, tinned milk etc, hundreds of rolls of cotton and other materials, plus tons of rice in bags. It is not long after finishing this task that we hear the promising sound of a train engine in the distance.

The engine is quickly coupled up to the empty vans. We are now aboard heading south in the direction of Oosthaven, which is quite a distance at the southern tip of Sumatra. The engine is typically fired by wood which necessitates a number of stops to replenish the bunker and also to take on board water for the boiler. We take advantage of these stops to stretch our legs as we are travelling in confined and very cramped conditions in the goods vans. I take the opportunity to make use of my previous experience of steam operating and make up a reasonably good "brew" of tea salvaged from the unloading job. I get the boiling water from the injector of the engine, which the rest of the unit are reluctant to try at first and I partake in the first drink to prove to the others that we will not be poisoned! I am pleased to say that all agree it is a good "brew".

151 MAINTENANCE UNIT DISBANDED – 153 becomes my new unit ... Destination BATAVIA (now Jakarta)

16th February 1942 – We finally arrive at Oosthaven, Sumatra after a very long journey. We noticed on the way in how the roads were lined with very expensive looking cars left abandoned by the Dutch Europeans. This indicates to us that the evacuation has been going on for some time.

We board one of the boats (it would appear that we are some of the last to do so), which is to take us across the **Sunda Straits** (separating Sumatra from Java) **to Batavia (Jakarta) on the North coast of Java** (Capital of the Dutch East Indies). There are units of the navy on escort duty.

Next morning we arrive at the docks in Batavia and disembark. We then board a train to take us from the docks to the city.

There are several allied headquarters in Batavia situated in large schools with the **Scholar Rahjah, Mr Cornelius** and various others. Our **151 M.U.** is taken to the **King William III School.** After cleaning ourselves up, which we certainly need, we are ordered on parade for inspection and briefing, joining up with many more RAF personnel. The first order given is that all men, who have completed their tour period on duty in the Far East Command, are to fall out in one party. The rest are to remain and reform in rank. We, the remaining, are given orders that **151 Maintenance Unit is now disbanded. 153 M.U. is now to be my new unit and we are to be posted to Yogyjakarta (a city South Java).** (It is believed that the other part of the original **151 M.U. are to go to India).** The time expired men are posted to the **"SS Orcades"** which is lying at the docks. SS Orcades was in our convoy on leaving "blighty", she has probably covered many more thousands of miles on convoy trips since May 1941 having left when the convoy split up in the Indian Ocean.

Letters from Joan to Tom – returned undelivered

432 Belchers Lane
Little Bromwich
B'ham

17th February 1942

My Darling Tom

Hello my sweet, how are you? I went to your house last Saturday to fetch some of my things back as they have worried me thinking they are in your mother's way. I went to the Cup with Gran for her 70th birthday. I have just been to try and buy a broom and do you think I can get one? I can't get one for love nor money. I am just waiting patiently to have another letter from you, one after December 6th. Goodnight my loved one and God Bless You.

Your Ever Loving Wife Joan xxxxxx

432 Belchers Lane
Little Bromwich
B'ham

19th February 1942

My Darling

Oh my goodness, can you possibly send me a cable? It would be such a relief to hear from you. I have sent 2 or 3 asking you to send me one. Have you received my photograph yet which I sent about a week ago? I sent an airmail card on Monday after I had written your letter and I will write you another. I enclose a letter from Fred received this morning, he says in his letter to me that he is definitely going to get married when he comes home but is very scared! I don't see what he has got to be scared about do you? It is so lovely. God Bless you and keep you safe.

From Your Ever Loving Wife Joan xxxxxxxx

Air Mail Postcard from Joan to Tom – returned by Air Ministry

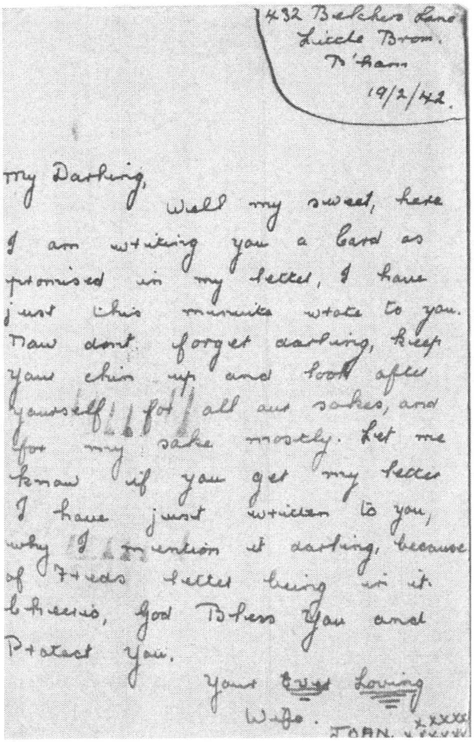

432 Belchers Lane
Little Brom.
B'ham
19/2/42.

My Darling,
Well my sweet, here I am writing you a card as promised in my letter, I have just this minute wrote to you. Now dont forget darling, keep your chin up and look after yourself!! for all our sakes, and for my sake mostly. Let me know if you get my letter I have just written to you, why I mention it darling, because of Freds letter being in it. Cheerio, God Bless You and Protect You.

Your Ever Loving
Wife.
JOAN. xxxxx

NEWS BACK IN BLIGHTY ... 25th February 1942 – *"King & Queen visit Birmingham"*

NEWS HEADLINES ... 27th February 1942 – *"Battle of Java Seas" (American, British, Dutch & Australian naval command attempts to stop the Japanese invasion of Java)*

Tom's story continues ... YOGYJAKARTA, JAVA – Camp Leader W.C. Groom

28th February 1942 – In my capacity of M.T.M. (Motor Transport Mechanic), our new unit, **153 M.U.** has now moved to Yogyjakarta, Java. Upon arrival we are billeted as usual in a school sleeping rough with no bedding. We should be heading for the drome but we learn later that the Americans, with their squadron of flying fortresses have plans in mind. During the night we hear the sound of many explosions and hear that all the fortresses have taken to the air in the darkness.

The following day we discover that the flying fortresses have left for some unknown destination to strike against the Japs from some other point. We are told that the reason for the mass explosions during the night was the delayed action of blowing up the runway. *(Little do we know what this means for us in the future!).*

2nd March 1942 – After yet another night in the school we are paraded and moved off by train to a small place called **Purbalingga, Central Java**; to be billeted yet again in an old rice barn. There are now many Jap aircraft roaming the skies and it seems there is nothing to stop them now gaining supremacy of the skies over Java. We are told by our C.O. that **Lord Portal** (Marshall of the RAF) has sent a wire to the RAF in Java informing all personnel that all remnants of the aircraft have left, we guess for Australia, and that the eyes of the world are upon us.

During our stay in the rice barn, we are issued with small fire-arms and given training in ground warfare. Apparently, we are to join forces with the **Dutch army**. The idea is to stave off, as long as possible, the intended Japanese invasion and of what is to be their last stepping stone, or words to that effect, to invade **Australia.** We are to leave tomorrow morning.

Reports Indicate *– By early* ***March 1942*** *the last airfield under allied control was on Java. Japanese forces were within twenty miles. On* ***2 March 1942*** *before midnight, the last flight of American aircraft departed Yogyjakarta.*

4th March 1942 – we are ordered to march at 14.00 hours to the nearest railway station and board a train at 20.30 hours after a long wait of six and a half hours. The train travels at a very slow speed in a southerly direction, towards the coast. At midnight we arrive at **Tjilatjap (South Coast of Java)** and spend the night sleeping on the train.

5th March 1942 – We march to a **Dutch army barracks**; a new experience for us as it is the first we have ever visited. We queue up for a very welcome breakfast of fried bacon and beans. On just polishing off same, the air raid siren starts wailing and in no time at all a large number of Japanese planes attack the small port and the barracks. We take cover where we can. The raid lasts approximately two hours and there is no opposition from any anti-aircraft guns. There are many Dutch and RAF personnel killed and wounded. The oil installations and storage tanks are all set alight and most of our time from now on is spent tending to the wounded and burying the dead.

Reports indicate: ***6th March 1942*** *– the town and harbour of Tjilatjap was destroyed by bombing.*

6th March 1942 – Leaving Tjilatjap for Jahmis (Java) - I am under the impression at this point that we are to join up with the Dutch army but this is not to be. We are to be moved to a small place called **Jahmis** and here we are again, we are awaiting another train; a wait lasting from midday until 02.30 hours in the morning. During this wait I recognise a very old familiar face, **Jack Greenall,** who used to work at **Fort Dunlop in Birmingham**, my last place of employment prior to joining the service. I remember him well because he had a very unusual job at the Dunlop, it was that of riding a bicycle, testing the cycle tyres. I remember he had been mentioned in the magazine "Cyclist" as having covered a record number of miles for the Tyre Testing Department. From now on we become pals (for what is to be a long time). I ask him how long he has been in the service and he replies "not very long". He shows me his five-figure service number which is due to him being an ex RFC in the 1914/18 War and having been called up on the 'Reserve'. I have a six-figure number, although the service numbers are now in the seven-figure bracket by this time. The train finally arrives and we are told that the delay has been caused due to the Javanese crews fleeing, owing to the increasing air-raids. I volunteer to drive as I have some knowledge and experience of steam engines but I am not needed as a still loyal crew arrive. The journey once again is in metal vans and the heat is terrific.

We reach our destination, Jahmis, the following day after an incredibly slow journey through the night. There is a heavy downpour of rain and we are ordered to assemble in the local picture house from which all the seating has been removed. Here we are to kip down for the night but just as we are settled, our Officers in charge inform us that **the Dutch have capitulated and we are to hand over all our arms, this being an Order. I keep my colt automatic hidden in my kit,** for some reason of my own.

Reports Indicate:* 7th *March 1942 *– three weeks after Singapore fell, the Dutch capitulated and Java surrendered to the Japanese. Approximately 3,000 combined forces were taken prisoner.*

NEWS HEADLINES BACK IN BLIGHTY ... 8th March 1942 - *The Capitulation of Java*

Chapter 10

OFFICIALLY "PRISONERS OF WAR" Tasikmalaya & Yogykarta, Java

Tom's story continues ...

Destination: Race Course, Tasikmalaya, Java – G C Ridgeway (Camp Leader)

8th March 1942 – Today is a day I shall never forget... We are moved to **Tasikmalaya (West Java)** and marched to the race course where we are ordered to billet in the stables, much against our will. It looks as though we are just going to hang about here to be taken by the Japanese; we believe our Officers in Charge are following orders from Head Quarters. **I have now buried my colt automatic under the floor of the stable.**

NEWS HEADLINES ... 9th March 1942 – *"Surrender of Java to the Japanese"*

Letters from Joan to Tom – returned undelivered by air Ministry

432 Belchers Lane
Little Bromwich
B'ham

10th March 1942

My Darling

Hello my sweet, how are you? I do wish I could hear from you, I am worried to death, wondering where you are and if you are alright. I told you I received a letter from you dated 14/11/41 but that was a month ago. Darling, the letters I have written to you, honestly you could open a library. Have you received my photograph? I do so hope you are getting my mail now.

Everything in Birmingham is pretty much the same, especially plenty of queues, which of course is a terrible nuisance. I was certainly just in time to get my pyjamas wasn't I?

Mom and Dad send their love. You are always in my prayers each night and I am just living for the day when you come home to me for good. What a tale you will have to tell us all when you do come, what a day that will be. GOD BLESS YOU AND PROTECT YOU.

Your Ever Loving Wife Joan xxxxxx

432 Belchers Lane
Little Bromwich
B'ham

12th March 1942

My Darling Tom

I have just come home from work and what should I see on the dresser but a letter from you dated Dec 1st and enclosed was a photograph of you standing by a car… is it? By the way, it is the first letter I have had from you for a month!

I have just spoken to your mother on the phone and I am going over on Sunday. She asked whether I had heard from you, it was strange that while I was reading your letter, the phone should ring. Mrs Stockton the girl in the other office has been away, so I have had to do her job, the operators' clock cards putting the number of hours they have worked, giving the bonus sheets out, oh and writing all the sheets out concerning their jobs. If she doesn't come back tomorrow, Friday, I shall have to do the same again and dish the wages out as well!

I have your photograph in front of me and I just can't see whether you have still got your moustache, have you? Haven't you gone thin my duck? But still never mind I will soon fatten you up when you come home, which I don't think will be long. I will be with you again tomorrow night so Goodnight, God Bless you and protect you. ALWAYS IN MY THOUGHTS

Your Ever Loving Wife JOAN xxxx

432 Belchers Lane
Little Bromwich
B'ham

17th March 1942

My Darling Tom

How are you these days? Oh I do hope you are alright and well. The girl in the other office is still away and I am still doing her work. I have never in all my life done so much writing. I have had to do all the operators' clock cards in the shop and their sheets plus give the wages out on a Friday. I also worked last Sunday, only until 12.30 though, from 8.00 am. Mom has been in town today and I told her anything she sees that she thinks will do for us, bring it. Well, she came back with a fruit bowl and some drinking glasses, every little helps doesn't it?

I have not told you before but I will break the news to you now, now that Dad is a lot better. He is still in hospital but there was such a big improvement in him when mom and I went to see him last Saturday. Mom found dad unconscious in the back kitchen on Saturday morning early in February. If he had been left another 5 minutes, he would have been dead.

Alf Lewis rang up to ask how he was and I thought how nice it was of him. Goodnight and God Bless you.

From Your Ever Loving Wife Joan xxxx

Joan's father attempted suicide in his home – February 1942.

During the early hours Joan's mother awoke sensing something was wrong as there was a strong smell of gas coming from the kitchen below. She found her beloved husband lying on the floor with his head resting on a small cushion inside the gas oven and immediately switched off the gas, flinging open the windows. Thankfully he was unsuccessful but this incident tragically led to his admission to a psychiatric hospital in Rubery, Birmingham. Joan's father sadly passed away just 15 months later on 31st May 1943 aged 56 years. The Death Certificate stated the cause of death as 'cancer' and the location as: 1959a Bristol Road South, Rubery, Birmingham. There is no mention of a "Psychiatric Hospital".

Joan's parents in their younger days

Joan's father with his pride & joy

Tom's story continues ...

Destination Yogyakarta (Java South)

21st March 1942 – After much speculation it turns out that our thoughts are to be proven right. The Japs roll up in great numbers! We are paraded and a meeting takes place between our Officers and quite a number of Jap Officers. (Officer in Japanese is 'Shoko' and Japanese for Sergeant we learn later is 'Gunso'). The Japanese Shoko's and Gunso's strut about with their traditional swords hanging from their belts, trailing the ground in most cases as most of them are noticeably very short in height, especially the privates. A few Shoko's and Gunso's are on the taller side, although I am pretty sure I could ground any of them with a good right hook! We have been living "rough" for some time but I think I am still in pretty good shape helped by the fact that I am quite disciplined and always attended PT (physical training) parades. The 'Nips', which we have now nicknamed them, have told us that Japan is now to be called 'Dai Nippon' (Great Japan). We decide to use other names!!

They move us to, of all places, **Yogyakarta, Java South** where upon arrival we are searched and put in an empty hanger. Our beds are just straw mats on the ground, which we are by now used to sleeping on.

Work on the drome – We are given orders to fill in the craters on the aerodrome runway, which the Americans had blown up during our previous visit as "free men". We soon find that the work is to be done in the Nips' time, of course, not our's! They start to use the butts of their rifles to jab us and any malingering has to be done when their backs are turned! Our main aim is to work using the 'Go Slow' method of course, as we still remember the previous orders from **Lord Portal**. Although we have not yet had an opportunity to have a go at the Nips, under orders, we have been well briefed that the Nips intend to invade **Australia** and must be sabotaged as much as possible.

We soon begin to realise that all the go-slow methods and new tactics are used with time. We are a 'mixed bag', Canadians, Australians, Scots, Welsh, Irish plus a mixture from all over England. The main topic of conversation is "how long are we to be in the bag" and "what is happening regarding the progress of the War?" Everyone is of the same opinion... the Far East has to be sacrificed! There is no possible chance of sending arms and supplies to us on the other side of the world, at the same time as being tied up with "Jerry" and the "Iti's" in the Middle East. We do, however, kid ourselves that we will be free in about six months!

Our next task is to load hundreds of sixty-gallon drums of aviation spirit, which have not been destroyed from the dump on the drome, on to railway trucks standing at the sidings. They have to be handled two or three times on and off motor trucks before being loaded on to the rail wagons and we manage to damage (on purpose) quite a number by dropping them off the lorries on to large pieces of rock. On one occasion a Nip guard asks why we are doing this and we make signs that this is to prevent large holes being made in the ground through the continual dropping of the drums. He just nods in approval – such is the mentality of some of them! One thing we have achieved is to damage a few hundred drums which have been loaded are now have leaking rims on the railway trucks, (*we are totally unaware of what further damage is to be caused by our actions later on).*

Two of our fellow prisoners, one British, the other Australian, attempt to escape to the hills but it is not long before they are reported by some anti-European native and rounded up by the Nips. **After torture and interrogation, they are made to dig their own graves and then, with hands tied behind them, shot at close range.** After this the Nips make it the responsibility of the RAF Officers to count us each morning.

Chapter 11

ARRIVAL AT OUR FIRST PRISON CAMP – Jaarmarkt (Surabaya) Java The barbaric torture begins … Introduction to Gunso Mori "The Bull"

23 March 1942 – Today we leave the drome at **Yogyakarta, Java South** and travel cramped up in railway trucks eastwards to the far end of Java, arriving at **Surabaya (a port city in Java North**).

Our first "proper" prison camp is called the **"Jaarmarkt"**, the name we are told means 'Yearly Market' in Dutch. *(the Jaarmarkt is where they held the Annual trade Fair over an area of approximately 4 acres.).* Most of the camp consists of the original buildings with quite a few long billets built in bamboo and atap, the latter being palm leaves, forming the roof and sides. The billets are about the same size as the old wooden barrack rooms back in 'blighty'. Down each side in the interior there are sleeping shelves, approximately two and a half feet wide, made of split and flattened bamboo stems (baleh-baleh) stretching the whole length. This platform is to be our bed. The floor was the earth. We very soon discover that the bamboo bedding platform, was infested with bugs and lice, as this is a transit camp where prisoners have been coming and going for some time. The Nip quarters are in the large brick building at the entrance of the camp. All around the perimeter is a high brick wall with barbed wire crowning it. Sentry boxes are mounted on towers all around with machine guns and searchlights which are able to cover the whole camp for would be escapees.

It is here we first have the company of **Dutch European prisoners** and the Nips waste no time in using our labour for their War effort. Working parties are taken out on lorries, standing room only, where we are shown off to the natives in the city. The work to be carried out involves the salvaging of all the steel and machinery from the oil refineries and factories, which the Dutch have carried out an excellent job in making unserviceable. **Up until this time the Dutch European women and children have not been interned.** On occasions, if the Nip in charge is one of the few decent ones, he will throw us a few small items, such as packets of cigarettes, packets of sandwiches or bags of fruit. On one dreadful occasion, however, **one poor unfortunate woman is knocked down and kicked after attempting to get something to us *(what made it worse for us to witness was the fact that she was pregnant!)*.** We could gladly slit that individual's yellow throat on the spot but we are fully aware of the repercussions if we do. ***(One Canadian struck a Nip back previously because he had received a blow in the back for some trivial thing whilst on working party. The very same Canadian ended up having his hands tied behind his back with barbed wire and given the first beating of which we were to see many more. These were administered in front of the whole camp with the guns trained on us).*** The camp rations provided by 'Dai Nippon' consist of boiled rice for breakfast, (similar to the paste used for putting wallpaper on the wall!), a small portion of steamed rice, plus thin green vegetable soup for 'tiffin' (Malay for lunch). The same again for dinner at night. This is the menu and reward for working like 'coolies' from sun up until sun down *(and will continue to be for 365 days a year, something we are unaware of at the present time).*

For some unknown reason, the Nips suddenly begin to show signs of generosity, giving us 10 cents per day for our slavery! We learn by this time that all the machinery and metal that we are humping with bamboo poles and slings is to be shipped off to Japan for use towards their War effort in making the people of Asia 'free' *(this turns out to be the joke of the century! Even the native population have no idea what they are in store for).*

Letter from Joan to Tom – returned undelivered

432 Belchers Lane
Little Bromwich
B'ham

24th March 1942

My Dear Tom

Here I am again asking you if you can possibly write to me yet as you might know how I feel not hearing from you since the trouble started over there. As you can guess I am writing this at work, oh dear the girls are pulling my leg terribly by saying "go on, tell him how much you love him", why my treasure if I was to tell you that I should fill a book.

Mom and myself went to see Dad in hospital again last Saturday and he is still going on fine, thank goodness. By the way, have you received my photograph yet? I know I have asked you several times but I would like to know. I shall have to close now as the boss could walk into the office any minute. God Bless you and protect you.

From Your Ever Loving Wife Joan xxxxx

NEWS HEADLINES ... 28th March 1942 - *"Sumatra Fallen – Dutch Major Surrendered".*

Tom's story continues ...

11th April 1942 – We are still at the Jaarmarkt receiving 10 cents per day for our slavery as 'coolies' and now beginning to feel the strain of carrying out the heavy physical work for long hours, day in and day out. The payment enables us to buy little extras to augment the vitamins we are so lacking in our meagre rations. Many of us are still comparatively fit, although some are suffering with tropical ulcers mainly on feet and legs.

We are informed that we are to be moved to another camp ...

After being formed into different companies, we are issued with one loaf and a half of bread, two pairs of cheap looking rubber boots and a bundle of toilet paper with strict orders that we must only take what kit we can carry.

The worst is about to happen ... We're ordered into the big hall at the front of the camp where we are told to rest on the tiled floor. Having by this time witnessed many horrific brutal acts, we are becoming fully aware as to what the opinion of the Nips is towards us and their evil methods of discipline. We witness our officers being subjected to harsh discipline and being humiliated in front of us. (On a previous occasion, during the time we were paraded for the issue of the rubber boots, rations etc, **an RAF Wing Commander was beaten up in front of us**. He ended up on the ground with his arm broken by a Nip Gunso, who we had nicknamed **"The Bull"**). A big issue up until now has been the language problem, as most of our guards speak only Japanese, a few speak very little English with only a few words of Malay. *(It becomes evident that the language barrier and poor level of communication are the main reasons for most of the "beating up" ceremonies, one of which I personally become the victim at a later date).*

GUNZO MORI also known as "The Bull" or "Bamboo Gunzo". He was muscular and usually armed with a cudgel of split bamboo.

Letter from Joan to Tom – returned undelivered by Air Ministry

432 Belchers Lane
Little Bromwich
B'ham

26th April 1942

My Darling Tom

Hello my sweet, I trust to God you are fit and well. I have not heard from you since last December, so you can just imagine how I feel. There is no need to worry about me or anybody else as we are all o.k. just waiting for the day when you come home for good.

Do you know how much cigarettes are now? 1/- for 10 Players, 9d for 10 Woodbines, oh and beer has gone up as well, 11d for a pint of mild ale! Your mother bought us a kettle and a colander last week and I have also managed to buy a few other things for our home together.

I have been altering two of my summer dresses tonight and this afternoon I blacked your shoes and polished your slippers. Goodnight, God Bless You and Protect you.

From Your Ever Loving Wife Joan xxxxxxx

Letter to Joan from The British Red Cross Society Dated 30th April 1942

WAR ORGANISATION
OF THE
BRITISH RED CROSS SOCIETY and ORDER OF ST. JOHN OF JERUSALEM

President: HER MAJESTY THE QUEEN. | *Grand Prior:* H.R.H. THE DUKE OF GLOUCESTER, K.G.

WOUNDED, MISSING AND RELATIVES DEPARTMENT

Chairman: THE DOWAGER LADY AMPTHILL, C.I., G.B.E.

TELEPHONE NO.: SLOANE 9696
TELEGRAPHIC ADDRESS: "WOMINEL, KNIGHTS, LONDON"

7 BELGRAVE SQUARE
LONDON, S.W.1

30th April, 1942.

KO/RHT
RAF/L.6202.

Dear Mrs Orton,

We have received your letter of the 24th of April, which has been forwarded to us from our Foreign Relations Department, in which you make an enquiry for your husband, Leading Aircraftman T. Orton, No.849112.

We are sorry we have no news of him here, and we realise how anxious you must be. If your husband has become a casualty his next-of-kin will be notified by the Royal Air Force Record Office with the least possible delay, and the registered next-of-kin will also be notified if he proves to be safe.

The only enquiries we are able to make are for those men in enemy occupied territory who have been officially reported

P.T.O.

\- 2 -

"missing" or "believed to be prisoners of war". Then we are able to make enquiries for them through the International Red Cross Committee at Geneva.

Please accept our sympathy in your anxiety.

Yours sincerely,

Margaret Ampthill
by NM
Chairman.

Mrs J. Orton,
432 Belchers Lane,
Little Bromwich,
Birmingham.

LAST Letter from Joan to Tom – returned undelivered

432 Belchers Lane
Little Bromwich
B'ham

4th May 1942

My Darling Tom

I am still desperately waiting patiently to hear from you, it has been 6 months since I last heard.

Mom and I went to your house last Saturday and called in to see Gran in her new cottage, it is a lovely little place in Duke Street, Sutton. We then went to the Duke with your Mom, Dad, Gran and Harry, you know Gran's lodger but had to leave at 9 p.m. on account of the buses. The Sunday before, I left Sutton at about 8.45 p.m. and had to walk to Chester Road. I caught a tram alright but I was in a bus queue until 10.40 p.m. I managed to get the last bus and to crown it all, I had to walk from the Fox & Goose, it was 11.40 p.m. when I finally got home.

The gentleman next door but one, Mr Bennett, is trying to get us some pastel green blankets straight from the factory. I thought it would be best to have green on account of the mattress being green. I know you wanted blue but it would be nice to have everything to match, don't you think? We can have a blue sitting room can't we?

Goodnight my treasure, God Bless you and protect you. Speedy Return.

From Your Ever Loving Wife Joan xxxxx

p.s. Mom & Dad send their very best love

ALWAYS IN MY THOUGHTS

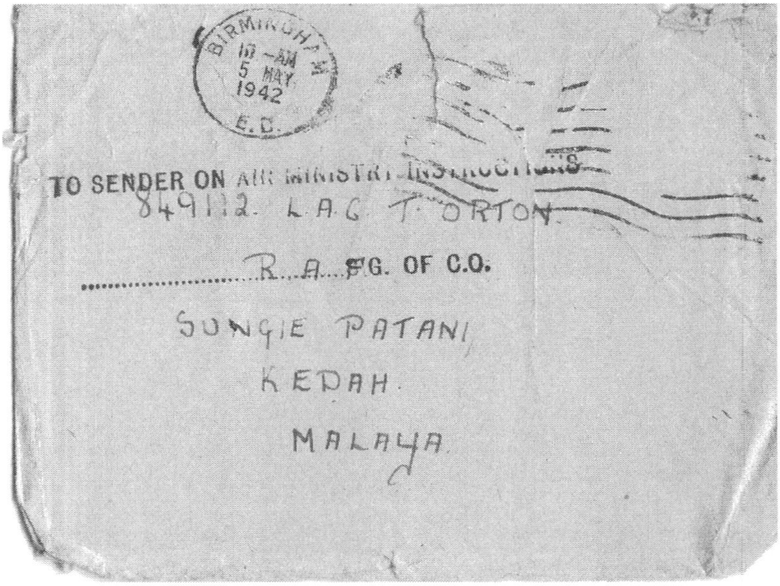
BIRMINGHAM
10 - AM
5 MAY
1942
E.D.
TO SENDER ON AIR MINISTRY INSTRUCTIONS
849112. L.A.C. T ORTON
R. A. F G. OF C.O.
SUNGIE PATANI,
KEDAH.
MALAYA.

Letter from Air Ministry to Joan Dated 6th May 1942

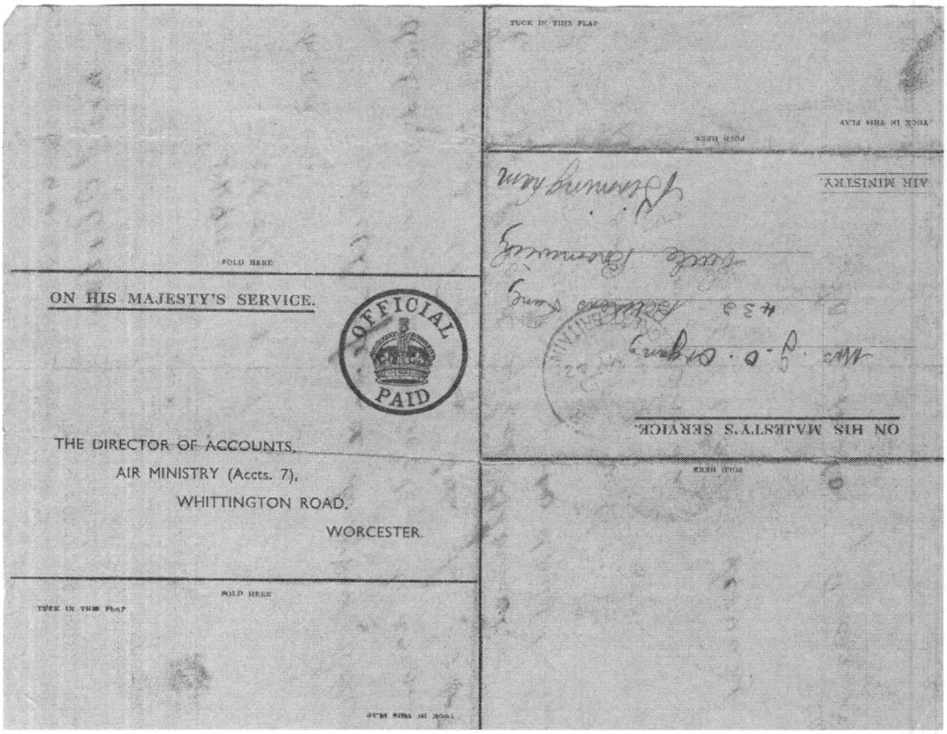
ON HIS MAJESTY'S SERVICE.
OFFICIAL PAID
THE DIRECTOR OF ACCOUNTS,
AIR MINISTRY (Accts. 7),
WHITTINGTON ROAD,
WORCESTER.

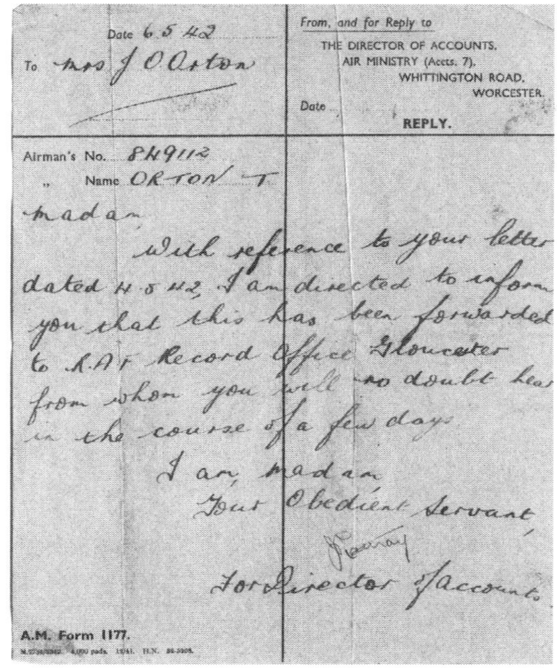

Date 6.5.42

To Mrs J O Orton

From, and for Reply to
THE DIRECTOR OF ACCOUNTS,
AIR MINISTRY (Accts. 7),
WHITTINGTON ROAD,
WORCESTER.

Date ...
REPLY.

Airman's No. 849112
" Name ORTON T

Madam

With reference to your letter dated 4.5.42 I am directed to inform you that this has been forwarded to R.A.F Record Office Gloucester from whom you will no doubt hear in the course of a few days

I am, Madam
Your Obedient Servant

For Director of Accounts

A.M. Form 1177.

Letter to Joan from Record Office – R.A.F. Gloucester Dated 19th May 1942

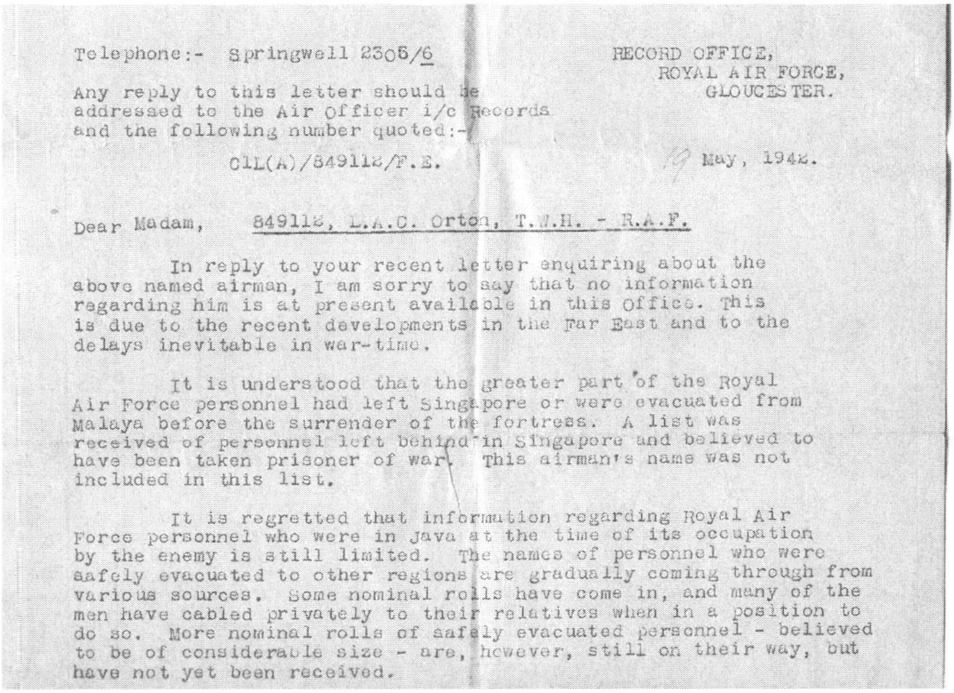

Telephone:- Springwell 2305/6

RECORD OFFICE,
ROYAL AIR FORCE,
GLOUCESTER.

Any reply to this letter should be addressed to the Air Officer i/c Records and the following number quoted:-

C1L(A)/849112/F.E.

19 May, 1942.

Dear Madam, 849112, L.A.C. Orton, T.W.H. - R.A.F.

In reply to your recent letter enquiring about the above named airman, I am sorry to say that no information regarding him is at present available in this Office. This is due to the recent developments in the Far East and to the delays inevitable in war-time.

It is understood that the greater part of the Royal Air Force personnel had left Singapore or were evacuated from Malaya before the surrender of the fortress. A list was received of personnel left behind in Singapore and believed to have been taken prisoner of war. This airman's name was not included in this list.

It is regretted that information regarding Royal Air Force personnel who were in Java at the time of its occupation by the enemy is still limited. The names of personnel who were safely evacuated to other regions are gradually coming through from various sources. Some nominal rolls have come in, and many of the men have cabled privately to their relatives when in a position to do so. More nominal rolls of safely evacuated personnel - believed to be of considerable size - are, however, still on their way, but have not yet been received.

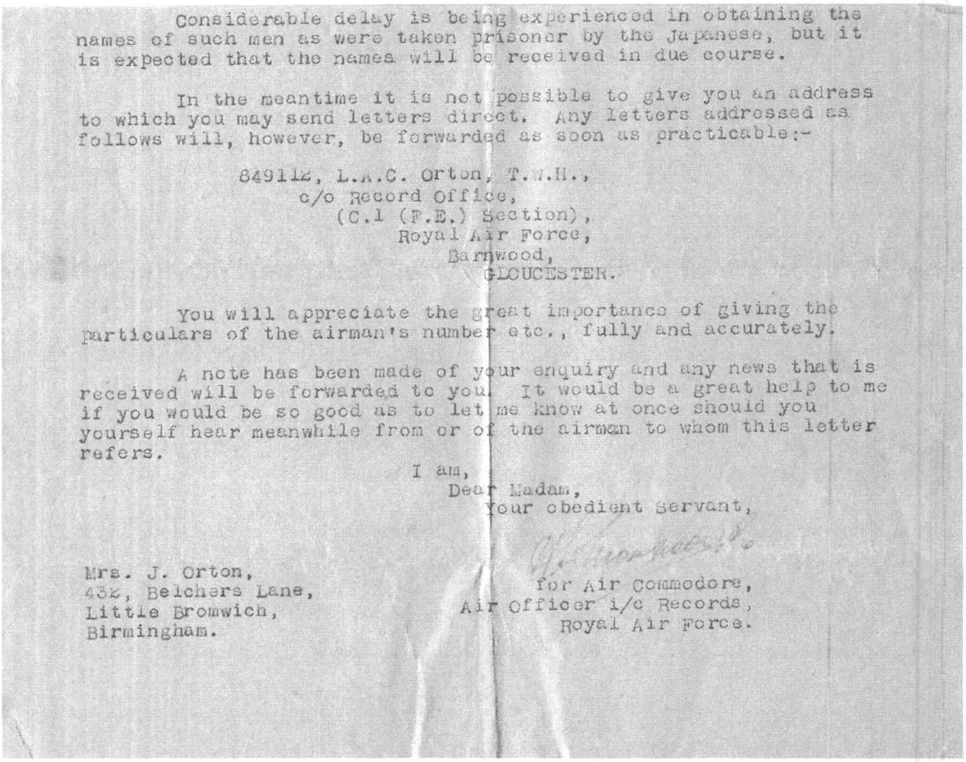

Considerable delay is being experienced in obtaining the names of such men as were taken prisoner by the Japanese, but it is expected that the names will be received in due course.

In the meantime it is not possible to give you an address to which you may send letters direct. Any letters addressed as follows will, however, be forwarded as soon as practicable:-

849112, L.A.C. Orton, T.W.H.,
c/o Record Office,
(C.1 (F.E.) Section),
Royal Air Force,
Barnwood,
GLOUCESTER.

You will appreciate the great importance of giving the particulars of the airman's number etc., fully and accurately.

A note has been made of your enquiry and any news that is received will be forwarded to you. It would be a great help to me if you would be so good as to let me know at once should you yourself hear meanwhile from or of the airman to whom this letter refers.

I am,
Dear Madam,
Your obedient Servant,

for Air Commodore,
Air Officer i/c Records,
Royal Air Force.

Mrs. J. Orton,
432, Belchers Lane,
Little Bromwich,
Birmingham.

Letter from Tom's brother Fred to Joan:

No. 7264089 Sgt F. Orton
Military Hospital
Gibraltar

12th June 1942

Dear Joan

Maybe by now you are under the impression I have forgotten all about you, on the contrary, after my last letter to you I did not think it would be necessary as I was hoping to see you in person; unfortunately, my wishes have not yet materialised so I decided it was high time I picked up the old pen and scribbled a few words to you. I do not think it will be very long before we meet. The letter you wrote to me in January was sent to Malta by mistake and arrived here last night – better late than never what?! Thanks Joan, much appreciated. So you liked mother's kimono? Well I see no reason why our Joan shouldn't have one, in fact I will try to bring one home with me. How tall are you, what colour do you prefer? – something to go with the pyjamas Tom sent you I should imagine. Shall have to be pretty smart at buying it as they are beginning to tighten up out here now.

The Sunday before last I went to Algiers which is at the extreme south of Spain just opposite Gibralta. It is quite a decent place although the large numbers of Spanish soldiers were inclined to spoil the scenery although they are a very quiet crowd. We had about nine hours there altogether, tasted their excellent cognac, saw the bullring, their fleet (a destroyer) and returned fully satisfied with our first escape from this Rock in three years.

Yes! May (her second name) and I certainly intend to have a good time when I do return, she has waited a long time and it is up to me to repay her for her patience. You will come to the wedding won't you Joan?

Well Joan, as they will insist in interrupting me by ringing the telephone, I'm afraid I must close for now – see you soon – keep the folly old chin up.

Adios – hasta la vista!!
Your Loving Brother in Law Fred xxxx

Chapter 12

MY FIRST "BEATING" for not bowing to "Yellow Boots"– Jaarmarkt Camp (Surabaya – Java)

Tom's story continues ...

On walking out of the improvised shower house *(this turns out to be the end of such a luxury, as Surabaya is to be the last of what is to be considered as "civilisation" for some considerable time hereafter),* I hear the familiar shout of "currha" (the equivalent of "hey you") coming from the sentry in the lookout tower. Stopping in my tracks with my tattered towel around my girth, I have no idea what the sentry is yelling at but he continues to bellow even louder with a lot of gesticulating. He eventually charges down from the tower and confronts me, still bawling in Japanese "kiotsuki", *(which I later learn means "stand to attention").* My reward for my innocent ignorance is a vicious blow across the left ear which is already infected (we have now nicknamed this common injury from a beating as "Singapore ear"). My ear becomes numb with pain and I try to get the message across to him in English, Malay and by sign that my ear is already causing me severe pain from all the previous blows across the head. He either fails, or chooses not to understand and I have no choice but to stand and take the punishing blows for what seems like an eternity. I am frantically trying to work out what exactly he wants from me but I simply cannot understand him. After about twenty minutes of continual blows across my ear he struts off back up to his perch on the tower. ***(I later learn that my punishment was for not bowing to him. This particular Nip actually becomes one of the most notorious guards for brutality who becomes promoted, not only in rank but to the nickname of "Yellow Boots". Many of the prisoners witness an incident on one of the prison ships whereby he executes a prisoner by decapitating his head in one blow of his not long issued sword. An execution for an offence we are told was for stealing a small portion of dried fish!)***

Japanese guard

NEWS BACK HOME IN BLIGHTY … 26th June 1942 – *Air-raid alert for Birmingham 1.03 a.m. to 2.29 a.m.*

Letter to Joan from Tom's Brother Fred:

No. 7264089 Sgt F. Orton
Military Hospital
Gibraltar

6th July 1942

Dear Joan

Here we are again, fit and well, turning brown thanks to weeks and weeks of beautiful glaring sunshine (aren't you jealous?). You ask whether it will still be July? well if you will promise to tell no one the awful truth, I will tell you. Unfortunately, a few things unforeseen have turned up which may put it back a few weeks, may be a few months! I cannot state the cause in a letter but I sincerely hope everyone will understand, especially May as I know how much she is looking forward to "The Day" and she has certainly waited a long time.

Dear Joan, do not worry too much about Tom for I feel convinced he is alright, the trouble being the Japanese will not allow the British Red Cross to get in touch with Singapore but I feel sure it is only a matter of time before they do.

Thanks for the measurements of the kimono, I really think I shall have to nickname you "Titch" being only 5' 4", you see I am 6' 2", ok Titch? I think May is due for a shock when I return as when I came away, I was only 5' 11" and haven't told her anything about the change. I shall have to buy her a pair of stilts. I cannot recall what I did put at the bottom of my last letter but it is a bad habit of mine to include a few words of Spanish in my letters. Have been sitting back in my chair trying to think what I put but cannot call it to mind, never mind Joan I will teach you some Spanish when I return.

I have bought May a 3-piece set of underwear, 3½ yds of material, some Evening in Paris and a bottle of something. For mother at No. 84, a pink frock and for dad cigarettes and tobacco. The latest letter from May tells me that we have another member to the family, namely a baby to Len & Gladys, I had better make another trip to the town (?village) to obtain a present for "Baby Joyce". Gosh!! I'm beginning to think I am an old man, being an uncle.

GOOD NIGHT! GOOD LUCK! AND MAY WE ALL MEET VERY SOON!!
Fred xxxx

NEWS BACK HOME IN BLIGHTY ... Air-raid alerts in Birmingham

16th July 1942 – 6.18 a.m. to 6.30 a.m. **23rd July 1942** – 11.59 p.m. to 1.05 a.m.

Letter to Joan from British Red Cross dated 24th August 1942 – STILL NO NEWS!

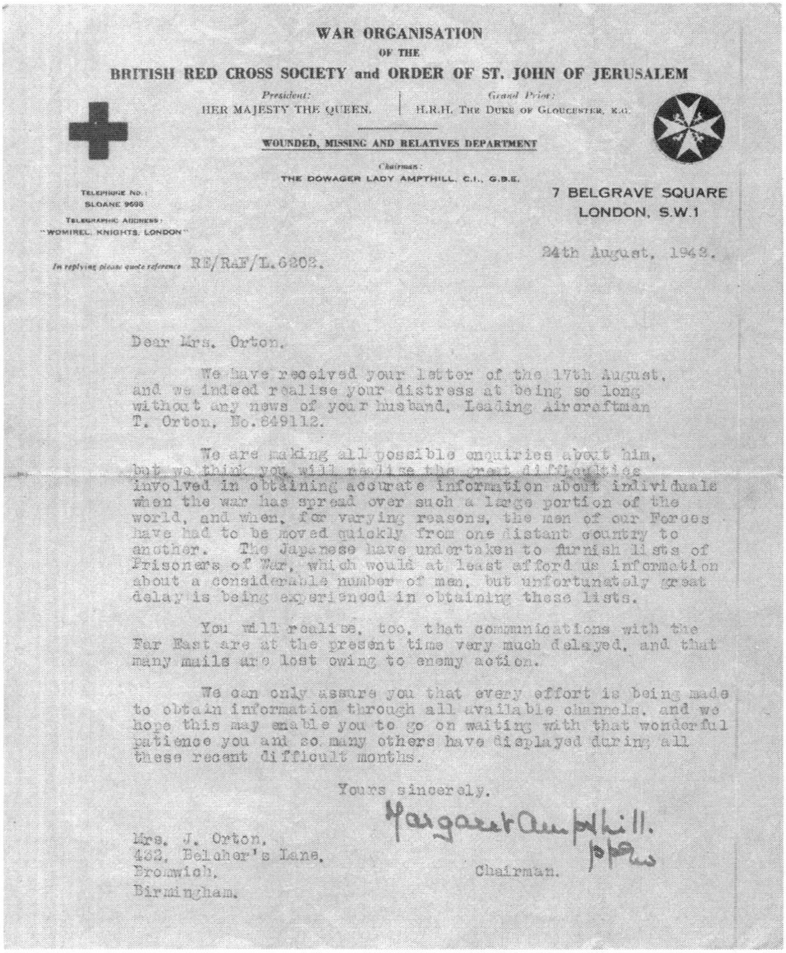

WAR ORGANISATION
OF THE
BRITISH RED CROSS SOCIETY and ORDER OF ST. JOHN OF JERUSALEM

President: HER MAJESTY THE QUEEN. | *Grand Prior:* H.R.H. THE DUKE OF GLOUCESTER, K.G.

WOUNDED, MISSING AND RELATIVES DEPARTMENT

Chairman: THE DOWAGER LADY AMPTHILL, C.I., G.B.E.

TELEPHONE NO.: SLOANE 9696
TELEGRAPHIC ADDRESS: "WOMIREL, KNIGHTS, LONDON"

7 BELGRAVE SQUARE
LONDON, S.W.1

In replying please quote reference RE/RAF/L.6202.

24th August, 1942.

Dear Mrs. Orton,

We have received your letter of the 17th August, and we indeed realise your distress at being so long without any news of your husband, Leading Aircraftman T. Orton, No.849112.

We are making all possible enquiries about him, but we think you will realise the great difficulties involved in obtaining accurate information about individuals when the war has spread over such a large portion of the world, and when, for varying reasons, the men of our Forces have had to be moved quickly from one distant country to another. The Japanese have undertaken to furnish lists of Prisoners of War, which would at least afford us information about a considerable number of men, but unfortunately great delay is being experienced in obtaining these lists.

You will realise, too, that communications with the Far East are at the present time very much delayed, and that many mails are lost owing to enemy action.

We can only assure you that every effort is being made to obtain information through all available channels, and we hope this may enable you to go on waiting with that wonderful patience you and so many others have displayed during all these recent difficult months.

Yours sincerely,

Margaret Ampthill.
pp

Chairman.

Mrs. J. Orton,
432, Belcher's Lane,
Bromwich,
Birmingham.

Tom's story continues ...

LYCEUM Prison Camp, Surabaya, Java - Moved here 5th **September 1942**

19th October 1942 – Epidemic of dysentery. 4 deaths. Food very poor but permitted to buy sugar, coffee and salt.

2nd November 1942 – Epidemic worsening. Double funeral today was attended by high Jap official. Japs questioning more food coming into camp. 6 ox carts of food unloaded.

7th November 1942 – All extra food supplies stopped.

13th November 1942 – In hospital with dysentery.

DARMOC Prison Camp, Surabaya, Java – Moved here 2nd December 1942

JAARMARKT Prison Camp, Surabaya, Java – Moved back here **10th January 1943**

16th January 1943 – In sick bay with septic foot.

17th January 1943 – My birthday. Hit by guard – late on parade. All working party ordered to slap each other's faces.

Letter to Joan from India Office, Whitehall Dated 19th January 1943

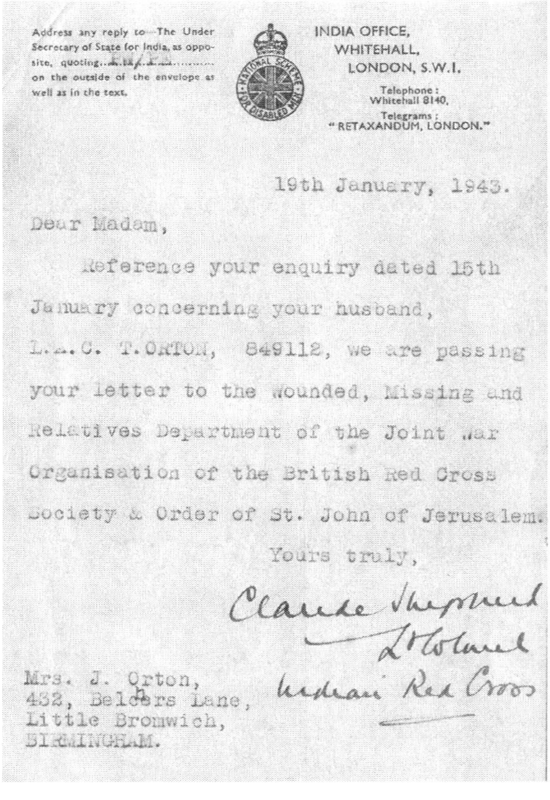

Address any reply to—The Under Secretary of State for India, as opposite, quoting [illegible] on the outside of the envelope as well as in the text.

INDIA OFFICE,
WHITEHALL,
LONDON, S.W.1.

Telephone: Whitehall 8140.
Telegrams: "RETAXANDUM, LONDON."

19th January, 1943.

Dear Madam,

Reference your enquiry dated 15th January concerning your husband, L.A.C. T.ORTON, 849112, we are passing your letter to the Wounded, Missing and Relatives Department of the Joint War Organisation of the British Red Cross Society & Order of St. John of Jerusalem.

Yours truly,

Clarke Shepherd
Lt Colonel
Indian Red Cross

Mrs. J. Orton,
432, Belchers Lane,
Little Bromwich,
BIRMINGHAM.

Letter to Joan from the British Red Cross Dated 21st January 1943 – PRISONER LISTS!

WAR ORGANISATION
OF THE
BRITISH RED CROSS SOCIETY and ORDER OF ST. JOHN OF JERUSALEM

President: HER MAJESTY THE QUEEN. | *Grand Prior:* H.R.H. THE DUKE OF GLOUCESTER, K.G.

WOUNDED, MISSING AND RELATIVES DEPARTMENT

Chairman: THE DOWAGER LADY AMPTHILL, C.I., G.B.E.

TELEPHONE NO.: SLOANE 9808
TELEGRAPHIC ADDRESS: "WOMIREL, KNIGHTS, LONDON"

In replying please quote reference:

7 BELGRAVE SQUARE
LONDON, S.W.1

RE/RAF/L.6202.

21st January, 1943.

Dear Mrs. Orton,

Your letter of January 15th, in which you make a further enquiry for your husband, Leading Aircraftman T. Orton, No.849112, Royal Air Force, has been passed on to us by the Indian Red Cross Society in London.

We do indeed realise your anxiety to have some definite news after such a very long time, but we fear there is very little we can add to the letter we wrote to you on August 24th last.

The Japanese, after much delay, are now releasing a certain amount of information about prisoners in the Far East. Lists of the majority of prisoners in Hong Kong have already come through, and now limited lists of prisoners in Singapore are gradually being received from Tokyo through the International Red Cross Committee at Geneva. The next-of-kin of these men are being notified as soon as possible.

p.t.o.

- 2 -

We ask you, once again, to accept our assurance that every effort is being made by the Government and the International Red Cross Committee to obtain further information, and we very much hope that some news will soon come through about your husband.

We feel so much for you in your continued anxiety, and we wish to offer you our renewed sympathy.

Yours sincerely,

Margaret Ampthill

Chairman.

Mrs. T. Orton,
432, Belcher's Lane,
Little Bromwich,
BIRMINGHAM, 9.

Casablanca Conference January 1943 – US President Franklin D. Roosevelt, British Prime Minister Winston Churchill plus leading military advisors including Vice Admiral Lord Louis Mountbatten

Chapter 13

CONFLICTING NEWS FOR JOAN from Air Ministry … Captured 8 March 1942 – Reported Missing 14 April 1943?

NEWS HEADLINES BACK IN BLIGHTY … 9th March 1943 –
General Montgomery visits Birmingham

Letter to Joan from Air Ministry Dated 25th March 1943 – TOM PRISONER OF WAR!

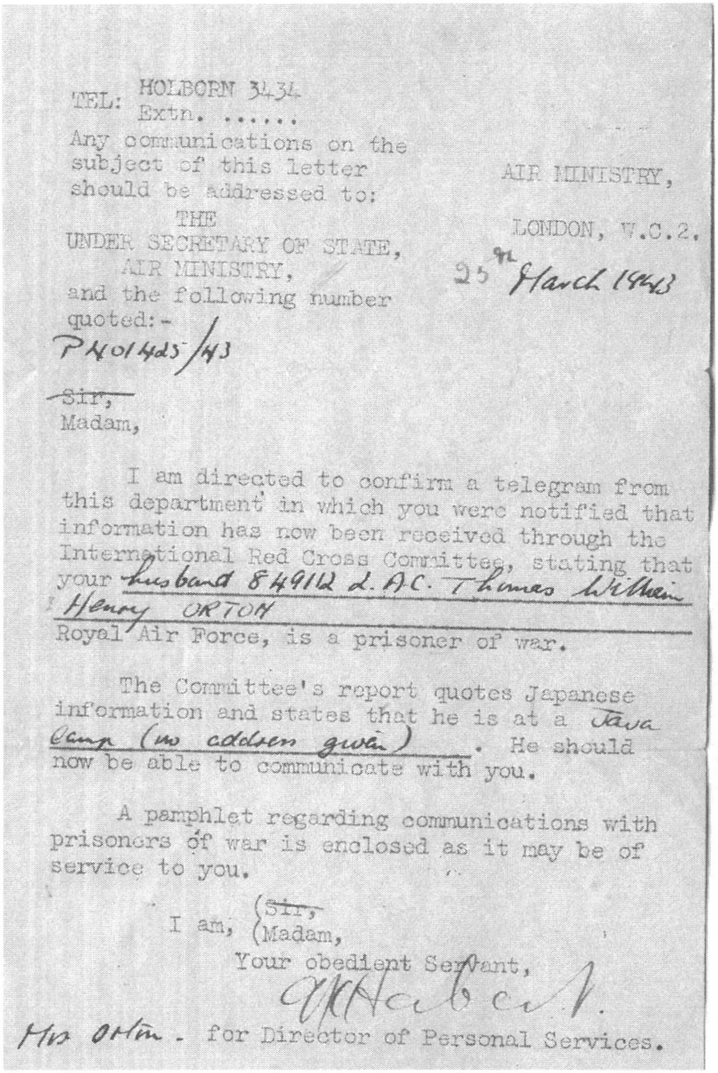

TEL: HOLBORN 3434
Extn. ......

Any communications on the subject of this letter should be addressed to:
THE
UNDER SECRETARY OF STATE,
AIR MINISTRY,
and the following number quoted:-
P4 01425/43

AIR MINISTRY,
LONDON, W.C.2.
25th March 1943

~~Sir,~~
Madam,

I am directed to confirm a telegram from this department in which you were notified that information has now been received through the International Red Cross Committee, stating that your husband 849112 L.A.C. Thomas William Henry ORTON Royal Air Force, is a prisoner of war.

The Committee's report quotes Japanese information and states that he is at a Java Camp (no address given). He should now be able to communicate with you.

A pamphlet regarding communications with prisoners of war is enclosed as it may be of service to you.

I am, {~~Sir,~~ Madam,
Your obedient Servant,

Mrs Orton. for Director of Personal Services.

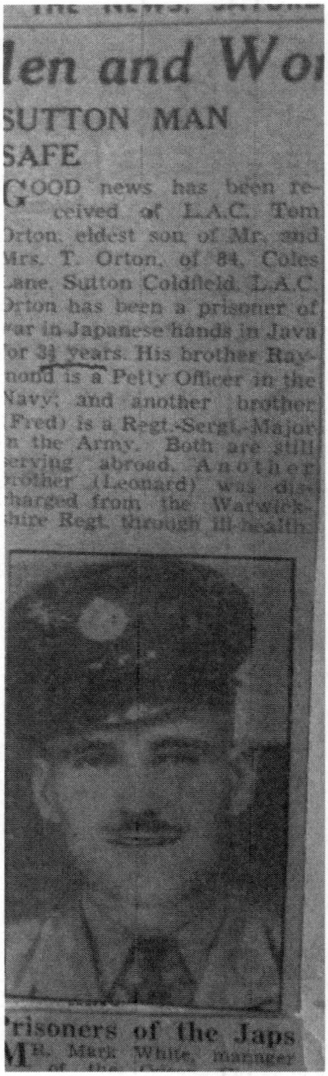

len and Wo

SUTTON MAN SAFE

GOOD news has been received of L.A.C. Tom Orton, eldest son of Mr. and Mrs. T. Orton, of 84, Coles Lane, Sutton Coldfield. L.A.C. Orton has been a prisoner of war in Japanese hands in Java for 3½ years. His brother Raymond is a Petty Officer in the Navy; and another brother (Fred) is a Regt.-Sergt.-Major in the Army. Both are still serving abroad. Another brother (Leonard) was discharged from the Warwickshire Regt. through ill-health.

risoners of the Japs

MR. Mark White, manager

Local press cutting

Letters of Support to Joan from friends & relatives

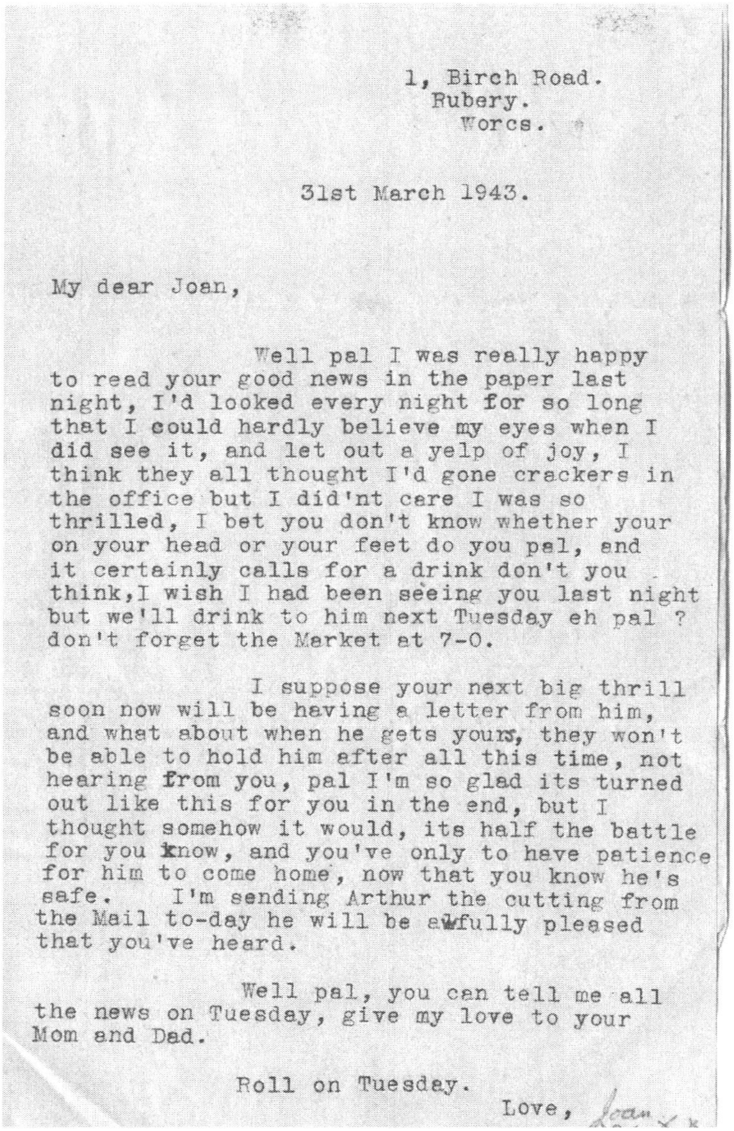

1, Birch Road.
Rubery.
Worcs.

31st March 1943.

My dear Joan,

Well pal I was really happy to read your good news in the paper last night, I'd looked every night for so long that I could hardly believe my eyes when I did see it, and let out a yelp of joy, I think they all thought I'd gone crackers in the office but I did'nt care I was so thrilled, I bet you don't know whether your on your head or your feet do you pal, and it certainly calls for a drink don't you think, I wish I had been seeing you last night but we'll drink to him next Tuesday eh pal ? don't forget the Market at 7-0.

I suppose your next big thrill soon now will be having a letter from him, and what about when he gets yours, they won't be able to hold him after all this time, not hearing from you, pal I'm so glad its turned out like this for you in the end, but I thought somehow it would, its half the battle for you know, and you've only to have patience for him to come home, now that you know he's safe. I'm sending Arthur the cutting from the Mail to-day he will be awfully pleased that you've heard.

Well pal, you can tell me all the news on Tuesday, give my love to your Mom and Dad.

Roll on Tuesday.

Love, Joan

Selly Oak
Birmingham

4th April 1943

Dear Joan

I hope to express my thoughts to you by these few lines. The news of your dear Husband being safe is indeed a great blessing to you. I don't expect you know yet how and where he is but the news that he is alive and well is good enough for a little time and I know you have to be a very patient girl for news. I hope you will soon receive a full report. Now Joan you can look ahead with brighter outlook. How glad we all shall be when the world is at peace and all will live their lives as they wish, what a day Joan when Tom smiles his broad grin. I can always see him on his Wedding Day, I guess he is very upset not hearing from you, I should like to have seen you when you received the great news. Now Joan, again I want you to know how glad I am to know of your good news, Tom is always amongst my prayers for his safety and hope soon to hear that you have had a letter from him, and Joan please mention my name when you write.

I hope this letter will express my thoughts to you. Hope your mother and Dad are well. Will close with love.

Auntie Blanche

Letter from Air Ministry to Joan – "ASSUMED MISSING!!!"

Gerrard 9234

TELEPHONE: [illegible]

Extn. ....

Any communications on the subject of this letter should be addressed to:—

THE SECRETARY,

and the following number quoted:—

P4/FE

AIR MINISTRY,

LONDON, W.C.2.

14 April 1943

848112 L.A.C. Y. W. H. Orton

Madam,

I am directed to inform you that the position of personnel whose whereabouts have been unknown since the evacuation of the Malaya, Java and Sumatra area has been under review.

While there was reason to believe that the Allied Forces in certain parts of the Netherlands East Indies were still fighting, personnel who might possibly have joined these forces were not officially regarded as missing. In view, however, of the absence of any recent news of them, it can no longer be assumed that they are still operating.

It is regretted therefore that your husband must be regarded as missing with effect from 1st February, 1943.

It is desired to emphasize that this action has not been taken on account of any fresh news of him having been received. Although a number of names of officers and airmen who are prisoners of war have been received from the Japanese, it is believed that there are as yet many more to come. He may therefore eventually prove to be a prisoner of war, or possibly, still free and at large on one of the islands. Any information relating to him that is received will be passed to you at once.

Mrs. Orton

/I

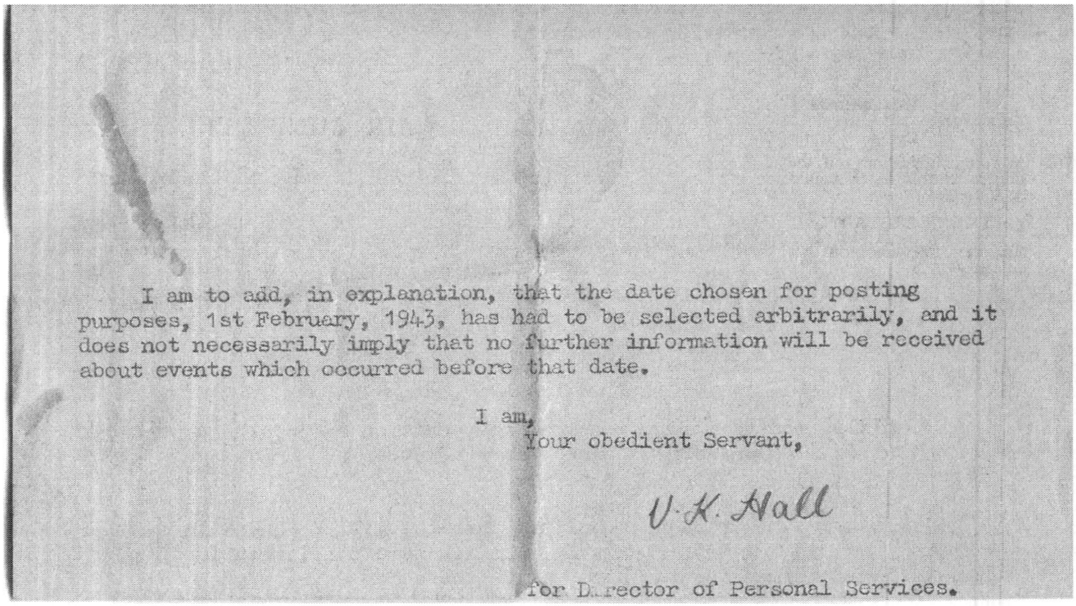

I am to add, in explanation, that the date chosen for posting purposes, 1st February, 1943, has had to be selected arbitrarily, and it does not necessarily imply that no further information will be received about events which occurred before that date.

I am,
Your obedient Servant,

V. K. Hall

for Director of Personal Services.

Chapter 14

MY FIRST "HELL SHIP" EXPERIENCE – The Amagi Maru ... "Unknown Destination – a 2-week voyage"

*It is reported that prior to departure from **Jaarmarkt** Prison Camp, a large medical parade was conducted by a number of Japanese medical officers sitting behind a table. Prisoners were ordered to file past stripped to the waist and approximately 2,070 so-called 'fit' men (those who were not lame or seriously ill at that stage and mainly RAF, were selected to board ships to an unknown destination. As part of the selection process, Prisoners were subjected to a glass rod being inserted into the rectum to check for the presence of blood and signs of dysentery, which turned out to be a futile, undignified and degrading exercise as the samples were at no time actually ever looked at!*

Tom's story continues ...

Departure from Jaarmarkt prison camp to the Amagi Maru prison ship in Surabaya (North Java).

15th April 1943 – We are paraded at 04.30 hours, after very little sleep, and marched into the darkness to the railway station. We are then conveyed to the docks. (During any movement of this kind there is always frenzied hysteria amongst the guards; probably due to our 'go slow' tactics which obviously cause a certain amount of frustration for them).

On arrival at the docks, we are paraded in front of what is to become known to us as the **'Hell Ship' named the 'Amagi Maru'.** Our main kit is taken from us and stowed aboard. The majority of us are left with just our side pack of the RAF webbing; most of those without this pack are in possession of the service gas mask bag. These bags are essential to us for carrying our enamel plate, mug and spoon, as well as any meagre rations we have been allowed (needless to say the bread has already been "scoffed"!) Each prisoner is ordered to stand to attention at the foot of the gang plank to be sprayed from head to toe with disinfectant. We are then ordered to proceed up to the deck where we scuffle to try and get the best spot to "doss down" which ends up as a waste of effort, as we are all ordered to go through a small hatchway! Once through the hatchway, we climb down a single stairway into the top compartment of the battened down hold. The first men down choose a spot as near to the foot of the stairs as possible as naturally they have in mind the idea of stretching out on the tarpaulined covered planks, which actually doesn't happen because the Nips at the top of the hatchway keep forcing and cramming more and more men down, all at bayonet point. "Our non-luxury cruise" experience begins!! I am sitting squatting and squashed amongst hundreds of men on the tarpaulin covered planks; we are packed in like sardines, unable to stretch out or lie down. The unbearable tropical heat is immense and our bodies stink with perspiration. After what seems like hours, the Amagi Maru pulls out and anchors in the harbour. It's the first of the prison ships to be loaded and has been awaiting the rest of the small convoy.

I have an uncontrollable strong urge "to pay a visit" as I desperately need to get rid of some of the bloating and excess fluid in my body. (Our diet consists mainly of water and rice; the rice is the main cause of the bloating). I ask my comrades if there is anyone in the same predicament but it seems that I am the only one that is far from being a camel and unable to continue holding. I am allowed to crawl over the mass of perspiring bodies and warned of what reception I may receive at the top of the stairway! I am prepared and, as expected, I am greeted with a snarling Nip and a bayonet pointing at my rice distorted belly. Clearly, he cannot understand me but it is critical that I reach the latrine, which is slung over the deck rail. In the end I do manage to get him to understand my dilemma and I guess he begins to realise that he will not frighten me back down into the hatchway... so he gives in! He gestures and threatens me about my speedy return though!

Walking the few yards across the deck to the latrine, **I spot another prisoner ship slowly leaving the port and as it departs to join us, it is blown up into small pieces, parts of which soar hundreds of feet into the air.** I am conscious of the fact that I must not slow down or stop in my tracks and watch, as I am more than aware that there are many eyes on me and the Nip is quite capable of either striking me down with one blow of his rifle butt or using his bayonet. Hastily, I pay my visit to the latrine and scurry quickly back down the hatchway stairs to tell my fellow prisoners of my disastrous eye witness account on deck.

The ship sails out of Surabaya harbour at approximately 17.30 hours. We remain battened down in the hold, packed in together like sardines and still in the same cramped positions when a somewhat unexpected couple of four-gallon petrol tins are passed down to us for toilet purposes.

(This is to be the start of a memorable journey, as we later find out).

The following day we are told that we are to be allowed on deck but only in limited numbers and only for a short period of time. We are desperate to breathe some fresh air albeit it's only for a short time and whilst on deck I take the opportunity to try and have a good look round as far as possible. The first thing that catches my eye is the plate on the super structure of the Amagi Maru, although it has been painted over, the wording is still legible **'Built on the Clyde'**, estimated to be within the region of 1,500 tons.

There are three other ships sailing with us in convoy, Amagi Maru, Matsukawa Maru and Kunitama Maru, plus one small naval vessel as escort. We're sailing in a westerly direction north of the **islands of Madura and Bali.** There is a cook house galley on the aft of the upper deck and I notice two large 'wajans', large cast iron cooking pans, one for boiling rice, the other for the seaweed soup. These are to become our daily rations for lunch and dinner at night; breakfast is the usual rice ('pap' as it is called) which is boiled to a paste. Nothing else accompanies the pap.

JAPANESE PRISONER OF WAR "Hell Ships" – *These were "old abandoned hulks" bought by the Japanese during the depression which included ships built in the Clyde. Ships which had previously sailed with pride ending their final years as tombs of the seas for the descendants of the fathers who had built them.*

These Japanese "Hell Ships" provided not only inhumane living conditions but tortuous cruelty by their crew. Used for transporting Japanese Prisoners of War to destinations to be worked as forced labour. The Prisoners of War were crammed into cargo holds which can only be described as much worse than conditions used for cattle. Once at sea the hatches were closed Once at sea the hatches were closed allowing little air and no ventilation. Little food or water was provided for journeys which could last weeks, resulting in many deaths due to lack of oxygen, starvation or dysentery. They were stacked on sleeping platforms, 3 feet above one another, forced to sit cross-legged for the duration of the journey, some became delirious or unresponsive due to such cruel conditions.

Some ships carried a mix Prisoners of War, Japanese Troops and cargo and were not eligible to be marked with a red cross to indicate they were carrying just Prisoners of War. This resulted in allied submarines and aircraft mistakenly attacking and sinking the ships before reaching their destination. More than 20,000 Prisoners of War died at sea when ships were erroneously attacked by the allies.

STERN ORDERS FOR PRISONERS AT SEA:

These orders were issued by the 'Commander of the Prisoner Escort, Navy of the Great Japanese Empire'. The threat of the death penalty covered such breaches of discipline as 'talking without permission and raising loud voices' and 'using' more than two blankets.

~ *REGULATIONS FOR PRISONERS* ~

1. *The prisoners disobeying the following orders* ***will be punished with immediate death****.*
   a) *Those disobeying orders and instructions*
   b) *Those showing a motion of antagonism and raising a sign of opposition*
   c) *Those disordering the regulations by individualism, egoism, thinking only about yourself, rushing for your own goods*
   d) *Those talking without permission and raising loud voices*
   e) *Those walking and moving without order*
   f) *Those carrying unnecessary baggage in embarking*
   g) *Those resisting mutually*
   h) *Those touching the boat's materials, wires, electric lights, tools, switches etc)*
   i) *Those climbing ladder without order*
   j) *Those showing action of running away from the room or boat*
   k) *Those trying to take more meal than given to them*
   l) *Those using more than two blankets*

2. *Since the boat is not well equipped and inside being narrow, food being scarce and poor you'll feel uncomfortable during the short time on the boat. Those losing patience and disordering the regulation will be heavily punished for the reason of not being able to escort.*

3. *Be sure to finish your 'Nature's call', evacuate the bowels and urine, before embarking.*

4. *Meals will be given twice a day. One plate only to one prisoner. The prisoners call by the guard will give out the meal quick as possible and honestly. The remaining prisoners will stay in their places and wait for your plate. Those moving from their places reaching for your plate without order will be heavily punished. Same orders will be applied in handling plates after meal.*

5. *Toilet will be fixed at the four corners of the room. The buckets and cans will be placed. When filled up a guard will appoint a prisoner. The prisoner called will take the buckets to the centre of the room. The buckets will be pulled up by the derrick and be thrown away. Toilet papers will be given. Everyone must co-operate to make the room sanitary. Those being careless will be punished.*

6. *Navy of the Great Japanese Empire will not try to punish you all with death. Those obeying all the rules and regulations, and believing the action ad purpose of the Japanese Navy, co-operating with Japan in constructing the New Order of the Great Asia which led to the world's peace will be well treated. (This provoked smiles – not merely on account of its pidgin-English!!)*

The End.

Chapter 15

THE PROMISE OF A "TROPICAL ISLAND REST CAMP" DESTINATION ... Amboina Island (Ambon), Ceram (Seram) & Haroeke (Haruku)

The Amboina Island (now Ambon) lies off the South West Coast of Seram Island. The Japanese arrived on 30th January 1942 and occupied the island until their surrender.

It is recorded that on Ambon Island a number of prisoners were slaughtered for accepting food from the local inhabitants.

Seram (Ceram) showing Haruku (Haroekoe) and Ambon (Amboina)

Tom's story continues ...

17th April 1943 – The option we have during this day is to either roast on deck in the unbearable blistering heat of the tropical sun, or stay in the hold yarning about where we are bound for, or lie and dream of home. There is talk that the Nips have told some of the chaps that we are bound for a "rest camp on a quiet tropical island" and that England is 'abyss", (finished) and bombed out by the Germans. *(We later learn this is all part of their scheme to further demoralise us in spite of our position).* The long nights are spent crammed back into the stifling hold with rain leaking in. We are still sailing east and surprised to learn that we are only approximately seven hundred miles or so from Australia.

BACK HOME IN BLIGHTY ... An AIR MINISTRY ERROR! - Letter of Apology to Joan

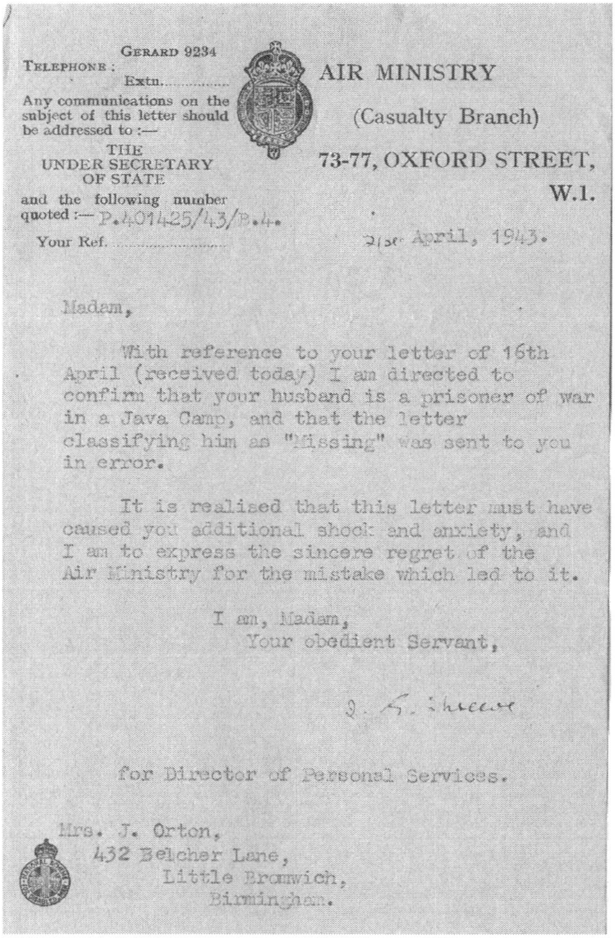

TELEPHONE: GERARD 9234
Extn. ....

Any communications on the subject of this letter should be addressed to:—
THE UNDER SECRETARY OF STATE
and the following number quoted:— P.401425/43/P.4.

Your Ref. ....

AIR MINISTRY
(Casualty Branch)
73-77, OXFORD STREET,
W.1.

21st April, 1943.

Madam,

With reference to your letter of 16th April (received today) I am directed to confirm that your husband is a prisoner of war in a Java Camp, and that the letter classifying him as "Missing" was sent to you in error.

It is realised that this letter must have caused you additional shock and anxiety, and I am to express the sincere regret of the Air Ministry for the mistake which led to it.

I am, Madam,
Your obedient Servant,

for Director of Personal Services.

Mrs. J. Orton,
432 Belcher Lane,
Little Bromwich,
Birmingham.

Tom's story continues ...

22nd April 1943 – The Amagi Maru ship finally reaches the Amboina Island and anchors in the harbour. (*We later learn this is a former* ***Dutch naval base***). After spending yet another long night cramped in the hold, a number of invasion boats pull in alongside us. It looks as though various supplies are being unloaded from the forward hold by the prisoners confined there. We have been unable to have any contact with these prisoners during our voyage but it looks as though there are fairly large amounts of supplies being unloaded.

23rd April 1943 – Today turns out to be quite memorable ... the air raid sirens are sounded and an allied reconnaissance plane appears over the harbour; the first we have seen! A magnificent sight which raises our spirits and boosts our morale. It feels so good at last to have something positive to talk about as there are always a few of us that get down in the dumps at times (we later learn that the main reason for this in most cases is that it is one of the first signs of malnutrition). We hear that a nearby aerodrome was bombed.

We leave **Ambon** the next day, continuing to speculate and deliberate our unknown destination.

NEWS HEADLINES BACK IN BLIGHTY ... 23rd April 1943 – *2 Bombs fall on Bordesley Green" (very close to Joan's home - Tom is totally unaware)*

Tom's story continues ...

25th April 1943 – The Amagi Maru approaches a large island which we think is the village of **Amahai, Ceram (North of Ambon)** and, as there's no landing quay, the ship is taken as close to the shore as possible. The Nips start their usual behaviour of frenzied hysteria, bawling and screaming orders at us. We are ordered to take the tarpaulin and planks off the top of the holds and the derricks of the ship are prepared for action. It is at this point that we discover the nature of the cargo we have been sitting on since leaving Surabaya. Sixty-gallon drums of aviation spirit! It now makes sense - the fumes from these drums must be the reason for the dreadful sickness suffered by most of the prisoners on the ship.

All prisoners are lined up in parties and each prisoner is ordered to roll one drum over the side of the ship, jump into the water and swim the drum ashore which is quite a distance. I have to admit I am amongst the poor unfortunates who is not a strong swimmer and beginning to feel quite anxious! It turns out ok though as the drum acts as a buoyancy aid making it not too difficult a task. As the prisoners reach the shore the drums are taken from us. We are ordered to swim back to the ship and it occurs to me straight away that I will not have the aid of the drum and the Nips are sitting on the shore watching us very closely holding their machine guns at the ready. The weaker swimmers are in no position to argue ... it is a matter of being gunned down, sink, or swim! Needless to say, after this experience, my swimming somewhat improved! We have lost count of the vast number of drums we are ordered to swim ashore but we begin to appreciate the welcome cool soothing effect of the water on our tired bodies after so many long weeks crammed like sardines in the stinking hold of the hell ship.

The forward hold is now empty of the drums and we are ordered to upload the hold aft of the ship where high numbers of our fellow prisoners have also been confined in cramped conditions. Sickness and many other illnesses have taken their toll on many men which has cut the number of fit men quite considerably. This results in the fit men from our hold being ordered aft to carry out additional work and it is here that we make a disturbing discovery .... **the contents of the hold are crates of bombs!**

Standing "uneasy" on parade, we are somewhat fearful about how we are going to get these crates of bombs ashore ... obviously not by the swimming method! We do not have to wait long before we receive such orders. Two invasion barges appear from nowhere and we are instructed to load the bomb crates onto the barges in readiness for them to be taken to the shore. We are constantly being screamed and bawled at by the Nips .... "lekas", "speedo" and other words such as "bahgaro", the former being Malay for "hurry", the latter meaning "B" fool. Their favourite weapon and form of chastisement now is **the bamboo pole across our backs.**

The unloading of the Amagi Maru takes nearly three days. The absence of the other ships becomes noticeable and we give thought as to where they could be and how they are contributing to "Dai Nippon's" War effort. It appears that our tasks here are now complete and we are to be transferred to another ship.

4th May 1943 – Whilst awaiting on the quay we are told that we are not staying at Amahai, Ceram as we are being taken to a "jasme", Japanese for "rest camp – a camp to rest up". Asking about the whereabouts of our main kit off the Amagi Maru, we are told that it will be waiting for us at the "rest camp". (We never do cast eyes on our kit again). My only possessions are the things I stand up in, my side pack containing eating utensils and a few other small items, including my tattered towel. Our numbers are now reduced somewhat as many of our comrades were put ashore at Ceram (Seram).

Sailing into the darkness, scarcely anything can be seen and we are totally exhausted. We chat about recent incidents and events, drawing us to our own conclusions. We think perhaps the ship that blew up in Surabaya harbour may have been as a result of our damaging the aviation sprit drums at Jakarta, perhaps caused by someone lighting a cigarette! We may, however, be completely wrong! Another thought is that if the ship was similar to the Amagi Maru, then it is pretty certain that tragically there were prisoners aboard.

It is our understanding that the Nips are using allied prisoners for slave labour in **constructing an air strip on the Ceram Island**. We do know that before our arrival, they had Dutch prisoners there.

Chapter 16

HAROEKOE (Haruku) "Hell Camp"

The tiny island of Haroekoe (Haruku) – known as the Nutmeg Island of the Spice Islands, is just east of Ambon Island, south of Seram in the Molucca Archipelago (the Moluccas).

It is reported that after a voyage of approximately 17 days more than 2,000 British and Dutch prisoners reached their destination ... ***the Coral Island of Haroekoe*** *(Haruku).*

Prisoners of all ranks, including officers, doctors and soldiers were beaten and kicked throughout the voyage without knowing the reason for their punishment.

The prison camp on Haroekoe was built on un-drained swampy slopes. There were a few bamboo structures but without sides and inadequate roofing. A previously dug latrine trench ran parallel with each hut but due to a heavy downpour of rain over several days, the latrines became full to the brim with human excrement floating on the top. A repugnant welcome for the prisoners! The prisoners dug around each hut in a desperate attempt to divert the streams of rain water but it still flowed over the prisoners as they slept! The Japanese would only allow the use of a small number of inadequate tools which made little impact in helping the prisoners attempt to create a new drainage system.

The prisoners of war were transferred from ***Surabaya to Haroekoe with the intention of using their labour to construct a new Japanese military airfield to be used as a Japanese launch pad to strike Australia.*** *Known as 'white coolies' the prisoners were ordered to slice down two large solid humps which rose above the surface in the coral spine of the island, using the spoil to fill the valley inbetween. They were issued with a native tool called a pachul, pickaxe and a chisel to hack away the coral by hand to make the land level.*

During the first few months, ***dysentery claimed 1 in 5 Prisoners on Haroekoe island. Approximately 400 men were carried by their comrades to "Boot Hill" where they were***

laid to their final rest on the sandy shores of what would have been a paradise island. The nauseating stench of death permeated the whole camp. *The final death rate was approximately 63 per cent and only approximately 750 survived their ordeal.*

Lieutenant Kurashima was the Camp Commandant.

Tom's story continues ....

6th May 1943 – After approximately seventeen days at sea aboard the hell ship, we reach our destination the Coral Island of Haroekoe (Haruku), (later to be known as "Hell Camp").

In the early hours of the morning, we are taken ashore via small motor boats onto a small jetty on a very muddy shore with dense rain drenched vegetation. Experiencing a tropical downpour of rain and suffering from exhaustion, we are ordered to march, with the aid of the light of torches carried by our guards, for a long trek through the jungle path to our promised "rest camp". I am wearing my RAF peaked cap, a towel around my naked shoulders and my khaki drill shorts. I have bare feet. It is during this march that I experience the first symptoms of dysentery; severe crippling abdominal pains and the strong sensation of desperately needing to go to the toilet.

Arriving at the camp our spirits sink even further as we are welcomed by the disheartening sight of partly-built bamboo billets which are supposed to house us! These billets have only been started on providing little cover from the torrential tropical rainstorm; just bamboo uprights with an atap roof and no sides. We are to spend our first night here in what the Nips have described as our "rest camp"!

There are no latrines and many of us are in excruciating pain. The only option is to rush to the nearest undergrowth to excrete blood and slime from our bodies (symptoms and courses of action which soon result in the loss of the coating of our stomachs and bowels). Cursing the Nips, we pray for the light of morning to come.

We have spent the night lying on the wet muddy ground contaminated with human excrement. Daybreak arrives and we are paraded and issued details by our officers who are under orders from the Nips. We are told that we are the advance party and our first task is to complete the building of the billets and prepare the camp in readiness for more prisoners expected to arrive very soon. If our officers do not carry out the orders of the Nips, or if the orders are not carried out by the prisoners, our officers suffer the consequences of a beating-up in front of us!

It is reported that six days after the prisoners' arrival, ***Squadron-Leader Pitts*** *was ordered to have two shifts of six hundred men ready for work on the airfield. A hopeless task due to the serious outbreak of dysentery and many hundreds being unfit to do any type of work. The dysentery outbreak grew into an epidemic, making it impossible for the officers to meet the Japanese demands. These officers were paraded and beaten in front of the prisoners.*

Tom's story continues ...

The first completed billet is set aside and made out of bounds by using barbed wire as it is to be used as sick quarters for the dysentery cases. The roof and side walls are made of dried coconut leaves providing no protection against wind or rain. Each hut accommodates approximately 100 – 125 patients with a bed space measuring approximately 1 metre across. Patients lie in rows on baleh-baleh (split flattened bamboo) sleeping platforms and I have now become one of the many severe cases of dysentery myself. The toilets outside are small bamboo huts built over a large deep pit with a large bamboo pole rigged up across for the seat. One certainly has to keep one's balance as the lack of doing so could be distasteful! The drainage system is not working! There are not enough tins to serve as bedpans for the seriously ill and many are left to lie outside in the open air on the bare muddy ground.

8th May 1943 – There are even more dysentery cases, many men have become delirious. What little water we have is fetched from the small polluted river quite a distance away, which is contaminated with human excrement coming from the open trench latrines. There is an epidemic of hundreds of flies hatching from the maggots. Much contaminated drinking water is being consumed and due to the water shortage many have become dehydrated.

10th May 1943 – After being examined by Japanese doctors, many sick patients are beaten with bamboo sticks and set to work scrubbing. There are approximately 400 very sick and 150 near to death. A number of our own Medical Officers have been beaten for not allowing sick prisoners to work!

13th May 1943 – After nearly a fortnight on **Haroekoe** I am still in the sick bay. The only treatment I have received for my dysentery is one spoonful of charcoal and one of tannic acid. The Nips have told our Medical Officers that this is the only treatment available. The fit men are busy at work on the camp including those skilled in many trades, especially carpenters; there is now no malingering, which is to be for our own benefit. During the last few nights we have heard the sound of aircraft, possibly heading east. The guards are shouting "skorkhi" (planes), "apphi mahtti" (lights out). We fail to understand their panic as we have very little light anyway ... the lights we do have are made from a small tin containing whatever we are able to scrounge, such as any type of oil used for cooking, (if anyone is lucky enough to pinch with any food worth cooking), an old piece of string, or even bootlace, serves as a wick poking through the small hole in the top of the tin.

15th May 1943 – The dysentery epidemic has now got a real grip on the camp, resulting in two or three deaths. The first graveyard is prepared in the undergrowth a few yards from the camp. (We have no idea at this time as to the number of bodies there will be buried here before our departure). It is my view that the Nips are beginning to become more and more anxious about the numbers of deaths as prisoners are beginning to die daily. Our officers tell us that the food alone, despite the lack of medical supplies, will almost certainly eventually wipe us out altogether. Four goats arrive at the camp; we assume this is as a result of the loss of so many prisoners. They are immediately slaughtered and added to the watery soup. The Nips also try to soften us up with a small amount of sugar and one sago cake each!

17th May 1943 – Three more men have died during the night and the carpenters are kept busy making rough wooden coffins. We are now experiencing a number of malaria cases, a potentially lethal parasitic disease. The workload for the medical officers and medical orderlies is increasing at an alarming rate with few medical supplies left.

18th May 1943 – An incredibly horrifying sight ... The plague of flies is worsening! The buzzing of millions of flies can be heard alongside the groaning and howling of sick men now lying like skeletons on the baleh-baleh bed spaces, many with deep gaping sores on their hip bones and some of the mortally sick just lying in a coma. Many are dehydrated and maggots are crawling over bedspaces covered in excrement. Any clothing, blankets, eating utensils are being boiled and sterilised. Lists of deficiencies are made out for the fit men and we must now wear the clothing of our dead comrades.

19th May 1943 – Men are still dying! Our **RAF Camp Commandants, Squadron Leader Pitts and Hopkins** are given permission to go to a kampong (native village) to buy food for the camp cookhouse under the supervision of Korean guards. **The Nip camp interpreter 'Kasiyama' has visited the sick bay along with 'Gunso Mori' (The Bull).**

21st May 1943 – 2 more men die. The death toll is 17, increasing to 65 by the end of May.

British Red Cross Instructions to Joan for sending mail

PW/FE/2a/42.

WAR ORGANISATION
of the
BRITISH RED CROSS SOCIETY and ORDER OF ST. JOHN OF JERUSALEM.

PRISONERS OF WAR DEPARTMENT
FAR EAST SECTION.

9, Park Place,
St. James's Street,
London, S.W.1.

Telephone No.
REGent 0111.

Letters and postcards addressed as shown below may be sent post free to Service personnel known or believed to be in Japanese hands. They should be posted in the ordinary way and should not be sent to the British Red Cross Society to be forwarded. The name and address of the sender should be shown on the back of the envelope: members of H.M. Forces should, however, give a civilian address to which replies should be sent. Only letters and postcards may be posted, and parcels and other packets cannot be forwarded. In order to avoid delay in Japanese censorship, no one should write more than once a week. Letters should be brief (i.e. not exceeding two sides of an ordinary sheet of notepaper). They should be clearly written and whenever possible, should be typed. No enclosures are allowed. There is at present no air mail service.

All letters and postcards must invariably bear the two phrases:-

"Prisoner of War Post,
Service des prisonniers de guerre."

in the top left-hand corner.

I. If the camp address is known, address your letter this way:-

(1) Write in the top left-hand corner:-

"Prisoner of War Post,
Service des prisonniers de guerre."

(2) Write personal particulars (see below).
(3) Write "British Prisoner of War" and the Camp address.

The personal particulars to be furnished under (2) are:-

NAVY	Officers.	Rank, Initials, Name (in block letters).
	Ratings.	Rating, Initials, Name (in block letters), Official No.
ARMY	Officers.	Rank, Initials, Name (in block letters).
	Other Ranks.	Army No., Rank, Initials, Name (in block letters).
AIR FORCE.	Officers.	Rank, Initials, Name (in block letters).
	Airmen.	Personal No., Rank, Initials, Name (in block letters).

II. If the camp address is not known, address your letter this way:-

(1) Write in the top left-hand corner:-

"Prisoner of War Post,
Service des prisonniers de guerre."

(2) Write personal particulars (see below).

(3) Write "British Prisoner of War"
C/o Japanese Red Cross,
Tokyo.

P.T.O.

\- 2 -

The personal particulars to be furnished under (2) are:-

NAVY

Officers. Rank, Initials, Name (in block letters), R.N. (or R.N.R. or R.N.V.R.)
Name of Ship.

Ratings. Rating, Initials, Name (in block letters), Official No.
Name of Ship.

Examples:-

Cmdr. K. JONES, R.N.
H.M.S. Exeter,
British Prisoner of War,
C/o. Japanese Red Cross,
Tokyo.

Stoker J. SMITH, 123456,
H.M.S. Exeter,
British Prisoner of War,
C/o. Japanese Red Cross,
Tokyo.

ARMY

Officers. Rank, Initials, Name (in block letters).
No. of Unit and particulars of Regiment or Corps.
Locality where last serving or last heard of.

Other Ranks. Army No., Rank, Initials, Name (in block letters).
No. of Unit and particulars of Regiment or Corps.
Locality where last serving or last heard of.

Examples:-

Captain J. SMITH,
~~6th Btn. Warwickshire Regt.,~~
Malaya,
British Prisoner of War,
C/o. Japanese Red Cross,
Tokyo.

123456 Corporal T. ATKINS,
~~100th A.A. Battery, R.A.~~
A.P.O. No. ....
British Prisoner of War,
C/o. Japanese Red Cross,
Tokyo.

AIR FORCE

Officers. Rank, Initials, Name (in block letters).
No. and particulars of Unit, Squadron or Wing.
R.A.F.
Locality where last serving or last heard of.

Airmen. Personal No., Rank, Initials, Name (in block letters).
No. and particulars of Unit, Squadron or Wing.
R.A.F.
Locality where last serving or last heard of.

Examples:-

Squadron Leader J. EVANS,
R.A.F., H.Q.,
Malaya,
British Prisoner of War,
C/o. Japanese Red Cross,
Tokyo.

123456 Leading Aircraftman C. TAYLOR,
200 Squadron,
R.A.F.,
A.P.O. No. ....
British Prisoner of War,
C/o. Japanese Red Cross,
Tokyo.

Chapter 17

THE EVIL AND BRUTAL "GUNSO MORI" & OTHERS ~ EXAMPLES OF JAPANESE ATROCITIES ~

Tom described an example of the atrocities he had witnessed in the local press a few years before he passed away under the headlines of "Veterans recall VJ Day – What price freedom? The nightmare will haunt him for the rest of his life."

On one occasion, a Canadian prisoner lost complete control and struck a Japanese guard; he was punished with barbed wire being tied around his neck. Another example of inflicting cruel and harsh punishment on the prisoners would be to put them in what was to become known as 'the 'oven' which could only be described as "a corrugated iron dog kennel". They would have rope tied around their necks and a bowl of water would be placed just out of reach leaving them to suffer for three or four days until they were almost dead.

NEWS REPORT:

The Japanese Guard Gunso (Sergeant) Mori *was one of three cruel and sadistic individuals responsible for making life in Haruku camp an everlasting hell. The other two were* ***Lieutenant Kurishima****, the camp commandant and Gunso Mori's sidekick* ***Kasiyama****, the camp interpreter. It is reported that the evil Gunso Mori really ran the camp and that Kurishima was just a lazy, insignificant nobody. Gunso Mori was in charge of the discipline of the prisoners... not a difficult task as the majority were far too ill and weak to resist.*

Gunso Mori and his sycophantic Korean sidekick and interpreter Kasiyama were known as "Blood and Slime" (two of the symptoms of dysentery). Gunso Mori was to blame for the epidemic of dysentery and large number of deaths. For example he would not allow a latrine to be built over the sea fearing it would 'sully the ocean belonging to His Imperial Emperor'. This callous behaviour resulted in the ground of the camp becoming sodden with infected human excretion, attracting disease-spreading maggots and flies into the billets.

Gunso Mori, also known as "Bamboo Gunzo" on account of his use of a split bamboo pole and a three inch leather belt, was a sadistic bully who derived pleasure from acts of killing and brutal torture. He would repeatedly beat the prisoners and embraced an audience. Many of these beatings would regularly be carried out during a parade of the whole camp. Prisoners were often subjected to brutal beatings for the most trivial offences, often for nothing at all, which included prisoners who were too sick and frail to fend for themselves. It was reported that he beat officers responsible for dismantling a hut built of rotten bamboo just because once the main supports were removed, the rest of the hut collapsed. He was known to have slapped the face of a Senior British Officer sixteen times (a strong Japanese slap would leave deep cuts and bruises) for refusing to accept boots issued to his men that were far too small and painful to wear.

A much decorated War hero, it has been said that Mori's state of mind and brutal behaviour may have been due to the fact that he was an ex-China veteran who had contracted syphilis which made him insane. Whatever the cause of his sadistic behaviour, Gunso Mori was a merciless brutal mass murderer who paid for his crimes by hanging in Singapore in 1946.

"Lieutenant Kurishima – Camp Commandant" *had what could have been construed as an almost fair reputation amongst the prisoners at Sourabaya (Surabaya) for example he would help them to obtain extra food and cigarettes, he would never use violence. However, such behaviour changed after his arrival at Haroekoe where he delegated to Gunso Mori and maintained a callous indifference to the suffering of the sick and dying prisoners. It is thought their appalling condition gave him derived pleasure! An official report on this camp states "not even the dead escaped his jocularity" as he suggested that the dead bodies of prisoners be taken to the kitchen and made into beef steak. Such evil remarks may have been in jest but they were an indication of his contempt to the atrocities and tragedies taking place.*

Tom's photograph and notes:

Pictured from left to right (back row) Squadron Leader Pitts, unknown. (front row) "the Bull", Camp Interpreter Kasiyama, Gunso Mori.

> ***We are the Knights of Bushido,***
>
> ***of the Order of the Rising Sun***
>
> ***We do not execute at sunset,***
>
> ***but at sunrise***

~ JAPANESE ATROCITIES ~

It is well recorded that *the Japanese behaved with the utmost brutality. Prisoners were often ordered to beat other prisoners and many were even flogged to death.*

WARNING! ... described below are just a few examples which some readers may find distressing.

WATER TREATMENT – Bound with barbed wire, water would be forced through the prisoner's mouth and nostrils into his lungs until he lost consciousness. Guards would then jump on to his stomach to force the water out, only to be repeated once the prisoner re-gained consciousness

BURNING – The prisoner's body would be burned with either lighted cigarettes, cigars, lighted candles, hot irons, burning oil or scalding water, often to sensitive parts of the body such as the nostrils, eardrums or sexual organs.

ELECTRIC SHOCK – An electric current would be applied to the most sensitive parts.

KNEE SPREAD – The prisoner would be forced to kneel with his hands tied behind his back. A pole would be inserted behind both knee joints so as to spread them and pressure would be applied to his thighs, sometimes by jumping on them causing the knee joints to become separated.

SUSPENSION - The prisoner would be suspended by his wrists, arms, legs or neck sometimes leading to strangulation or the joints being pulled from their sockets.

TIED TO A TREE - The prisoner would be tied to a branch of a tree by his thumbs and suspended with his toes just touching the ground for a considerable period of time, or the prisoner would be tied to a tree with barbed wire for approximately 2 days and nights without food or water. A bucket of water would be placed in front of him.

KNEELING ON SHARP IMPLEMENTS – The prisoner would be ordered to kneel on sharp implements whilst holding a heavy rock for a period of 1 to 2 hours. If the prisoner moved, he would be flogged.

REMOVAL OF NAILS – Usually with pliers, the prisoner's finger and toe nails would be removed or small bamboo chips would be driven under his nails.

FINGER BANDAGING – The prisoner's fingers would be bandaged together with a stick placed between each finger. Extra pressure would then be applied by tightening the bandage with a cord.

OTHER ATROCITIES – The mutilation of dead and living bodies was not uncommon. It is recorded that vivisection by the Japanese medical authorities was also practised upon prisoners. A prisoner was tied to a tree surrounded by a Japanese doctor and four Japanese medical students who cut open his chest, removing his heart. The consumption of enemy flesh was not considered a crime and sometimes made into something of a festive occasion in the officers' mess. Admirals and generals took part in these festivities and the flesh of murdered prisoners, or soup made from such flesh, was served to the other ranks.

Extract from the diary of a Japanese officer: *"Discovered and captured two prisoners who escaped last night in the jungle. To prevent their escaping a second time pistols were fired at their feet but it was difficult to hit them. The two prisoners were later dissected while still alive by a Medical Officer. Their livers were taken out and for the first time I saw the internal organs of a human being. It was very informative".*

Chapter 18

JOINING THE WORKING PARTY – HAROEKE (Haruku)

Tom's story continues ...

Although still pretty weak, I am now out of the sick bay and join some of my pals in my allocated billet. We have lots to talk about and I am to join the working party tomorrow. My comrades do not hide the fact that they are concerned I may still be carrying the dysentery bug! Having a reputation for being a particular sort of a clean chap in my habits, much to my relief, I'm accepted into the "gang".

I am updated about what is going on in the sick bay, for example, **Kasiyama has told every patient in the sick bay in his pigeon English that if they cannot work through sickness, or any other reason, they may as well die as they are no good to him. There is also a reminder that there are no means of escape.**

I am on **Tenko** working parade today, my first time since the unloading of the Amagi Maru. I must say, the camp working party have certainly done some good work on the camp. There is a pathway down to the river where we are allowed to wash, which I manage to do now that I am out of sick bay. There is also a **Padang**, parade square, on which we form up to number in Japanese. It's my first Tenko and I learn quickly that **any man that cannot shout out "san, shi, gho, rohco, shishi etc" receives a blow across the head.** I also gather what is the best form of action to take on being given the order to fall out for the different working parties, most important of all, which are the worst guards to work under. I soon discover that the best type of work to go for is that of carpentry and I do manage to succeed in joining these working parties.

We are ordered to march along the jungle-path towards, what we call "the drome" (aerodrome/airfield) which is just under 2 miles from the camp, through the village of Pelauw. For a reason unbeknown to us, the party is split up and I end up at the Nip barracks, situated near the shore of the island. These barracks are occupied by army Nips, most of whom are supposed to be specialists in all trades appertaining to the construction of airstrips. The Nip in charge of our small party of about a dozen is a professional carpenter and he doesn't appear to be too harsh as far as Nips go. He is able to speak a little Malay, which makes it easier for me to understand what is to be done and enable me to carry out his orders. **The prisoners are to build a bungalow for the Officer Shoko**, who is to be in charge of the drome when it is completed. We are a little bemused as to how the Nips think building a bungalow can possibly be of any significant importance to the Nip war effort! Timbers of strict dimensions must be sawn and planed. Up until now it is quite noticeable that there has not been any of the usual shouting of "lakhas" and hysteria experienced on previous working parties. Our 'tiffin' is sent up from the camp by lorry at about 13.00 hours; a small measure of steamed rice with a ladle of pumpkin soup, sometimes, but very rarely, we may come across the smallest fragment of meat.

I'm not sure whether it's my imagination but the food appears to be better than that given to us in whilst in sick bay. It would appear that **Kasiyama's** comments made to the patients in sick bay are somewhat true. **"If you are in a reasonable state of health to work, you get a little more nutritious food."** Better food turns out to be not the only benefit of working on the drome ... by the time I arrive back in camp, my "cherhy cherhy" bag, as our side packs are called, is packed with wild spinach collected from amongst the wild vegetation. The name "cherhy cherhy" given to my side pack means "search" in Malay and although we are a long way from Malaya, I manage to make myself understood by the natives and in some cases the Nip guards, (I discover later – they speak better Malay than English).

It is the end of our first day at the Nip barracks on the drome and we are allowed, much to our delight, the pleasure of a "mahndi" (Malay for "washing ourselves") in the sea before we return to the camp. The routine upon returning to camp is to go down to the river for a "mahndi" but as we have already been allowed to do this in the sea, we are first in the "makhan" (food) queue.

After our meal we have the usual chinwag about the day's events and discuss the concoction I have cooked on the fire. I offer some boiled spinach around but it is taken advantage of by only some ... those who trust my talents as an horticulturist! The camp is scattered with palm trees and the sight of the "clahpers" (Malay for coconuts) makes one's mouth water.

Orders of the camp are that the coconuts must not to be touched by prisoners but I do manage to get my hands on one during a storm one night. Lying awake I heard a thud on the ground where the coconut had fallen and although it was pitch black outside, (living in the conditions we have had to endure for so long, one's senses, well at least mine, have become very sharp!). Moving slowly and quietly out into the darkness of the night and only having to grope within a small radius, I put my hands straight on to the coconut and scurry quickly back inside. What a find? What a luxury? Feeling very pleased, I manage to keep the coconut well-hidden and during the next day I get to cut it out from the husk, drink the milk and shred it on an old tin, which had been punctured all over with bodged holes. There may be opportunities to exchange goods with fellow prisoners, as someone has always got something, by hook or by crook, whether it is in the food line or otherwise.

Over 129 men have died since setting foot on Haroekoe. This is not to be wondered at as we are without vitamins and there is a serious lack of medical supplies and drugs. **The policy of the Nips is "no work so you die".** Prisoners are now suffering from even more serious medical conditions, such as **tropical ulcers**, which can be caused by the least scratch or knock on the legs or feet and **pellagra,** which is a painful condition due to continual exposure to the hot sun. **Vitamin deficiency** causing burning feet, blurred vision, numbness around the mouth and ears – resembling someone who has been injected with Cocaine! (A typical example I can describe is that of one of my friends named **Alan Guest** who came from my home town **Sutton Coldfield**. Alan developed an inflammation of the mouth which became so infected that he was unable to sip water through his lips due to the stinging sensation to his mouth. This meant that he could not take advantage of what little nourishment, if any, there was in the camp food.)

Chapter 19

COMING INTO CONTACT WITH A "NATIVE" – Haroeke (Haruku)

Tom's story continues ...

Today, I will later learn, that I am fortunate in being selected for the carpentry work as I am soon to come into contact with a native. Although such contact is strictly forbidden, I do manage to communicate with one.

I persevere and try to explain to the native the symptoms my friend **Alan Guest** has contracted. The native responds in a hurried manner, saying he will come back later – as soon as he can. Although I have warned him of the danger of us being caught, he just grins and disappears. Any amount of confidence we may have is possibly boosted by the fact that there is only the one Nip Guard around.

The native returns and I tell the Nip Guard that I am going into the undergrowth to "pigghi benjo" (spend a penny!), taking with me, as we always do, my cherhy cherhy bag. The friendly native hands me six "pisangs" (bananas), which are really over-ripe with very dark brown skins and he explains to me what to do with them for medicinal purposes. I give him my thanks and hastily rejoin the working party to carry on with my work.

On our return to the camp we are always subjected to a search but with a bit of shuffling and heart pounding, I manage to get through with the "swag" covered with wild spinach in my bag. Heading towards the bed space of my pal **Alan Guest,** as soon as I am able, I convey the instructions given to me by the native. It turns out that the dark brown, soft, ripe and mushy bananas are the only things that he can suck without stinging his mouth and throat. He is to make them last as long as possible and to suck them for as long as he can. **Alan** follows the instructions and eventually his mouth recovers and gets back to normal. Thankfully Alan is now able to eat the camp rations, plus the little extras that I am able to smuggle into the camp. I soon learn that this is to be the first of many benefits to be gained as a result of my lessons in the Malay language.

It is reported that strong allegiances grew amongst the prisoners. They would carry their comrades when sick and many would often share rations to the point that they themselves would become unwell.

Still on the increase, there are now many more cases of dysentery, malaria, pellagra and large open tropical ulcers, the latter being on the feet and legs. The least scratch or blow received on working parties from flying coral or blow from a guard's rotan (bamboo pole) can fester to huge proportions and in a few days turns into a gaping ulcer. Mosquito nets are disappearing as they are required to be cut up and used for bandages.

A further billet has been set aside as a sick bay for the increasing number of prisoners going down with horrific diseases. **The latest despicable order of the Nips is that every sick man is to catch fifty flies to entitle him to his meagre rations. "No flies – no food."**

Letter from British Red Cross to Joan Dated 26 May 1943 – Tom Japanese POW

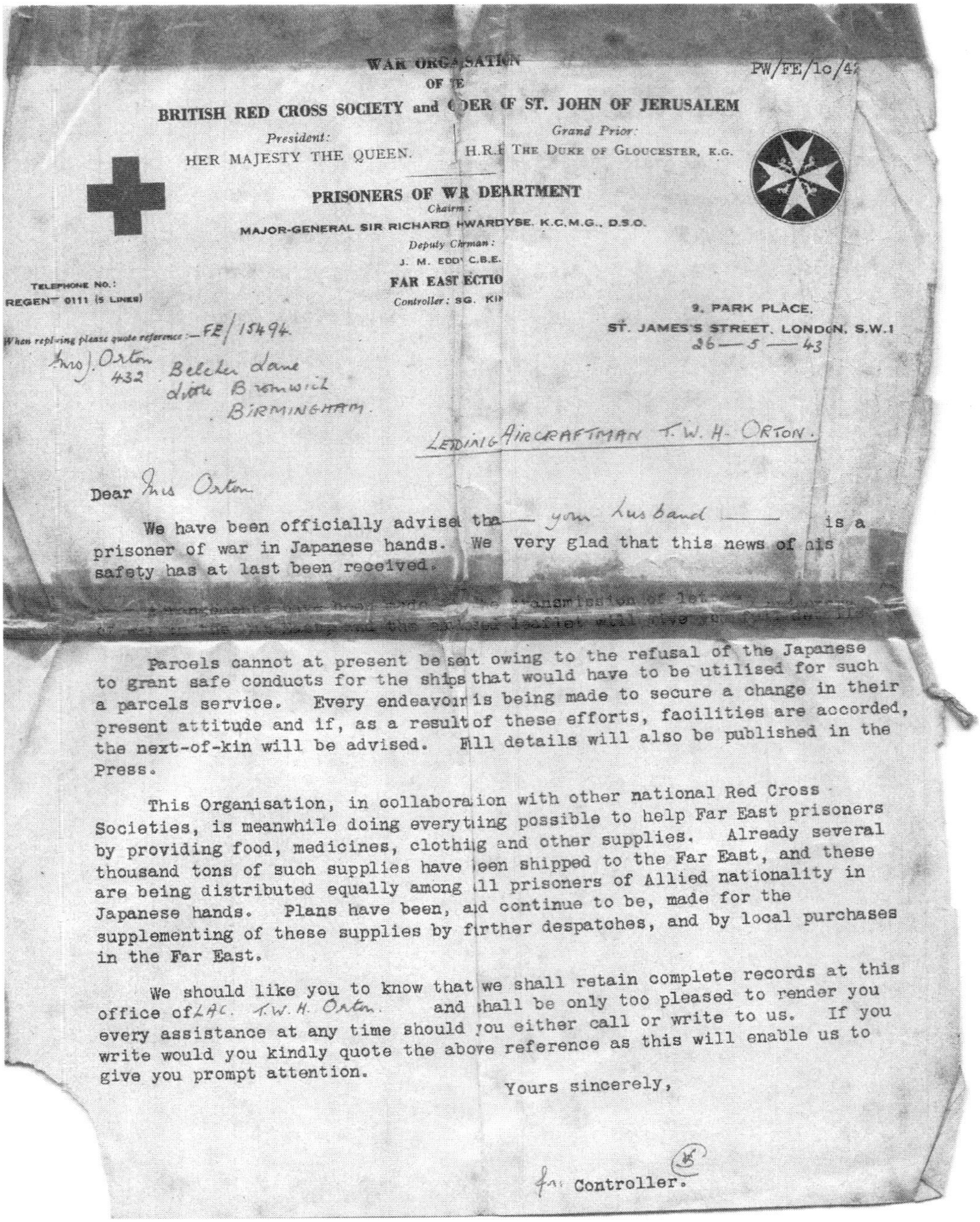

WAR ORG SATI
OF
BRITISH RED CROSS SOCIETY and DER F ST. JOHN OF JERUSALEM

President: HER MAJESTY THE QUEEN.

Grand Prior: H.R. THE DUKE OF GLOUCESTER, K.G.

PRISONERS OF WR DE ARTMENT
Chairm: MAJOR-GENERAL SIR RICHARD HWARDYSE. K.C.M.G., D.S.O.
Deputy Chrman: J. M. EDD C.B.E.
FAR EAST ECTIO
Controller: SG. KI

PW/FE/1c/42

TELEPHONE NO.: REGENT 0111 (5 LINES)

When replying please quote reference:— FE/15494.

9, PARK PLACE,
ST. JAMES'S STREET, LONDON, S.W.1
26 — 5 — 43

Mrs J. Orton
432 Belcher Lane
Little Bromwich
BIRMINGHAM.

LEADING AIRCRAFTMAN T.W.H. ORTON.

Dear Mrs Orton

We have been officially advise tha— your husband —— is a prisoner of war in Japanese hands. We very glad that this news of his safety has at last been received.

[illegible] transmission of let[illegible] leaflet will give you [illegible]

Parcels cannot at present be sent owing to the refusal of the Japanese to grant safe conducts for the ships that would have to be utilised for such a parcels service. Every endeavour is being made to secure a change in their present attitude and if, as a result of these efforts, facilities are accorded, the next-of-kin will be advised. All details will also be published in the Press.

This Organisation, in collaboration with other national Red Cross Societies, is meanwhile doing everything possible to help Far East prisoners by providing food, medicines, clothing and other supplies. Already several thousand tons of such supplies have been shipped to the Far East, and these are being distributed equally among all prisoners of Allied nationality in Japanese hands. Plans have been, and continue to be, made for the supplementing of these supplies by further despatches, and by local purchases in the Far East.

We should like you to know that we shall retain complete records at this office of LAC. T.W.H. Orton. and shall be only too pleased to render you every assistance at any time should you either call or write to us. If you write would you kindly quote the above reference as this will enable us to give you prompt attention.

Yours sincerely,

for Controller.

Tom's story continues ...

27 May 1943 – The death toll of fellow prisoners has now reached fifty-two, with many more lying in the sick bays in a very serious condition. **Gunso Mori and Kasiyama** continue to pay their daily visits to the sick bays dragging out men they consider fit to send out for work, if not on the drome, they must work on the camp.

There is Good news we think! ... The arrival of two small supply boats bringing a few medical supplies and food but unfortunately, as usual, most of these supplies end up in the Nip billets! Prisoners are given a few bags of soya beans, which even when boiled in the soup for midday and evening meals, we are unable to digest properly.

The latest whim of **Mori** is that we dysentery diseased prisoners are contaminating the Nipponese country, so the light duty sick men are tasked to make a small jetty from the shore. In constructing this, a pile driver is roughly made from tree trunks with a thick rope and pulley. It is just so barbaric using the manual labour of poor sick men to pull on the rope! Palm tree trunks are put onto the shore when the tide is out and the job takes a week to finish. When the job is complete, it resembles a small foot-bridge going out for around forty yards into the clear water of the sea. It has a small atap roofed hut, which is to be the "benjo" (latrine) for all the prisoners that can walk. This now means that every visit to the "benjo" by a prisoner will involve passing the guardroom but only after standing to attention, bowing to the guard commander and shouting "banjo ni ickemus" (I go to the latrine). On our return, we must go through the same procedure but shouting "banjo kari karimus" (I come back from the latrine).

31st May 1943 – There are now eighty prisoners buried in the cemetery alongside the camp. I am admitted to the sick bay by the RAF Medical Officer suffering again with the return of dysentery, something I have been dreading, as the sanitary conditions are nauseatingly filthy, even after all the attempts of the medical staff, who do their utmost to address these conditions. A terrible sight ... there are now so many patients just lying there dying who cannot help themselves in any way. The stench is unbearable.

Tom's story continues ...

10th June 1943 – Discharged from sick bay once more, I form up for the working party but the carpentry job is finished, so I find myself on the drome. We are ordered to scoop and chop at the surface of earth and hard coral and we are subjected to the blinding sun reflecting mercilessly off the pale coral. We load the sacking ready to be carried by the sling and bamboo pole method. Working at the hands of the Nips with their usual hysterical bawling of "lahkass" and "speedo", they are belting the prisoners filling the slings across their backs if they do not put sufficient earth and coral into the slings. They treat the two carriers the same if the bamboo pole breaks whilst they carry the load away. We hear that the runway is behind schedule for completion due to so much sickness and dying amongst us, so they are to bring in more prisoners from another area.

The guards on the drome are as hysterical as ever and the work is relentless. Our go-slow tactics are no longer tactics, as the heat of the sun and glare from the coral is now really telling on us. We have no spades available, picks and the chunkal (similar to a large garden hoe), are the main tools. I am drawn to the tools which bear the crocodile, the trade mark of a Birmingham firm by the name of **Martindales.** *(I have fond memories of Martindales who were based at Crocodile Works, Alma Street, Birmingham, as prior to the War, I was a transport mate with my father who drove the lorries containing hundreds of tons of these tools to the Liverpool docks. Little did I dream that one day I would be working with these as a slave to the Nips.)* The "parang", a large knife used for cutting away the clearings in the jungle also bears the same trade mark.

*It is reported that on **21st June 1943** – Haroekoe camp was inspected by a major in the Japanese Army Medical Services. All Officer prisoners were paraded and informed that the rising numbers of dysentery was all their fault! They were told that all they had to do was to "kill all the flies and cut their finger nails" to prevent the epidemic from worsening!*

*On **1st July 1943** – the 200th death was recorded which was that of a British prisoner.*

*During **July 1943** – the death rate was increasing rapidly and many prisoners were suffering in extreme pain from sores and ulcers. Prisoners who passed away were buried not far from the camp. Their comrades made coffins from odd planks where available but as these ran out, they attempted to make boxes from green bamboo. At times during incessant torrential downpours, prisoners too sick and frail to march to the aerodrome would scrape out shallow hollows in the hard coral ground for graves. When the dysentery epidemic was at its worst, one grave could contain up to 14 men. A burial would be led by an Officer and attended by a Japanese guard, probably to ensure that no one escaped rather than to honour the dead! The evil Gunso Mori appeared at one funeral very drunk and was subsequently sick into the open grave before the body was covered.*

The sick list and the death toll increased rapidly at Haroeke camp. At one time there were more than 1,300 prisoners in sick bays. Many others were considered fit for work but they were desperately in need of daily treatment.

At one point in time there were no more than 200 "healthy" men available to work on the drome and depending on Gunso Mori's mood, men would be removed from the sick bays. When Mori was promoted to Sergeant Major, his evil behaviour worsened. For example, he would regularly beat the sick, forcing them to drag their frail bodies to work. Guards were heard to say "the sick would soon be dead, leaving more food for the workers!"

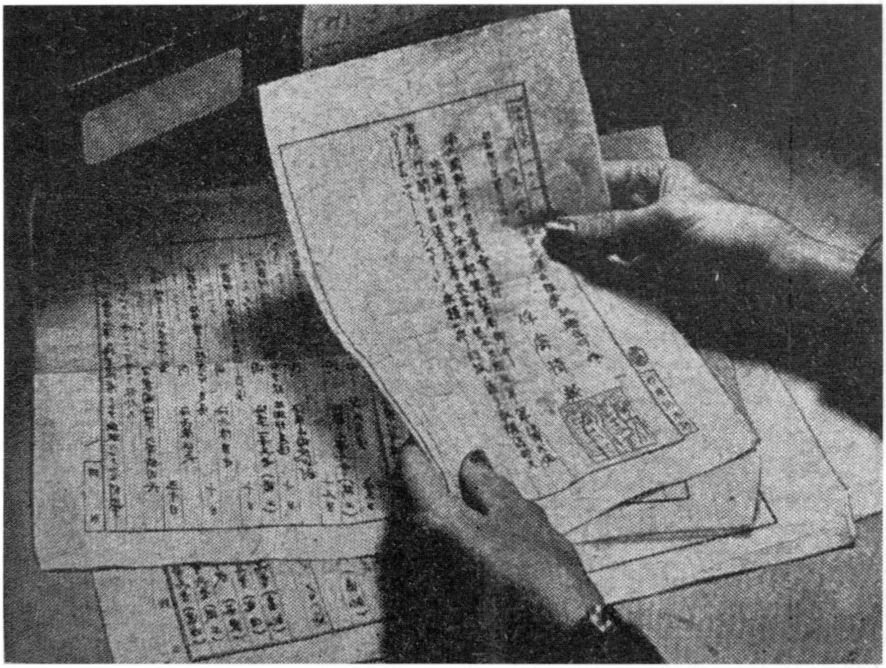

Examples of lists of prisoners

Letter to Joan dated 24 August 1943 – MISSING LETTERS!

WAR ORGANISATION SWD/SFO
OF THE
BRITISH RED CROSS SOCIETY and ORDER OF ST. JOHN OF JERUSALEM

President: HER MAJESTY THE QUEEN. | *Grand Prior:* H.R.H. THE DUKE OF GLOUCESTER, K.G.

PRISONERS OF WAR DEPARTMENT

Chairman: MAJOR-GENERAL SIR RICHARD HOWARD-VYSE, K.C.M.G., D.S.O.

Deputy Chairman: J. M. EDDY, C.B.E.

TELEPHONE NO. REGENT 0111 (5 LINES)

FAR EAST SECTION.
Controller: S. G. KING

9, PARK PLACE.
ST. JAMES'S STREET.
LONDON, S.W.1

When replying please quote reference: FE/15494

24th August, 1943.

Mrs. J.Orton,
432 Belchers Lane,
Little Bromwich,
Birmingham. 9.

849112 L.A.C. T.W.H.Orton.
Royal Air Force,

Dear Mrs. Orton,

Thank you for your letter of 15th August. We sympathise with you most sincerely in your having to wait so long for personal news of your husband. We know that letters, and some supplies have already reached Java, and we think that as you have not had your letters returned to you, you may assume your husband is receiving them.

A few letters have just begun to arrive from prisoners of war in Java Camps. Permission was given only in January of this year to the men detained in these camps to write to their relatives and friends. The difficulties to be overcome with regard to the despatch of correspondence from the Far East, and also to transport, have been enormous, and letters frequently take from six to nine months to reach this country. We hope in the course of a month or so a consignment will arrive from the Japanese camps generally, and when this does come, that it will contain good news of your husband for you. We anticipate an improvement in the posts from the Far East.

Thank you for your kind expressions regarding the help we give you. We are indeed glad if it brings you comfort. We assure you that should we have any news regarding your husband, we will inform you immediately.

Yours sincerely,

S.G.KING.

Controller.

Tom's story continues ...

"By now I have lost track of dates but the following pages continue to describe the relentless torture and endless days that are to follow"

More men arrive on the camp. They are from all three branches of the British Services and there are quite a few meetings of old friends who have been split up earlier. One of the newcomers is **Ronald Searle**, a clever cartoonist, *(Ron later becomes famous for his cartoons and drawings of prison life. One being that of a Prisoner of War squatting on the "benjo" on the end of the pier, relieving himself of the undigested soya beans (ground bait for the fish) whilst dangling a piece of thin string attached to a camp made fishing hook. It is unknown as to whether anyone was ever successful and managed to 'get a bite'.)*

The Nips are now resorting to "blasting" methods to speed up the work. All the surplus earth and coral is to be used for banking up dispersals for hiding the aircraft they are expecting to operate.

The airstrip is finally almost complete; mission accomplished as a result of brutal cruelty and forced slavery imposed upon prisoners of war.

The only plane spotted in the sky is a **Messersmicht German fighter** which looks very much the worse for wear, however, it does not hang around for very long.

5th September 1943 – *The state of the overall wretchedness of the camp worsened and the total deaths reached approximately 284. More and more men were reduced to skin and bone with numerous infected ulcers, sores, skin parasites, fungal infections, pellagra, mental disturbances, chronic diarrhoea, impaired movement/paralysis, swollen stomachs and legs. The sound of men howling and groaning in pain grew louder. Medical supplies were depleting with very little bandaging material available.*

Great loyalty between the men continued to develop, with groups carrying comrades as they fell sick and many sharing what little rations they had which resulted in them becoming ill themselves.

Chapter 20

BOMBING OF THE "DROME" & PELAUW VILLAGE – Haroeke (Haruku)

Mid November 1943 – early January 1944: *American air operations increased and during mid December 1943 the Haruku camp was bombed where approximately 500 prisoners were working on the aerodrome. The aircraft flew down directly over the drome and the first bombs were released over the nearby village of Pelauw (situated between the drome and the sea. The second attack was on the drome itself creating a dense cloud of dust and a shower of bomb splinters over a large area. Many prisoners fled with some choosing to lie flat on the ground. The prison camp itself was not damaged. Many prisoners were wounded from flying shrapnel and their feet suffered deep cuts from running across the sharp coral ground. It was reported that approximately 270 bombs were dropped on Haruku. This attack caused great panic and hysteria amongst the Japanese and Korean guards whereby they immediately ordered a burial squad to dig a mass grave and the working parties to fill in the bomb craters. The nearby village of Pelauw was on fire and some 70 villagers died from the bombing. The corpses of these villagers were soaked in petrol and burned. A special group of prisoners were selected to clear the village.*

The last day I spend on the drome is to become a memorable event ... the Nips are very edgy and excitable shouting "skori skori", they are scurrying like ants towards the jungle.

We are left on the drome when around **seven fortresses** come in from the direction of the shipping jetty over the native kampong (village) of Pelauw flying towards the long runway of the airfield, dropping a string of bombs. In a panic I start to run but stumble and fall down. I decide that the safest thing to do is to remain flat on the ground remaining still and quiet. I am wounded by a piece of flying shrapnel in my left leg from a **kite**, which is nothing compared to many other serious casualties and fatalities. I am surprised at the small amount of blood loss from my wound but this could be due to the amount of blood I have lost as a result of dysentery, or maybe because it is on the side of my very bony knee. We are all skin and bone anyway, except for puffed up and very swollen feet and ankles. These are the telltale signs of the onset of beriberi *(caused by a lack of nutrition and diet that consists mainly of polished white rice).* The camp itself suffers no damage and we do later wonder whether the Allies knew about the camp as it had not been deliberately hit. We hear that part of the nearby *kampong is in flames with many casualties.*

I have been treated by the Medical Officer with what little cleansing treatment is available and given orders by the Nips to do what they consider to be "light duties"!! **I am allocated the horrifying task of searching for the reams of dead natives among the ruins of the kampong. This merciless undertaking is to include the stacking of dead bodies and body parts into a large heap in preparation for disposal by burning to be aided with the use of "precious" Nipponese petrol.** During this search, we seize the opportunity to raid the wrecked pantries and eat our fill of food stored within them. Not everyone is able to participate due to the terrible stench but I am amongst the not so 'tickle stomached'!

A mass grave is to be dug and bomb craters on the drome are to be filled in.

Returning to the camp, the Korean guards and Gunso Mori are becoming increasingly hostile towards us. We would normally fall out, drop our bags at our billets and then go down to the river to wash our filthy, weak bodies but today **each prisoner must go down to the river and carry large rocks back up to the camp. No washing allowed. (These rocks are for the construction of a new road on the camp).**

Horrifying incidents are now on the increase. For instance: should a prisoner be caught carrying a rock not considered large enough, **he must return to the river and fetch the largest rock selected by a guard. The prisoner is then ordered to stand en-route, holding the large piece of rock above his head, arms fully outstretched.** This form of punishment, used to show an example to others, becomes a favourite mistreatment imposed upon us whilst out on working parties for so called "malingering". We witness many prisoners left standing in this position for so long, they collapse when released.

The relentless marching to and fro from the river lasts until the rage of the Gunso wears off. We are thus prevented from a desperately needed wash with the cooling effect of the river water on our bodies after many long hours toiling in the tropical sun, as once we have eaten our meagre evening rations, the bugle sounds for "lights out". Aircraft now pass over the camp each night and the "lights out" order has become much stricter. It becomes pretty apparent to us, due to the hysterical behaviour of the guards, that the aircraft are not Nipponese!

NEWS PRESS REPORTS BACK HOME IN BLIGHTY: 29th January 1944 - Daily Mirror

of escaped men flogged, then shot outright; of Indian soldiers in ... from behind; of a British officer ... and tortured; and of hundreds left ... a Japanese transport was tor-

★

...state of prisoners arriving from Java.

The refusal of the Japanese Government to permit neutral inspections of camps in the southern area is difficult to understand in view of the fact that they have allowed visits by neutral inspectors, although on a scale which we cannot regard as adequate, to camps in the northern area comprising Hong Kong, Formosa, Shanghai, Korea and Japan itself.

GOVT. WARNS TOKIO ON WAR CAMPS

Growing Brutality

The British Government are reasonably satisfied conditions generally in this area are tolerable, although as the Secretary for War has said on more than one occasion the scale on which food is provided is not adequate for long periods to maintain the health of the prisoners.

I should add that the conditions in Hong Kong appear to be growing worse.

The whole story would appear very bad indeed, but I have worse to come.

We have a growing list of cases of brutal outrage on individuals or groups of individuals. I cannot burden the House with full details of these, but in order to give an idea of their nature I must quote one or two typical examples.

First, two cases affecting civilians. The first is that of an officer in the Shanghai Municipal Police Force.

Flogged by Guards

With 300 other Allied nationals he was interned by the Japanese in a detention camp for so called political suspects at Haipong-road, in Shanghai.

He incurred the displeasure of the Japanese gendarmerie and was taken to their office in another part of the town.

When he emerged from the building he was practically out of his mind. His arms and feet were infected where ropes had left deep scars, and he had lost 40lb. in weight. He died within a day or two of his release.

The second case comes from the Philippine Islands. Here on February 11, 1942, three British subjects escaped from a Japanese civilian internment camp.

They were recaptured and flogged by the camp guard. Two days later they were sentenced to death by a military court despite the fact that international law prescribes the imposition of only disciplinary punishments for attempts to escape.

The firing party used automatic pistols and the three men were not killed outright.

Bayonetted

I turn to cases affecting soldiers. A number of Indian soldiers captured in Burma had their hands tied behind their backs and were made to sit in groups by the side of the road and then systematically bayonetted from behind in turn each man receiving apparently three bayonet thrusts.

By some miracle one man who collapsed recovered and escaped to our lines. That is how we know.

The other case concerns an officer of a well-known regiment of the line who was captured in Burma.

After being clubbed across the face with a sword he was tied to a stake and a rope was passed round his neck. Only by raising his body could he get enough air to keep him alive. He was then subjected to further torture.

Fortunately an Allied attack developed and the Japanese fled and the officer was rescued by a British tank.

The third case concerned the transport Lisbon Maru which was being used for conveying 1,800 British prisoners of war from Hong Kong. On board the conditions were almost indescribable.

The prisoners were seriously overcrowded; many were undernourished and had contracted diphtheria, dysentery, and other diseases; there was no medical provision and the sanitary arrangements were virtually non-existent.

Two of the prisoners died in one of the holds where they lay and no attempt was made to remove the bodies.

On October 1, 1942, the vessel was torpedoed by a United Nations submarine. The Japanese officers, soldiers and crew kept the prisoners under the hatches and abandoned ship forthwith, although it was twenty-four hours later before the vessel sank. There were insufficient lifeboats, rafts, etc., on board.

Japs Are Warned

Some of the prisoners broke out and swam to the land, and they were fired on. In all 800 prisoners lost their lives.

I have said sufficient to show the barbarous nature of our Japanese enemies.

He has violated not only the principles of international law, but all the canons of decency and civilised conduct.

The British Government have repeatedly made the strongest possible representations to the Japanese Government through the Swiss Government. Such replies as ...

...otests—

...'S

...ment Mr. Eden had made would be given publicity. Would he see that the power of the B.B.C. is used to broadcast it to the four corners of the earth?

21st July 1944 – The Birmingham Post 'JAPAN'S AFFAIRS AT A CRISIS' – *The resignation of General Tojo, Japanese Prime Minister since October 1941, with his entire cabinet, was announced by the Japanese News Agency yesterday and according to the Japanese Information Board, a stronger cabinet is to be formed "to infuse new life into our people and prosecute the War more closely".*

'AN ADMISSION OF FAILURE' – *One broadcast said the reason for the cabinet's resignation, to put it straightforwardly, is that the individuality of the cabinet was unable to keep up with the intensity of the burning war spirit of the people.*

Chapter 21

"DEPARTURE FROM "HAROEKOE PRISON CAMP" (Haruku)

Tom's story continues ...

During the next few weeks, there is much activity and a quite a lot of transferring of prisoners by boat from the island; destination, of course, which as always is the case 'unknown'. We are given the opportunity, through our own officers, to volunteer for the making up of different drafts. I personally decide that I would prefer to stick where I am with the friends I have made for as long as possible; the others also agree that we should stay together, however, it turns out that the official list, when issued, does include a few comrades in our company. These include: **Sergeant Bobby Burns** of Anderson Road, Erdington, Birmingham **and Alan Guest** of Sutton Coldfield, (the friend I had managed to help cure whilst suffering with vitaminosis). This reduces our little community from the Birmingham area. (We are never to meet again, as I learn later that tragically both ***Sergeant Bobby Burns and Alan Guest*** die on the prison ship that takes them from the Haroekoe Island; the cause of their deaths I believe may have been either as a result of one or more of the tropical diseases, plus malnutrition and living conditions on the ship, or that the ship was attacked by our own aircraft and sunk. The fate they meet I never learn, only the fact that they never reach their destination. I do know that on board one of the ships was the notorious Nip guard, who had beaten me and belted my infected ear at the Jaarmarkt. He had been promoted to the rank of "shoko" (officer) and nicknamed 'yellow boots' because of the colour of his pigskin boots. This notorious guard was known for cutting a prisoner's head off in one blow for stealing a small piece of dried fish!)

Some short time later we are told that we are the next to leave Haroeke island. It appears that now the drome is completed, there is no further useful work/slavery we can be put to.

(Sometime during the middle of July 1944 Haroekoe (Haruku) Prison Camp was broken up.)

Chapter 22

DESTINATION "WEIJAMI PRISON CAMP" Amboina Island (Ambon)

Approximately 500 prisoners were sent from Haroekoe to Amboina for further work and the remainder were returned to Java. It is believed that out of the original 2,070 British and Dutch prisoners who left Sourabaya (Surabaya) for Haroekoe in April 1943, less than 50 per cent were still alive at the end of the War.

Tom's story continues ...

12th July 1944 – Aboard a wooden fishing boat, we sail towards Ambon town but we are put off on the side opposite the town in the hamlet of Weijami back on the Amboina Island and as always seems to be the case, we arrive around the hours of midnight. We are marched in the darkness and torrential downpour of rain to the camp. On arrival we are herded into the billets which are of the now all too familiar design. We are soaked to the skin and in our bare feet. I notice the earthen floor is slippery and can only assume that this is due to the poor construction of the atap roof. Suffering from sheer exhaustion we just flop onto the bamboo platforms in the hope of getting some sleep, which unfortunately is not to be the case. We are subjected to the horrific sounds of what can only be described as the howling of human suffering of some sort from a billet. The billet appears to be not too far from us on the outside of the camp.

Next morning we discover the reason for all the screaming and howling during the night. We have been dumped into a camp in which the inmates, confined here before our arrival, were various natives from the surrounding islands. These natives have been used as a slave labour force, the majority of whom have been wiped out by starvation, disease, including cholera (something we have not, so far, experienced or come into contact with). The camp is in the midst of a dysentery epidemic.

The earthen floor of the billets is not all mud, as we had originally thought upon our arrival in the darkness of the night, it is mostly dysentery ridden excretion from the poor unfortunate occupiers. The Nips have moved most of them out; the ones who can walk anyway. The near to dying cases have been left to die in agony with no attention and disposed of the next day. We are ordered to wash down the baleh-baleh covered in excrement and clean the billets up. Flies are everywhere.

I have by this time lost most of my old gang comrades from Haroekoe. The only friends left together on what is now known as Weijami Camp are **Johnnie Blythe, Flight Sergeant Norman** and of course myself. **Flight Sergeant Norman** is a reservist who has been recalled by the RAF (his job in "civvy" life was that of Public Transport Traffic Inspector for Birmingham City Transport). **Johnnie Blythe comes from Southend.**

Our next task is to dig air-raid shelters for the Nips. Specifications are approximately 10 ft deep and 12 ft by 12 ft in floor area. We are then ordered to cut down palm tree trunks which are laid across the top of the holes in the ground and the surplus earth from the hole is then banked up in a large mound on top of the trunks. A large platform is then erected above the mound, with a small "funk hole" for the very "brave" Nips, which they like to be known as! (We later learn that this type of shelter is suitable for the anti-personnel bombs that have been used on the drome at Haroekoe. These bombs detonate on impact but a direct hit by any other type of bomb will bury them alive ... something we would welcome!). A benefit to us from cutting down the palm trees gives us access to what we call palm cabbage; the young shoots in the centre of the foliage, similar to young celery, but much sweeter.

After the work has been completed on Weijami camp, we get to know the reason for our visit and what is to become a "memorable stay".

The camp is situated on the opposite side of the harbour on Amboina with the docks of the port facing on the other side. Working parties of prisoners are taken across to the harbour in an invasion barge, which makes three trips. We are yet again crammed and packed in like sardines (something we are becoming used to!). The work required of us is of a different nature but still considered to be "coolie" work. It involves the unloading and loading of ships. The incoming cargo consists of supplies for the Nips, both food and medical. We now have the opportunity to learn plenty of survival tricks and take advantage but unfortunately a few horrific incidents happen when prisoners are unlucky enough to get caught and are subsequently beaten up by the guards. We find that the best policy is to attempt to get on the working parties listed for the loading of the slings in the holds of the boats, as here there are many cases and containers accidentally damaged ... on purpose!! We manage to disappear and hide amongst the cargo one by one and in turn hastily consume the "loot" on the spot. It is surprising the amount of 'swag' that gets back into the camp at night in spite of the regular searches we are subjected to. We have worked out that one of the best ways is the passing back method in the ranks.

One morning after our breakfast of pap, the barge had made two journeys leaving myself and two pals in the last party waiting at the camp for it's return. For this, we are later to count our blessings. We suddenly hear the sound of aircraft causing hysteria amongst the Nips. They are shouting as usual "skorki" and they bolt like rabbits down into the air-raid shelters. Looking up into the clear blue sky we see a sight that is to give us the biggest morale boost ... the first time since we have been in captivity. **We count fifty fortresses.** We do not feel threatened, we feel safe, as we are able to see any bombs dropping from the fortresses within range of the camp. The only dread we have is that they are heading for the docks where there are the two barges loaded with fellow prisoners, also heading for the docks. It seems by the terrific sound of the bombing that the docks are getting it but we are also aware of the Nip drome on the island.

Chapter 23

NEWS OF THE NIPS LOSING AIR SUPREMACY
Weijami, Amboina Island (Ambon)

Tom's story continues ...

We are now aware that the Nips have lost air supremacy, in this part of the Pacific anyway. We give a sigh of relief as the noise of the bombers and explosions dies out but on looking up into the clear tropic skies again, twenty-five fighters appear. These are the first twin fuselage aircraft we have seen (they later become known to us as Lockheed Lightnings – American fighter aircraft). Breaking up formation, they dive down strafing any buildings or installations they think are Nip barracks. Our prison camp must be one of their targets, although it is situated in amongst a thick plantation of palm trees. All we can do, as we had done previously on the drome at Haroekoe, is find the most sheltered spot and throw ourselves flat on the floor with hands over our ears. Many of us utter a prayer to the "Almighty". We pray that we should not be killed off by allied planes having survived all these years of starvation, disease and tortuous treatment of slavery from the hateful Nips.

We are now finished as a working party over at the docks but we are still not allowed to stand around idle doing nothing (no day passes without orders of work of some kind).

Worryingly, the attitude and behaviour of the Nips towards us worsens. They take great delight in telling us that they will never surrender and we will never be freed as they will gladly slit our throats first. We often talk amongst ourselves planning what action we would take to meet the occasion if need be.

It is here on **Weijami camp** that I am to have the first attack of Malaria *(a serious infectious disease caused by a mosquito borne parasite)* the worst kind of which is cerebral. I am struck down by this disease quite suddenly whilst on working party, which is the first time I have ever collapsed. Already weak, I begin to lose my vision and suffer an overwhelming sensation that I am taking my last few breaths. I am carried back to the billet with a fit of violent shuddering and the sensation of feeling frozen cold, which does not seem possible with the climate being so hot. These symptoms last for the best part of an hour. I then gradually being to feel as though I am enclosed in a Turkish bath with full steam on, perspiring profusely, at the same time wanting nothing but to 'guzzle' water. I know this is the not the best thing in the world to happen to me as the wet beriberi *(caused by a Vitamin B1 deficiency affecting the heart and circulatory system)* is now slowly creeping from my feet upwards causing me great discomfort and difficulty in walking, The painful swelling is causes the sensation of having weights tied to my feet and I literally have to drag them when trying to slowly walk.

The RAF Medical Officer has given me a dose of Quinine tablets. I am aware of the fact that these are in short supply as the Nips even ration these out in small amounts.

Within approximately three hours, my condition begins to improve. Thankfully, the Medical Officer has put me sick in quarters which, in my opinion, is better than the sick bay where men are still dying daily. By this time the Nip Commandant has given up bestowing his presence at the burials possibly we think due to the guilt he may be feeling at the number of so many losses. There is only the presence of an ordinary guard at the burials by now.

I feel fortunate to receive three days' treatment of Quinine but I am still suffering with the painful heaviness of my swollen feet and legs.

I hear that **Flight Sergeant Norman has gone down with dysentery and has become a patient in the sick bay.** I manage to get the opportunity to visit him but I am so shocked at the drastic change in his appearance! I can only imagine it must be as a result of the lack of nutrients in the food, which is far inferior to the already poor diet available outside of the camp. I must mention here that I have such respect and high regard for the Medical Officers and Orderlies, as they are constantly asking the Nips for more nourishing food for the sick. The food supplies may improve slightly but only for a very short period which does not allow the poor patient time to recover and get back on his feet. This is continually being drummed into the Nip Commandant by our Medical Officers but it seems that our Medical Officers are fighting a losing battle. (*The Medical Officers and Orderlies carry out wonderful work with what limited equipment and drugs they have at their disposal. Operations are performed under incredibly* *difficult conditions, for example, in a bamboo hut on a wooden operating table whilst Orderlies desperately try to keep the flies away).*

I try my utmost to rally **Flight Sergeant Norman** and get him back on his feet again but he is sinking lower with each night that passes and then it occurs ... that awful familiar sight of a glazed look! We have witnessed this so many times in the eyes of so many who have not been able to carry on with their fight for survival. The barbaric Nips may be the enemy but we must also endure the pain and suffering fighting another enemy ... fateful diseases such as dysentery, malaria, beriberi, tropical ulcers and pellagra *(Pellagra is described by the 3 d's, diahorrea, dermatitis and dementia. Symptoms also include high sensitivity to sunlight, aggression, alopecia, oedema, skin lesions, weakness, insomnia, mental confusion/emotional disturbances, leading to dementia. More will be discovered later!)*

We are now reduced to only two of our original team, **Johnnie Blythe** and myself. **Johnnie** has managed to avoid the various diseases so far, although he currently suffering with painful open tropical ulcers on his legs.

These painful ulcers have now become a very common sight. (On one occasion I suffered with a very large one on my left foot, which became very close to turning green but thankfully it was cured by the Medical Officer. It was cleaned out with a silver spoon, a smear of ointment made on the camp, the base being coconut oil, then two M & B tablets crushed up into a powder and sprinkled over the whole area of the ulcer. The only dressing available was a sterilised mosquito net bandage. I cannot recall having ever seen proper bandage whilst on any camp, apart from our last camp from which we are to be released.)

The only way to protect any scratch or minor wound from the flies is to cover it with some kind of green leaf, secured and tied with anything available.

(The best treatment and cure for these tropical ulcers I have seen so far was on the Haroekoe Island. It was a yellow powder salvaged from Dutch supplies and used by a **Dutch Medical Officer, Doctor Springer**. If I remember rightly this was pronounced something like "Yhoderform". As long as the ulcer was properly cleansed and the former applied, it completely healed within a few days. Nevertheless, the M & B treatment, which was applied to my left foot, was I think, just in time as it may have led to amputation. Many amputations are carried out on some camps without anaesthetic. I am thankful that I did not have to experience such treatment.)

The time has come, as is usual after air-raids, for us to be moved to yet another "rest camp"!! I am about to be split up from my pal **Johnnie Blythe**, despite our efforts to stay together.

It has rained for the first time in many days. Some of us are barefoot and some are wearing wooden sandals, marching in a sea of mud which covers the sharp coral surface of the road. We are being pushed and bullied and after marching for a few hours we are ferried across to a small ship. There are about 500 of us and I really don't think there will be room for us all.

Around September 1944 *– Allied aircraft raided the town of Ambon causing great damage. The Japanese decided, as a result of these raids, to move the prisoners of war.*

NEWS BACK HOME IN BLIGHTY ...

12th September 1944 – *"Birmingham's Fire Guard of 50,000 volunteers stand down"*

17th September 1944 – "Black Out Relaxation"

Chapter 24

DEPARTURE FROM "WEIJAMI CAMP" – Amboina (Ambon) DESTINATION ... Moena Island (Muna) 'Raha Camp'

Raha Prison Camp *was on the Moena Island at the foot of the Eastern leg of Celebes (Sulawesi) in the Strait of Butung ... treatment of the Prisoners of War by the Japanese was to become even more unbearable!*

CELEBES (now Sulawesi) showing Muna Island

There are many recorded atrocities on ***Moena*** *prison camp. Prisoners were ordered to climb trees, full of red ants, and remain there for a considerable period of time. Many prisoners were beaten into unconsciousness with the* ***camp commandant "Yoshida"*** *sometimes taking part in these beatings. The prisoners were also subjected to some of the standard Japanese Kempeitai tortures (tortured to the limit of human endurance, or to the point of death!).*

A ***Dutch prisoner*** *who was out on working party was spoken to by a Japanese guard, caught by surprise, the prisoner jumped up from his sitting position on the ground springing to attention holding his shovel in his hand. Allegedly, the guard was alarmed by this sudden movement and accused the prisoner of threatening him and his punishment was to crawl about like a lizard whilst being beaten approximately 30 times with a pick handle. After the working party returned to the camp, the incident was reported to the camp commandant and the Dutch prisoner was cruelly held up against a tree by his fellow prisoners and given a further 50 strokes. This act of brutality did not end at this point as it was followed by other prisoners being beaten.*

An English prisoner was given 70 strokes by ***Yoshida*** *personally as allegedly the prisoner had not given 'eyes right' to the commandant's satisfaction!*

A Royal Marine *was caught with a bag of eggs which he had smuggled in from outside the camp for sick prisoners. The entire camp was paraded to witness the Royal Marine suffer brutal torture. His working party were also tortured which included the British Officers and the Chaplain. The Royal Marine was then condemned to death. The Chaplain was ordered to say prayers for the dead, followed by a long period of solitary confinement whilst suffering from dysentery.*

During an inspection of the camp hospital, a Japanese doctor discovered remains of food in a dustbin. As punishment, a senior Dutch Medical officer and his two assistants were ordered to stand for a considerable time with their heads bent down over the dustbin whilst l the other doctors and orderlies were given a severe beating, some were beaten senseless.

7th October 1944 – *The reduced number of 435 surviving prisoners remaining on Amboina left the island on two boats with Major Gibson on one and Major Mossford on the other. (Major Mossford's boat was subjected to an allied air attack which resulted in the death of prisoners arrived on 14th October 1944). Tom is with Major Gibson.*

Tom's story continues ...

7th October 1944 – It is raining heavily and I am now aboard a boat with **Major Gibson** which is typical of the others but not as large. We are wet through and crammed into the holds with no air and inadequate sanitation. The boat is incredibly overcrowded and the sea is rough. We are exhausted and our frail bodies are becoming weaker having endured years working as slaves at the hands of the Japanese. The extreme burning heat of the sun is unbearable and we are only given just less than half a pint of water a day. At night, the air is filled with the yells and screams of those dying and the chronic hiccoughing of those about to die from beri-beri. I am witnessing many men dying like flies and their bodies callously being thrown overboard with sandbags tied to their legs.

13th October 1944 – The boat finally reaches the small Moena (Muna) Island. On disembarkation there are approximately 200 sick men incapable of walking unaided and they are left lying on the shore until we have finished unloading. After unloading, we are ordered to march 1.5 miles to a small camp at Raha. *(We later discover that this camp was previously occupied by the prisoners who were aboard the small boat sunk on 11th September 1944).*

The camp is small and the huts offer bug ridden bamboo platforms. Additional huts need to be built. A few Dutch prisoners have been kept here for the upkeep of the camp but without water! *(A bamboo pipe is later constructed to carry a very inadequate supply).* Our Camp Commandant, **Major Gibson,** is to be responsible for the discipline of all other officers, NCO's (Non-Commissioned Officers) and other ranks are under orders of the Nip Commandant and his Gunso (Sargeant) who is in charge of the Korean guards.

Major Gibson holds the higher rank in relation to the RAF Officers who are in charge of us, the new arrivals and the Medical Officers; the latter we have much admiration for, as they have done such good work in their devotion to duty. The Medical Officers are struggling under the great strain due to stress, over-work and lack of medical supplies. We often discuss amongst ourselves as to what the position would have been if the Medical Officers had not been with us, the death toll being bad enough as it is! (Mention must be made here of the RAF Dental Officer we left at Haroekoe camp and the extractions he had to carry out under very difficult conditions. Also, the Medical Officers who had no choice but to carry out operations without anaesthetic. An injection would be administered of some sort, possibly a placebo just for the psychological effect on the patient, with the comforting words "shout out if it hurts". I experienced two extractions under these conditions when I visited the small hut begging to be put out of my misery of raging toothache. Sitting in the camp carpenter-made dentist's chair, the Orderly put his knee in your chest whilst the Dental Officer carried out his 'cruel-to-be-kind' task. I am sure he was the type that felt almost as much pain as the patient but the continual pain over such a long period in itself almost became almost an anaesthetic!)

The health of all prisoners on **Moena camp** is still deteriorating rapidly with the lack of nutritious food and medical supplies. Tropical disease cases have vastly increased and now taken a large grip on the prisoners. Malaria has become particularly troublesome and many have succumbed to a type of fever, similar to Weil's disease. It is absurd how those cruel Nips still regularly make their rounds of the sick bay picking out patients they think fit for working parties whilst ignoring the pleas of the Medical Officers and **Major Gibson.**

The death toll is rising rapidly with the dawn of each day and we dread the thought of who will be next. Our captors no longer allow the rough wooden coffins to be made by the camp carpenters. The corpses of our dear comrades are now just wrapped and tied up in the straw mat in which they have lain and suffered. They are buried just a few feet below the surface of the ground in the cemetery adjoining the camp.

The cases of wet beriberi, which starts as swelling of the feet and legs, is now creeping up and causing bloated bodies. The main cause of beriberi is due to the poor diet of rice and lack of meat and vegetables, vitamins A, B, C and others. We are advised to sleep with our feet raised, resting on what little kit we possess. This poor advice results in horrific cases of excess fluid collecting in the scrotum, causing it to appear like a balloon filled with water. In these cases, the prisoner is taken to the sick bay where the fluid is drawn off by syringe. (*These are the severe cases and most of these men will die in the near future. My conclusion is that the fluid must have reached the region of the heart ultimately causing death.)* One desperate, dying prisoner turned to drink and eat the contents of a bedpan.

*It is reported that **Dr Alistair Forbes** suffered with malaria and beriberi whilst lying in the sick quarters. He was aware of the fact that you acquire a terrible thirst with a huge desire to drink water but he knew it was not good for the beriberi and this required extreme willpower. Dr Forbes, although not recovered, was ordered to go out on working party despite the fluid and swelling in his body.*

From 14th October – end of October 1944: 61 deaths reported.

NEWS BACK HOME IN BLIGHTY:

25th October 1944 – "BATTLE OF LEYTE GULF" *End of Japanese Sea Power*

26th October 1944 – The Birmingham Post "CRUSHING DEFEAT OF JAPANESE FLEET" *Philippines attackers driven off. US losses extremely light.*

Chapter 25

THE FRIENDLY NATIVE
Raha Camp – Moena Island (Muna)

Whilst out on working party, I manage to communicate with a friendly native, a benefit of being able to speak Malay. *(I must mention here that to hold a conversation with any native is a punishable offence leading to the minimum penalty of a beating up for both of us.)*

I try and explain my condition to the native. He replies "tidha bahgoos", meaning "not good" and signals that he will contact me later. Before he rushes off and disappears, I warn him "awhas" (beware of the Nips). I mention the latter as the Korean camp guards only perform duties inside the camps, the outside working parties are closely supervised by the Nips who were in the service in the capacity of a trade of some sort. The work on Moena is mostly road making, cutting through the jungle and swamps. Sometimes we are subjected to working up to our waist in the company of blood sucking leeches and malaria carrying mosquitoes.

The native keeps his promise and returns at the agreed time and hidden place, he hands me six small green limes, telling me to cut one in half each night and to suck out the juice. I must also, during the night, get up and go to the toilet immediately I feel the need to pass water. He gives me enough to last me twelve nights, I thank him in his native tongue and this is to be the last I see of him.

On return to the camp, the limes are carefully kept hidden under my collection of wild spinach and edible leaves which the camp guards are now accustomed to seeing in my side pack. *(Should these limes be spotted, I will certainly be due for some type of brutal punishment)*

There are no facilities for washing or bathing on Raha camp. The only time we are able to cleanse our filthy unhealthy bodies is during a not very frequent rainfall and this is the non-rainy season! Should we be lucky enough to get any welcome rain, off comes what bit of clothing we possess and there is a rush for the best spot under the eaves of the atap roofs of the billets. We don't care at this stage how we are able to dry ourselves. Should a chap be lucky enough to obtain a piece of soap, he will gladly share his luxury.

Chapter 26

OVER 3 YEARS IN CAPTIVITY

The conditions we have to live under can only possibly be conceivable to those who manage to survive this living hell. For the best part of three years, we have now endured the hostile and loathing Nips inflicting pain on innocent men whilst having to endure what can only be described as abhorrent and barbaric living conditions.

Experiencing the brutality of the Japanese can only undoubtedly bring out the best in a man or vice versa trying desperately not to lose one's spirit, which sadly does happen in hundreds of cases and many poor unfortunates just don't respond to the efforts of their comrades in their attempts to cheer them up. Strength, willpower and determination are so important. I often have thoughts about how one could quite easily shut oneself off, refuse help and stop eating what meagre rations are available. These thoughts are more prevalent when I am lying in the sick bay during a bad bout of malaria or dysentery. I could just give up, fade away and land up in the adjoining cemetery. The comradeship that has developed amongst us has grown to such an extent, irrespective of race or creed, that the losing of one's grip is, I believe, only dependent upon the individual's physical and mental make-up. The will to carry on and the strength required to participate in conversational topics is essential. We talk about various different things such as what life will be like when we eventually get back home. We discuss our strategy should the Nips try and carry out their threats to slit our throats in our sleep rather than free us if ever they are attacked. The Nips constantly remind us of these threats and they are spoken with such venom. These are just examples of the many speculative conversations and discussions one could start, which could at times lead to friendly arguments in the billets at night. We are, of course, fully aware and very cautious of guards creeping around listening, especially one or two that have gleaned a little English over a period of what seems like a lifetime to us.

Chapter 27

"THE BOY SCOUT" & THE FEAST
Raha Camp – Moena Island (Muna)

I will never forget the one Korean camp guard at Moena camp nicknamed the 'Boy Scout. Quite different to the rest of the Korean camp guards, he understands a little English and appears somewhat a little more refined. He is not so hostile and he behaves in a slightly more civilised manner than the others. Not sure why but I suspect he may have been, or may still be, a little on the Christian side. He does not shout and bawl like his counterparts but he is still very cautious in showing any sign of compassion towards us due to the rigid and severe discipline the Korean guards are subjected to under the command of the Gunso. It should be mentioned that the Nips have little respect for the Koreans, who are treated as second class citizens. Those recruited as guards are directly responsible for dealing with the prisoners.

I am not sure but the 'Boy Scout' is possibly either a member of the Nip cookhouse staff, or, in charge. One evening, he appeared at the barbed wire fence separating their billets from the camp and asks me in broken English if I can "mati" (kill) poultry. I answer "yes", not really understanding what he has in mind but one thing I do know is that the Nips are not partial to the heads, necks and innards of hens or cockerels; neither do they like blood of animals or birds in any way. The Nips eat mainly fish and white chicken meat and I am sure they certainly wouldn't look at a rare beef steak! Anyway, "sticking my neck out", I crawl through a small gap in the fence, which the 'Boy Scout' makes for me (ample for my very lean and malnourished body to squeeze through). He leads me to a pen containing about a dozen fowl; a fine sight for any prisoner! He asks me to enter the pen and select six of the most suitable birds for the pot; it would appear the Korean camp guards are keen to have a good feed tonight. I am quite experienced as I have caught various kinds of "delicacies" whilst out on jungle working parties, such as snakes, iguanas, reptiles etc, which the Dutch had told me was delicious eating.

Selecting the fattest six birds, I tie up their feet and wings. He offers me a knife to cut off their heads whilst still alive but I attempt to explain that this is not the best method of dispatching the birds. I proceed to do the job my way by pulling and breaking the necks; a quick and sudden death. I then hang them up to allow the blood to run to the break in the necks. Meanwhile I imagined how good the discarded offal would taste and the nutritious value desperately needed by my comrades when hopefully cooked in our hut later the other side of the wire. The guard is impressed by my method of scalding and plucking nice clean birds for the boil in a "wajang" (a large cast iron bowl) over a wood fire. These birds, I know only too well have been looted from the local natives in the surrounding "kampongs" (villages). This is the fastest I have ever moved during captivity. In a minimum of time all six chickens were in the wajang, (this large bowl reminds me of the old 'washing copper' my mother used for boiling washing and occasionally pig swill during my childhood just after the First World War). The guard asks me to let him know when the feast is cooked and ready. He left me alone with my nose enjoying the best aroma I had inhaled for many a long year.

Together with a handful of salt, which we haven't seen or tasted for a long time, the heads, necks and other discarded edible parts (edible to us prisoners anyway) are passed through the barbed-wire to my grateful pals standing with their mouths watering. Selecting the chap I feel is the best cook, I tell him to get cracking whilst I remain on the other side of the barbed-wire *(little do I realise that I am not to be included in the feast at this time.)*

A good hour has passed ... watching, waiting and stoking the wood fire to keep it going. During this time, I quickly fill as many mugs and cans with gravy as I dare and pass them through the wire to my pals. About to call the guard, I begin to feel the old familiar tension in my arms which I know is a worrying sign of the onset of an attack of recurring malaria. Within seconds my whole body starts to tremble uncontrollably and I am no more than a shivering physical wreck. The guard comes and taking one look at my condition, he allows me to pass groggily through the wire fence. Just about making it to my bedspace, I collapse on to the 'baleh-baleh' with my pals commiserating with me and promising to save me some of the cooked food for which I have taken a huge risk to obtain.

The Medical Officer **"Doc McCarthy"** is hauled in and I am given two Quinine tablets. It is obviously my fate never to taste the remainder of the chicken stew! In any case the Quinine tablets which are dispensed miserly by the Nips, are far more important as without them, this type of malaria can be fatal within an hour. The medication begins to take effect and I begin to drift off. I remain out for the count for the whole night until "Tenko" reveille. Ordered to stay in sick quarters, I struggle to swallow my plate of pap.

Chapter 28

WRONGLY ACCUSED & BEATEN
Raha Camp – Moena Island (Muna)

The working parties have all been grouped from the routine parade on the camp Padang, fit men to work outside of the camp (only considered 'fit' in the eyes of the Nips) and the not-so-fit are allocated to work on the camp itself.

Still lying in the sick bay on the bamboo platform, feeling extremely weak, I start to doze off with the after effects of the malaria attack and Quinine medication which always seems to induce a somewhat strange type of stupor. I begin to have thoughts about what the impact, both physically and mentally, from these tortuous prisoner of war years has upon us all, in particular the 'good' and the 'not so good' being brought out in one's character.

I am awakened suddenly by the rough hard jab of a rifle butt in my ribs by a very irritable guard. He asks "brapha whang adha?" (how much money have you?). I reach into the back pocket of the tattered, almost threadbare, shorts I am wearing and produce an old leather purse. *(This old leather purse was given to me by a former member of the RAF Police at Seletar named Powell, who tragically passed away at Haroekoe camp.)* I show the contents of the purse to the very angry, aggressive and increasingly agitated guard. It contains just over ten guilders in silver coins *(these are more valuable than the almost worthless Nip paper money).* The hostile guard asks me to explain as to how I have come to accumulate this sum of money. I try to focus and explain to the best of my ability, bearing in mind I am extremely weak and not able to think clearly. His understanding of the English language is very limited, making matters even more difficult. Unfortunately, I am unable to account for the whole amount, which does not help and causing him to become extremely dissatisfied with my explanation. He is yelling and storms out of the billet, returning with a Dutch prisoner we have nicknamed "Noah" who can speak Japanese and is the camp interpreter. Noah explains to me in English that I will be in serious trouble if I do not explain fully as to how I have come to be in possession of this money. *(I know the Dutch prisoner is more than aware of the bartering that goes on amongst the prisoners. We have become quite accustomed to 'dealing' in small personal items, plus other odd supplies acquired whilst on working parties, learning to conceal such dealings from the Nips.* I respond by saying that it is difficult for me to remember but desperately try to explain, in as much detail as I can, how I have obtained every penny of it. *This is the truth!*

The Korean guard continues asking many questions *(on reflection later I think he was suggesting that I had inadvertently infringed a rule prohibiting the possession of silver coins.)* He is now becoming increasingly agitated and impatient; I guess he thinks I am not telling the truth, so off comes his leather belt! Each time I am unable to answer a question, I receive an agonising blow, not on the body but across the head with the leather belt. This goes on for some time. *(If I knew the reason for the interrogation, I could probably clear myself of the crime I am supposed to have committed).* Eventually this brutality stops and I am escorted to the guardroom of the camp but without the company of Noah the interpreter!

My body is weak and I am barely able to hold myself upright but nevertheless I am ordered to stand in front of at least six aggressive Korean guards screaming at me in their unintelligible language. They can only speak their own tongue, not even Malay, never mind English! I have been struck about the head so many times that I am numb to further beatings and ill treatment which probably annoys my tormentors even more. *(I think maybe they expect me to cry out to them begging for mercy!)*

There is a short interval to this ongoing punishment upon the arrival of the 'Boy Scout' who tries to intervene. I can only imagine that he must be confident that I am telling the truth but the Korean guards choose not to listen to him as they then proceed to drag me to the Nip billets. (The very place that I prepared supper the previous night and it is here in one of the huts that I am further subjected to the shouting and bawling of the Korean guards in a language I do not understand). I am at a loss as they are insistent on asking me to account for every cent that I have accumulated but this is virtually impossible. (*Officially we are not supposed to have any Dutch silver money in our possession as we have only been paid the ten cents per day by the Nips. The ten-cent coin is made from cheap metal, mostly aluminium which they have circulated in the occupied East Indies, after calling in, as they had thought, all the Dutch silver coinage.)* Being in possession of the Dutch silver money in itself is a crime in their eyes but I suspect that this is not the real reason for the torturous beatings.

Weak and numb, I find the strength to remain standing upright whilst taking repeated violent and indescribable blows across the head for what seems like an eternity. My body can't escape but my thoughts can! I appear to have gained an inner strength which helps me to fight off the temptation to give in and collapse but my eyes have now become bruised, cut and swollen slits. I can just about see the cruel hatred on the faces of these inhuman specimens of mankind and standing like a punch-drunk boxer, I grin to myself, congratulating myself on still being able to stand up! This irritates the Korean guards as they become wilder and even more enraged.

The one Korean guard's face I shall never forget ... he holds his rifle and bayonet to my bare chest and utters the only Malay words I think he knows "mhow matti?" (do you want to die?). I look straight into his evil eyes and simply reply "tidahpa" (I do not care!). I have actually reached such a state that I am convinced should he choose to lunge the bayonet into my chest, I won't feel a thing. This evil guard becomes so humiliated by his grinning fellow tormentors that he stands back and brings his hobnailed boot up with a vicious blow into my bloated belly of rice and swollen spleen. The intense pain is beyond words but causes me to heave and wretch wanting to throw up. At this moment, I am tempted to give up by just letting go of myself and collapsing on to the earthen floor of the hut but once again that inner strength takes over. I still continue to stand but how this is possible I do not know. My jaws are set like iron, not knowing or caring, about their next intentions.

At the point of collapse, camp commandant **Major Gibson** appears in the doorway of the hut with the words "Orton get back to your billet". I am in no fit state to grasp these instructions immediately. He repeats them slowly and clearly two or three times before the order sinks in having been beaten almost senseless. Staggering out of the hut resembling a stupefied drunk, I am unable to say thank you to Major Gibson, the man who I believe has just saved my life. If I had collapsed and gone down, I would have quite possibly ended up as bayonet target practice for my tormentors. *I later learn this is why they took this matter into their own hands without orders from their superiors.*

Whilst leaving the hut, I do catch a glimpse of a prisoner off one of the HM Naval ships. He is standing, leaning on his walking stick wearing a boiler suit and straw-hat grinning! It crosses my mind that I could do with that stick more than him and staggering past him I do question why he is in the Nip compound? What has he been up to? Has he been up to some of his tricks? *(He has a reputation for keeping himself to himself, not speaking to anyone, also for kleptomania, pinching anything left lying around, even off his own comrades. Under these inhumane conditions, starvation, disease, filth and squalor, brutal beatings etc, the effect on any man is immense and has brought out both the good and the bad in us. On the whole we have fostered a comradeship that I am sure would not have perhaps been formed in normal life!)*

Whilst staggering to my bed space, I still cannot figure out how the possession of money still current in the Moluccas would lead to such a barbaric punishment. I flop down onto the bamboo platform in a state of collapse. I just need to drift off into a state of unconscious to relieve my poor battered body and mind from the agonising pain that the tortuous beatings have inflicted upon me. At the point of entering into a dream-like state, I am brought back to my senses by two of the camp workers who tell me that I have to return to the guardroom. In my attempt to focus and think clearly whilst in a punch-drunk state, I am at a loss as to why they have not yet finished with me! With a strong urge to tell them where to go and to take the guards with them, I utter a few curses to myself realising they are under strict orders to fetch me. The camp workers help me off the bamboo platform and hold me up, helping me to stagger to the guardroom to once again face the guards. I am convinced they are going to start again with their callous brutality but at this stage I am numb and not caring what becomes of me anymore.

On arrival at the guardroom, I am ordered to stand in front of the Guard Commander sitting on the bench, along with two or three others. The Guard Commander mumbles to me in broken English "I am sorry" ... "mistake" ... "kasi present (give present) and holds out to me a ten guilder note (Nip currency). Standing speechless and bewildered, my initial reaction is to take the ten guilder note, screw it up and throw it back at him. **Major Gibson** is also seated with two other British Officers standing behind him. I am sure he can read my thoughts as he stares at me intently and motions for me to take the note. I heed his warning and take the note. The next order comes directly from the guard, he says that I am to be taken back to my bed space in sick bay for a rest and to "get a lot of rice to eat". I certainly don't fancy anything to eat, it is the rest that I am desperate for! I reluctantly give my thanks and I'm helped back to my bed of bamboo where I fade out of this world into a state of unconsciousness.

I eventually come to and open my eyes to the harsh brilliant sunshine blazing through the opened flap of the hut at the head of my bed space. Looking through the slits of my painful swollen eyes, I can sense all eyes of my sick inmates are upon me. I receive many kind words of condolence from those men fit enough to take stock of the injuries sustained from the relentless torturous beatings. My face and body are covered in deep cuts and bruises with severe swelling and I am told that I have been out for the count for almost of forty-eight hours.

Flight Lieutenant McCarthy comes to visit and asks how I am feeling, although he says he thinks he has a pretty good idea. I respond by mumbling that my head feels as though it has been used as the ball at a football match. He proceeds to explain to me the reason for the interrogation and subsequent beatings ...

A prisoner in the sick bay had been showing alarming symptoms of malnutrition, including mental irregularities. One of the most serious was uncontrollable kleptomania whereby he would pilfer anything lying unattended. His mental state was well known and during each morning, whilst he sat or strolled outside, an orderly would check his bed space and remove any stolen articles. Anyone with anything missing would then check with the orderly and when the possessions were recovered, nothing more was said.

I was badly beaten and wrongly accused due to a wallet disappearing from a guard's army shirt which he had hung over an open shutter in his Nip billet. The guard's hut lay right by the Nip cookhouse and I had been spotted being taken inside the cookhouse area by the 'Boy Scout' to prepare the 'chicken feast'. From these observations, assumptions were made that I must have stolen the wallet!

During the course of my barbaric punishment Major Gibson had been told about the alleged theft, at which time he went straight to the kleptomaniac's bed-space and discovered the wallet, complete with contents, in the prisoner's knapsack. Major Gibson immediately intervened and was able to stop further brutal beatings. He was also able to explain about the mental illness so that the perpetrator got away with a simple box on the ears. Major Gibson made it abundantly clear that without his intervention, I would not have survived!

I bear this fellow prisoner no malice, even though I have suffered brutal beatings through his actions.

As my story continues, it still relates to the good and the bad being brought out of some of us at various times under prison camp conditions.

Lying nursing my cuts and bruises, I am having dark thoughts about those particular Korean guards and decide that I shall no longer continue to speak of the incident with my sick comrades just as I hear the familiar word "khurra" (hey you) at the flap of the window. I slowly turn my painful throbbing head and find myself looking into the smiling face of the 'Boy Scout'. He takes one look at me and mutters the words Nippon "bunja pukhol, tidha bahgoos" which means they have hit me very much and it is not good. I respond by referring to them as something else, including a four letter word, which most of the guards understand by now. He says "nanti syjai combhali" (wait, I come back). I smile to myself at this comment as it sounds a little comical... there is not much of me going any place in my condition! The 'Boy Scout' has made it his business to make a special effort to visit me as he is not a patrol guard of the camp, which I am pleased about. He is on the staff of the Nip cookhouse and I have never witnessed him on the camp bawling and shouting like his comrades. It is not long before he returns and he passes me the largest hand of bananas I have seen for a very long time. *(I presume they have come from the Nip cookhouse as we prisoners never even catch sight of such luxuries, never mind sample them!).* Taking the bananas I utter "terima-kasih" (thank you) and he makes his departure. (*I am sure he has taken a huge risk by bringing this gift to me!)* There are more than a dozen bananas and by the size of them, they could be described as "phisang rajha", the best type of that variety of fruit. They certainly would have been very expensive to buy even before the War started. This is an indication of how our captors are living off the fat of the land, whilst feeding us meagre rations and expected to carry out slave labour. My sick comrades' eyes almost pop out at the sight of these magnificent bananas. The sickbay rations are barely sufficient in vitamin quality to give a man a slow lingering death if he is in very poor health and spirit.

The attitude of the Nips is, "no work – no good – you may as well die". But malnutrition is the reason why so many prisoners are failing to survive disease and starvation.

I am pleased to be able to share the bananas with my comrades in the sickbay but many are lying almost unconscious. Surprised someone has such an item, I am handed a piece of broken mirror. Looking at the mirror through my swollen slit eyes, I am barely able to recognise myself!

Having come across the occasional prisoners who are quick to take advantage, it would appear that a few of these individuals are also resident in the sickbay. We nickname them "spivs". Naturally, owing to my painful injuries, my appetite is not good and when the rations are delivered, I am not always ready to eat straight away. I have been watching one particular patient, who strikes me that he is not as sick as he is making out and it is noticeable that he has more visitors than anyone else. He is also in possession of a collection of items that are almost impossible to obtain, least of all in the sick bay. Items such as tobacco and even 'tailor-made' cigarettes, (tobacco rolled in Nip toilet paper or dried palm leaves, looted whilst unloading a ship). It has become customary for us to take advantage whenever possible to rifle Nip supplies in order to survive but this prisoner is always the one to remind me that my grub is getting cold! What puzzles me is that he is fit enough to get up from his bamboo bed space and come across to both mine and others, asking if he can exchange anything for our meal ration. I also discover that he has a large bottle of valuable Quinine tablets; the bottle would hold approximately five hundred tablets. He offers me tobacco or cigarettes in exchange for unwanted meal rations and I tell him the only thing I will trade my rations for are Quinine tablets. He asks "how many tablets for a 'tiffin'?" (lunch). I ask for six tablets but he will only offer four in exchange for each 'tiffin'.

Having spent eight days in the sickbay, I have managed to collect a stock of twenty-four Quinine tablets on discharge. *(This later proves to be my guarantee of survival to fight against the type of malaria which will remain in my system.)*

Chapter 29

DISCHARGED FROM SICKBAY TO THE WORKING PARTY ...
An attempt to escape Moena Island (Muna)

The day after my discharge from sickbay I am straight back in the line up on working party parade on the Padang. We are standing to attention by the command "kiotski" numbering in Japanese, as is now the order of the day. We fall out into different working parties assigned to different Japanese army soldiers from outside the camp. I must mention here that some of these **Japanese army soldiers are notorious for their brutality, such as one nicknamed the "Mad Monk".** If possible, we try to avoid working on his party and it becomes increasingly obvious from our actions, as it is our sole intention to humiliate him in front of the Gunso and camp guards. He certainly doesn't appear perturbed as he just stands there with a broad grin on his face. Behind that grin but one can imagine, without a doubt, that he will be carefully scheming malicious attacks on those poor individuals who are unfortunate enough to land up with him.

November 1944 – There are about 180 patients out of a total of 425 suffering with Malaria.

Records show that at this time a group of prisoners made a desperate attempt to leave

Moena on two ships which managed to reach approximately 6 – 8 miles offshore before an air attack left both vessels ablaze, resulting in the death of 27 prisoners.

The survivors were returned to Raha camp. No further attempts were made to leave

Moena until 1945 when there were three drafts.

Chapter 30

WORK AT THE SAWMILL
... Getting to know the Natives
"America re-takes the Philippines"

Tom's story continues ... things are to be quite different for me from now onwards.

I have been discharged from sick bay and lined up for work selection. Adhering to the roll call order "bhango", (number) it is ascertained that the number of prisoners present actually tallies with the number of sick and light duty men available for camp work, this verifies that no one has escaped from the camp during the night.

During this routine check, the Gunso stands in front of me. He looks me up and down and asks me in Malay "sahkit abhis?" – "Is your sickness finished or are you better?" I reply "hi, yes" but in Japanese. *(Learning to speak basic Malay or Nip language is definitely an advantage, although not so much during my recent interrogation and accusation. It turned out that by not understanding the motive of the question put to me was definitely to my advantage at that time).* I always make a point of looking these people straight in the eye, as I've come to the conclusion that if you show any sign of weakness, you are more susceptible to being kicked and beaten. The Gunso asks me whether I am fit for work and I reply "yes". He then orders me to fall out and stand aside to await further orders leaving me feeling in a way somewhat uneasy. I can sense the eyes of all my fellow prisoners upon me and I begin to wonder whether I am to be subjected to a recurrence of those recent brutal beatings. Standing alone until all the working parties have marched off, a Japanese guard approaches and although he can only speak in Nip language, he is able to make me understand. He says that I had suffered an injustice through one of my own kind, unknown to the Gunso at the time and that I am to do a personal job for him outside the camp.

Ordered to march to the guardroom I have to go through the usual ceremonial ritual which is similar to the one we had at Haroekoe Camp. I face the guard commander, salute and shout "kerajia ni-ikemus" (I go to work). He salutes back and I am ordered to carry on accompanied by the Japanese guard.

We walk together to a large sawmill in the 'Kampong' (village), which is approximately one kilometre from the prison camp. We walk together for about just under a mile to the Raha sawmill. The presence of this particular Nip makes me feel uneasy, since the only men I can actually see here at the sawmill are natives who are busily going about their daily tasks. We are greeted by a look of surprise on the faces of the natives, as it is obvious that they are taken aback by our presence.

The Nip disappears into a building ordering me to wait outside. After a few minutes, he returns wielding a roughly cut cudgel with a hole in the handle through which passed a cord which could be slipped on the wrist for carrying or other use. I can only describe it as something that resembles a roughly made policeman's truncheon. The Nip informs me that the natives are wrongfully taking away wood from a large stack of off-cuts piled up in the grounds of the sawmill and my job is to be, in his words, "the same as a policeman in London". It is to be my duty to guard the large stack of wood, which is made up of teak, meranti etc and prevent any further theft. Perhaps he is making this comparison because of my RAF cap, or "cheese-cutter" as it is nicknamed and its well-polished badge. I acknowledge my understanding of this order. The guard then tells me that should I catch any native attempting to steal wood, I must give them a "banjak pukul" (beat him a lot) i.e. give the transgressor a whack with the weapon he has provided. He then goes on his way calling back to me that food will be sent to me from the camp at the usual time.

It is hard to believe that I am to be my own boss! (This turns out to be the best task of my three and a half years as prisoner). All that is required of me is to walk around the large wood pile ... no guards shouting those familiar words "lakas" and "speedo" (hurry – fast). It is world away from the usual hard labour to which my poor malnourished body has become accustomed.

I begin my new job by treating the natives with a certain amount of respect, as I am conscious that we are as good as foreigners to them in what is after all their country. The natives soon weigh me up, however, I am fully aware of the odd ones amongst them who would not hesitate to sell you out to the Nips for anything they can gain. After a while it soon becomes apparent that my weak ulcerated legs are not up to the continual standing and walking round, so I am forced to take the occasional squatting position; a position that is used by the natives for resting, with my arms completely encircling my knees. Natives walking past begin to address me as "tuan" (sir) with a friendly grin, asking "roko mau?" (do you want a smoke?). I am still trying to get used to not being watched by some Nip and wary that perhaps they may be hiding somewhere in the vicinity of the mill. The natives sense my cautiousness but they soon put my mind at rest with the words "Nippon pigi" (the guard has gone) and there is no danger.

Today is to be a memorable day for me ...

I now feel I am in a position to converse with the natives pretty freely and I ask if there are any small boats available on the island (the chance of escaping is one of the predominating subjects for discussion back at camp). They tell me that the Nips have destroyed most of them, even the fishing boats (used by the natives to bring food to the island). Apparently, this has been the case on each of the islands and all the fishing expeditions are tightly supervised by the Nips with a couple or three boats solely at their disposal. The Nips order a few of the local natives to take them to the most suitable fishing waters, hand grenades are then thrown into the sea and the floating dead fish are hauled in. The best part of the catch goes to the Nip cookhouse and the discarded remainder goes to the helpers.

The natives have told me not to worry about escape as the good news is that the '**Americans have retaken the Philippines**' *(20th October 1944).* Unbelievably good news, as this means that the Nips are now cut off from Japan here on the Moena Island. I am sure this must be true as the only aircraft spotted in the skies these days are certainly not displaying the rising sun or "fried egg" as we nickname it. One thing is for sure ... there is one activity of the natives that the Nips cannot control, namely the 'news drums' with which news is broadcast over the hundreds of small uncharted islands in this part of the Pacific and the natives are also well aware of this.

NEWS HEADLINES BACK HOME IN BLIGHTY ... Birmingham Post

6 November 1944 – "FIRST ALLIED AIR RAID ON SINGAPORE" – *Super-Fortresses in a record daylight mission. Substantial force achieves good results.*

25th November 1944 – "TOKYO HEAVILY BOMBED IN DAYLIGHT" – *Explosions and large fires in the Japanese capital. Enemy homeland will be attacked with decisive vigour.*

Tom's story continues ...

I am still at the sawmill and now having difficulty digesting all the small tasty morsels of food being bestowed upon me, such as "pisang goreng" (fried bananas), "tehlore" (hard boiled eggs), "ayam goreng" (fried chicken legs) and other native titbits. This is probably as a result of becoming so accustomed to having to quickly "scoff" any scavenged food items such as these on the spot in order to avoid the risk of the benefactor being brutally punished by the guards for their kindness with dire consequences! My meagre lunch ration of rice and watery soup arrives from the camp. I take it from the Guard but as soon as his back is turned, I dispose of it as I am now almost doubled up in excruciating pain with my stomach being so full and bloated. It takes me all my time to even look at it! All this food becomes too much for my poor digestive system and I am still in a state of disbelief!

It is now afternoon and I hear the drone of an aircraft. It turns out to be one lone American plane which circles the island, seemingly on reconnaissance. I imagine what will be going on back at the camp picturing in my mind's eye the guards shouting, full of panic and hysteria. I notice the look of hopefulness and anticipation on the faces of the natives knowing full well that they would be just as thankful as the prisoners to be rid of the Nips and for this all to end.

On my return to camp, I manage to spread the good news of the liberation of the Philippines amongst my colleagues. I also express my view that if we are still here on the Moena Island in a month's time, we will either have had our throats cut in our sleep, which by now we are prepared for, or we will be free men. I personally think perhaps the Nips will try and remove us from Moena.

The following day I am detailed to return to the sawmill again and as the days go by, I begin to gain confidence and start taking some of the food I have been given by the natives back to the camp hidden in my side pack covered with edible green leaves (allowed to be gathered during working fatigues). Thankfully, I have not been subjected to the routine search of the working parties on reporting to the guardroom. I have also managed to add a certain amount of tobacco to my bag of "swag" – a huge risk I am well aware of. If I am searched and caught out by the guards, it will not only be me that will be punished but I will be making it hot for the natives at the sawmill.

I am now becoming more and more popular with more friends than ever – something one would expect now that I have access to such goodies! I try and make sure that I look after those comrades who have done me good turns in the past and make a concerted effort to get some of my proceeds of the day to those poor individuals lying in the sickbay. It is quite disturbing that some of those in sick bay prefer a roll of tobacco as opposed to food but this is probably due to the fact that they're convinced they won't come out of the sick bay alive!

Out of the blue I am approached by the kleptomaniac prisoner responsible for stealing the guard's wallet and my subsequent tortuous beating up. He asks me for tobacco and I hand him a small amount which he takes from me without even mentioning the incident. (He is one of many mentally disturbed by malnutrition and does not survive).

It was reported that throughout the nights, over and above the sound of the drone of continuous singing and loud mutterings from those whose minds were crazily trying to escape the miserable existence, one could hear the monotonous and penetrating death rattle of the dying. The stench from the filth and amount of human excrement defied all description. Tormented by vermin prisoners were unable to sleep and scabies, now widely spread, developed into a mass of sores.

Chapter 31

LAST DAY AT THE SAWMILL (Raha Camp – Moena) Face to face with my Persecutor (War Criminal) – again

Tom's story continues ...

Today is to be my last day at the sawmill and upon my return to the camp, I am ordered to report to the Guard Commander. I immediately recognise him ... the evil individual who kicked me in my bloated stomach with his hobnailed boot. A day I shall never forget! After the usual ritual of saluting and waiting to be dismissed, he continuously glares at me with hatred in his eyes, angrily asking what is in my pack. I reply without any hesitation "makhan" (food). He curses me! He comments that Nippon give me plenty and reminds me that we are forbidden to bring anything into the camp. I remain standing to attention for what seems to be an eternity, convinced that anytime now he will order me to show the contents of my pack. My heart is pounding in my chest and I am sure he can detect the defiant look in my eyes but I am pretty sure that both he and all the guards are aware of the news that they are now in a sticky position being cut off from their motherland. Eventually the Guard Commander decides to let me go. I can only guess he decided he would be risking it if he got involved in any more trouble concerning me! (I do in fact later name this particular Guard Commander as a 'War criminal' on the atrocity list which we are invited to fill in upon our return back to Cosford RAF base, along with many others, during the latter end of 1945).

Postcard from the Red Cross to Joan Dated 5th January 1945

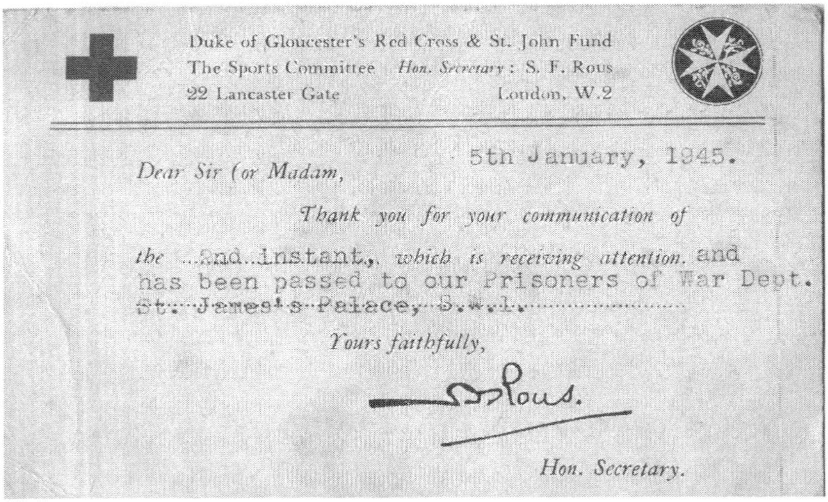
Duke of Gloucester's Red Cross & St. John Fund
The Sports Committee *Hon. Secretary*: S. F. Rous
22 Lancaster Gate London, W.2

Dear Sir (or Madam, 5th January, 1945.

Thank you for your communication of the ...2nd..instant.,. *which is receiving attention.* and has been passed to our Prisoners of War Dept. ~~St. James's Palace, S.W.1.~~

Yours faithfully,

S. Rous.

Hon. Secretary.

POSTCARD

-4 I 45
W.2

N 2D 11

Mrs. J. Oxton,
432 Belchers Lane,
Little Bromwich,
Birmingham.

EXTRACT from The Far East – Companion Journal to "The PRISONER of WAR"

(The official journal of the Prisoners of War Department of the Red Cross and St John War Organisation, St James's Palace, London S.W.1.

March 1945 - "Your Cables Begin Their journey - *Within a few days of the announcement of the new facilities for sending a ten-word telegram to prisoners of war and civilian internees in Japanese hands, the Far East Section at Park Place received nearly 20,000 applications and the number has since more than doubled. They came by letter, telegram, telephone, by personal call and in one day alone over 7,000 applications were received. The opening of the service was announced just before Christmas."*

Chapter 32

PRISONER SHIPS ATTACKED BY ALLIED AIRCRAFT
Depart Moena Island (Muna)

It is reported: *Approximately 263 surviving prisoners remaining on Muna were convinced they would be better off to remain on the island and they were relieved to hear transport by sea would be nigh on impossible as the Japanese ships were being closely monitored by the Allied aircraft.*

Tom's story continues ...

April 1945 – We make no bones about preferring to stay where we are to the bitter end, we are relieved to hear that transport by sea is almost impossible as every Nip ship is watched from the air.

However, at the beginning of April 1945 things change...

Two Nip ships arrive at Moena Island to take prisoners off to some unknown destination. (According to news we receive later in both cases these two ships are attacked by allied aircraft as they bear no marking whatsoever to show that there are prisoners aboard. Tragically most are lost at sea, others wounded or killed. All this is unknown to the pilots of the aircraft at the time as they are out to sink all Nip ships).

NEWS HEADLINES BACK HOME IN BLIGHTY ...

1st April 1945 – "CHEESE RATION CUT"

5th April 1945 – "JAPANESE CABINET RESIGNS"

12th April 1945 – "PRESIDENT ROOSEVELT DIES"

***It is reported:** On 13th **April 1945 the 1st of 3 drafts** of approximately 50 prisoners **leave** Moena Island with Flight Lieutenant Davis, Flight Lieutenant Allen, Flight Lieutenant Haddo, Dr Alistair Forbes.*

NEWS HEADLINES BACK HOME IN BLIGHTY …

23rd April 1945 – "BLACK OUT ENDS"

1st May 1945 – "ALLEGED DEATH OF ADOLF HITLER". *Hitler kills himself and his mistress.*

8th May 1945 – Daily Mail "VE DAY – IT'S ALL OVER". *The War's greatest day of suspense. Germany surrendered unconditionally to the allies yesterday. But there will be no official announcement of victory until 3 pm today when Mr Churchill will give the news to the world.*

I SMELL PINEAPPLE

Daily Mail

VICTORY EDITION

ONE PENNY — FOR KING AND EMPIRE — TUESDAY, MAY 8, 1945

3 POWERS WILL ANNOUNCE GREAT SURRENDER SIMULTANEOUSLY

VE-DAY—IT'S ALL OVE[R]

The King to speak to Empire: Victorious generals will follow Premier on radio

All Britain stood by for news

How it broke—hour by hour

THE WAR'S GREATEST DAY OF SUSPENSE

By WILSON BROADBENT, Diplomatic Correspondent

GERMANY surrendered unconditionally to the Allies yesterday. But there will be no official announcement of victory until 3 p.m. to-day—officially described as VE-Day—when Mr. Churchill will give the news to the world. He will follow this with an address to the House of Commons, and at 9 p.m. the King will speak to Britain and the Empire.

To-day's announcement will be made simultaneously in London, Washington, and Moscow. To-day, therefore is the first of the promised two-days V-holiday for the country. Broadcasts will also be made by General Eisenhower, and Field-Marshals Montgomery and Alexander.

Mr. Churchill's two statements to-day will not affect his intention to broadcast at length on Thursday night, the fifth anniversary of his assumption of the Premiership.

Before and after the King's speech, London will be floodlighted, searchlights will fill the sky, and it is now possible that there will be a victory salvo of guns, but this point had not been finally settled at a late hour last night.

THE KING THANKS C-IN-C

GOEBBELS' BODY IN A SHELTER

Took poison

GOEBBELS, the German Propaganda Minister, his wife, and five children have been found dead in Berlin.

MONTY MEETS ROKOSSOVSKY

4 toasts at lunch

THE WAR GOES ON HERE—

Prague bombed as SS men shoot Czechs

8th May 1945 – The Birmingham Mail 6.30 STOP PRESS … **PREMIER'S BROADCAST – END OF THE WAR ANNOUNCED.**

Mr Churchill in his broadcast to the nation this afternoon said:

"Hostilities will end at one minute after midnight, but in the interests of saving lives the case fire was sounded yesterday". "Channel Islands are to be free today". "It is not surprising that on such long fronts and in the existing disorder of the enemy the German High Command should not in every case have been able to obey the cease fire immediately".

"The German war is therefore at an end. But JAPAN remains unsubdued, and her cruelties call for retribution". The Premier concluded …. "Advance Brittania. Long live the cause of freedom. God Save the king".

8th May 1945 – Daily Mirror "VE DAY!" *Public holiday today and tomorrow official. This is VE Day after 5 years 8 months and 4 days of the bloodiest war in history. Britain and her allies have gained Victory in Europe.*

Daily Mirror

MAY 8

VE-DAY!

PUBLIC HOLIDAY TODAY AND TOMORROW—OFFICIAL

Massacre goes on in Prague as war ends

Celebrations delay due to a 'technicality'

By BILL GREIG

THIS IS VE-DAY. AFTER FIVE YEARS, EIGHT MONTHS AND FOUR DAYS OF THE BLOODIEST WAR IN HISTORY BRITAIN AND HER ALLIES HAVE GAINED VICTORY IN EUROPE.

Capitulation of Germany to the Allies was announced by Doenitz yesterday—but a mere technicality in the arrangements made with Russia and America delayed the British people's celebration.

One result of the delay is that Britain's workers get two clear days' holiday—today and tomorrow. This Cabinet decision was disclosed last night.

Originally it was intended that the first day's holiday would not begin until the Prime Minister had spoken.

Spend VE in camp, CO's say

"Daily Mirror" Reporter

COMMANDING officers of Army and RAF camps all over Britain told their men yesterday: "Spend VE-Day how you will, but PLEASE spend it in camp."

War winners may broadcast today

The Prime Minister will broadcast at 3 p.m. today.

It is probable that later in the afternoon General Eisenhower, Field-Marshal Montgomery and Field-Marshal Alexander will also speak over the radio to the Allied world.

At 9 p.m. the King will broadcast.

NORWAY AWAITS ALLIED LANDINGS

Goebbels and his family are found, poisoned

On top of the

In the heart of London an Allied soldier — he climbed the Eros statue in London's Piccadilly—gets just as high as he

THE WAR IN THE FAR EAST GOES ON! "BETTER EQUIPMENT IS NEEDED IN PACIFIC "WAR AGAINST JAPAN"

"WAR GOES ON AS USUAL IN ROOM 109" – Japs still on run in Burma.

22nd May 1945 – "RATIONS CUT AGAIN"

23rd May 1945 – "CHURCHILL RESIGNS AND FORMS CARETAKER GOVERNMENT"

28th May 1945 – "NAVAL AIR ATTACKS ON JAPAN"

Article from FAR EAST Companion Journal to "The PRISONER of WAR" – dated May 1945 (Issued to Joan)

Far East 11

Our Time – and Theirs

When you are listening to the one o'clock news, prisoners in camps in Japan and Korea (Chosen) are on the point of going to bed. Early nights are the rule in the camps, as also is early rising, and lights are usually turned out at 9 or 9.30 p.m.

Somewhere about the time that we are going to bed, prisoners in Formosa (Taiwan) are getting up, for reveille is at 5.50. a.m. and their clocks are seven hours ahead of ours. In Borneo, Hong Kong and Shanghai the time is the same as in Formosa.

As the children are coming home from school at midday in this country, out in Malaya the sun is beginning to set and by half past six night has fallen. For in Malaya, as also in Siam, Java, and Sumatra, the clock is six hours ahead of us here at home.

The above calculations are based on pre-war time systems.

Back Home in Blighty ... A Friend's Letter of Support to Joan

14th June 1945

Hello Joan

I was very pleased to hear from you again and I did wonder what had happened to you. I'm awfully sorry to know you are not well. I could see how you were when I saw you last, so I am not surprised. I don't think you will be any better Joan until you go away. Why don't you make up your mind to go convalescent. I'm sure it would do you the world of good. I mean, you shouldn't have to pay any fees for your keep but I am going to make a suggestion Joan. I hope you won't feel too badly about this, but I would like to let you have the cash for your expenses. Please let me know what you think, but I hope you are feeling much better for your rest.

I am rather busy lately Joan. I am helping the Conservative Party with the forthcoming election and go one or two evenings a week so when we meet Joan, I hope you can let me know in good time.

I can understand you worrying Joan because I know I should be the same but I was thinking how nice it was to hear how fond you are of him still, as its not many girls who would remain faithful and in love with someone they haven't seen or heard from for a long time. Anyhow, it will all be worth waiting for I'm sure and it won't last much longer, so keep smiling.

Bob is alright apart from a little gastric he has had. He doesn't complain much about anything but then he's lucky to be where he is and he says he appreciates it.

Let me know when you are coming down to see us and so, until I hear from you.

Sincerely Dulcie xxxx

NEWS HEADLINES BACK HOME IN BLIGHTY ...

15th June 1945 – "PARLIAMENT DISSOLVED"

5th July 1945 – "GENERAL ELECTION"

22nd July 1945 – "TEA RATION INCREASED TO 2½ oz WEEKLY"

26th July 1945 – "LABOUR SWEEP TO POWER; ATTLEE PRIME MINISTER"

It is reported: *On* ***26th July 1945 the 1st Moena Island draft of prisoners leave Macassar*** *(Sulawesi) with Flight Lieutenant Davis, Flight Lieutenant Allen, Flight Lieutenant Haddo, Dr Alistair Forbes.*

On ***28th July 1945 the 2nd Moena Island draft of prisoners leave Macassar*** *with Major Mossford.*

NEWS HEADLINES BACK IN BLIGHTY …

6th August 1945 – "ATOM BOMB DROPPED BY U.S. ON HIROSHIMA"

9th August 1945 – "ATOM BOMB DROPPED BY U.S. ON NAGASAKI"

(These atom bombs killed more than 110,000 civilians)

14th August 1945 at Midnight – Daily Mail Headlines "UNCONDITIONAL SURRENDER OF JAPAN"

15th August 1945 – "JAPAN SURRENDERS" *(some Japanese soldiers commit suicide)*

15th August 1945 – Daily Mail … PEACE – OFFICIAL *(Japan has surrendered)*

Daily Mail

FOR KING AND EMPIRE

ONE PENNY

Answer to atom bomb: *British scientists already at work* See Page Two

PEACE—OFFICIAL

World's vigil broken at midnight by Jap reply

160 WORDS END SIX YEARS OF WAR

From Daily Mail Correspondent

JAPAN has surrendered. In an official announcement from No. 10, Downing Street at midnight the news was given after a day of delays, rumours, premature reports and denials. The Japanese Note containing the acceptance of surrender to the four Allied powers was contained in a code message of 160 words sent by Tokio to Berne for transmission.

In a visit of less than five minutes the Japanese Minister in Berne last night handed over the Tokio reply which Mr. Leland Harrison, the U.S. Minister telephoned to President Truman. The Note consisted of only 160 code words.

The official Swiss communiqué said: "A 8.10 p.m. to-day the Japanese Minister in Berne handed to the Foreign Office the Japanese Government's reply to the Allied Declaration transmitted to Japan by the United States, Great Britain, Russia, and China on Saturday.

"The reply was addressed to the United States Government for forwarding to the four Allied Governments. The reply was handed over to the American Minister at Berne at 8.25 p.m. and was cabled from the Swiss Legation to Washington at 9.5 p.m."

U.S. refuses to wait and lifts the roof

'War over' fever

JAPS WAIL OUTSIDE PALACE

'Our efforts fail'

ATOBOMB NO PEACEMAKER

Vatican warns

Call-up halts on VJ-Day

And 'war' direction ends

U.S. promises end

'TAKE MY LIFE, NOT MY HONOUR'

Jury retire in Pétain treason trial

MARSHAL'S LAST PLEA

From WALTER FARR, Daily Mail Special Correspondent

Paris, Tuesday.

THE Pétain jury late to-night had retired and were deliberating the fate of the aged marshal. Their verdict was expected in a few hours.

Labour bid for 'Modern Times' policy

Higher wage riddle

PLANS for increasing the efficiency and productivity of British industry are being examined by the Labour Government.

Radar men may pick up the moon

'JAPAN HAS SURRENDERED'

—ATTLEE

WOMEN OF A HOME

World's vigil broken at m

160 WORDS END SIX YEARS OF WAR

From Daily Mail Correspondent

JAPAN has surrendered. In an official announcement from No. 10, Downing Street at midnight the news was given after a day of delays, rumours, premature reports and denials. The Japanese Note containing the acceptance of surrender to the four Allied powers was contained in a code message of 160 words sent by Tokio to Berne for transmission.

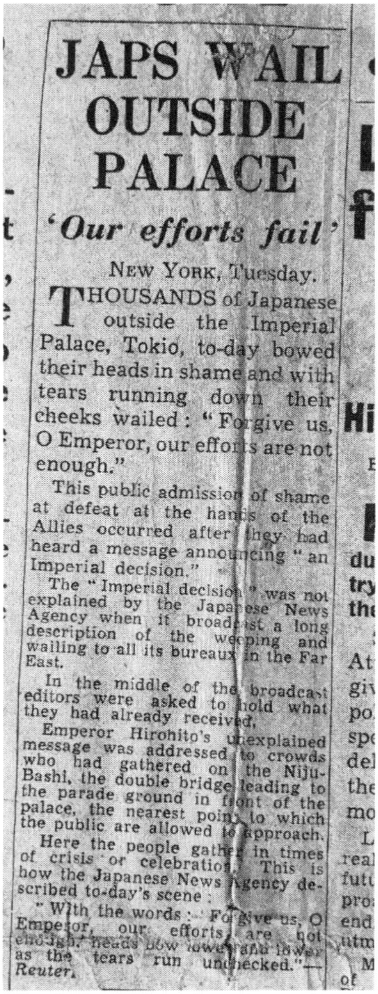

JAPS WAIL OUTSIDE PALACE

'Our efforts fail'

NEW YORK, Tuesday.

THOUSANDS of Japanese outside the Imperial Palace, Tokio, to-day bowed their heads in shame and with tears running down their cheeks wailed: "Forgive us, O Emperor, our efforts are not enough."

This public admission of shame at defeat at the hands of the Allies occurred after they had heard a message announcing "an Imperial decision."

The "Imperial decision" was not explained by the Japanese News Agency when it broadcast a long description of the weeping and wailing to all its bureaux in the Far East.

In the middle of the broadcast editors were asked to hold what they had already received.

Emperor Hirohito's unexplained message was addressed to crowds who had gathered on the Niju-Bashi, the double bridge leading to the parade ground in front of the palace, the nearest point to which the public are allowed to approach.

Here the people gather in times of crisis or celebration. This is how the Japanese News Agency described to-day's scene:

"With the words: 'Forgive us, O Emperor, our efforts are not enough,' heads bow lower and lower as the tears run unchecked."—Reuter.

'JAPAN HAS SURRENDERED'
—ATTLEE

Mr. Attlee, broadcasting at midnight, said: "Japan has to-day surrendered. The last of our enemies is laid low."

15th/16th August 1945 – "VJ CELEBRATIONS IN BIRMINGHAM"

It is reported: *On* ***Early August 1945 the 3rd draft*** *of prisoners* ***depart from Raha Camp, Moena Island*** *with Major Gibson and *Captain (Dr) Shimada unaware that the war has ended. They leave 182 graves.* ***(Tom's draft)***

At this time, prisoners were still unaware of the fact that the day before, Emperor Hirohito had announced the surrender of Japan over the radio. ***Major Gibson****, although he had been the camp commander for quite a period of time, was too sick and frail to take responsibility* ***for the departure of the last group*** *and he handed over the command to Lieutenant de Haan. The Japanese medic Dr Shimada left with them. Out of the three boats to leave Muna, one capsized (close to the shore) due to a leak which was eventually repaired. The other two boats sailed on and arrived in Bajoa mid-August 1945.*

Tom's story continues ...

Early August 1945 – The Nips have now decided to attempt to use another form of transportation of prisoners, which does prove to be successful. We are ordered to march to some invasion barges in the darkness of night. These invasion barges are moored up close to the most available tree sheltered islands, thereby keeping out of sight of the now numerous allied planes which are searching out and sinking all Nip shipping. (The allies are still unaware of the fact that these ships may have prisoners of war aboard. The Nips continue to make sure they don't display any markings of any description to indicate that allied Prisoners of War are stowed away in the holds of these "hell ships").

The invasion barge is packed full and we lie cheek-by-jowl keeping as still as possible. Nothing can be cooked on board and we are given meagre rations of cold steamed rice. We are only able to drink what little water we may have in our water bottles. The dampness and cold have made many of sick men even worse. The conditions are beyond words but at least our weak and malnourished bodies are not subjected to any form of physical labour. We all try and support one another by trying to give help, wherever possible, especially to the fresh cases of sickness and disease still occurring amongst our comrade prisoners. I cast my mind back to the sick men at Haroekoe and Moena prison camps, having to catch all those flies in order to receive their meagre rations. (*I later learn that they do eventually become free men in Australia long before we are freed – those prisoners that survived of course).*

The Nips quite often mention that in Japan if a buffalo is unable to pull a plough, he is no longer working for the Emperor and not entitled to any food – the same applies to prisoners of war.

Chapter 33

DESTINATION... MACASSAR, Celebes (Sulawesi) Via Bajoa –Watampone (Rice Barn Collapses on Prisoners)

Macassar is the largest city on Celebes which has several large peninsulas (known as arms).

It is reported that the appalling conditions of indescribable squalor in all the prisoner of war camps in this region were the same as everywhere else, however, the conditions at the prison camp at Macassar were particularly abysmal. The camp was extremely overcrowded with poor and inadequate accommodation with no bedding or clothing available. Many of the prisoners were dressed in rags at this time.

Each day the prisoners were subjected to horrifying acts of torture and beatings. The ***Camp Commandant "Yoshida"*** *appeared to enjoy such brutality as he was usually present at the time they were carried out, sometimes becoming actively involved. Prisoners were terrorised with severe, frequent, brutal punishments and recreation was totally forbidden*

The prisoners, which included the frail and infirm, were cruelly overworked. They were exposed to appalling sanitary conditions and scant medical supplies, hence the rapid spread of dysentery and malaria. The death rate caused by malnutrition and disease was extremely high and on the increase.

British Red Cross parcels and mail continued to be withheld and did not reach the prisoners.

It is reported: *Early* ***August 1945 – 3rd Moena draft*** *with Major Gibson, Captain (Dr) Shimada and prisoners arrive at Macassar* ***(Tom's draft).***

Tom's story continues ...

Mid-August 1945 – I am part of the 3rd draft to arrive at Bajoa, a coastal village in **Watampone** – Western leg of Celebes (now Sulawesi). We have become accustomed to the disembarking of our stiff, weak and starved bodies in the hours of darkness and a tropical rainstorm. Many collapse, panting for breath from sheer exhaustion. Groping and stumbling our way forward through the deep mud we are ordered into a rice store which is meant to be our resting place for the night, at least it is shelter from the tropical rainstorm. Our bed spaces are on the earthen floor of the barn and instinctively I pick myself a spot near the entrance, which for some unknown reason has become my usual practice.

Our night of rest is soon disturbed by the animal like screams of a guard beating up a prisoner caught urinating up the outside of the barn, but this is merely a prelude to a much louder and disastrous disturbance.

I am lying with my head towards the entrance of the rice barn when suddenly, completely out of the blue, I hear a sound resembling that of some kind of aircraft gliding across the roof of the barn. Looking upwards it slowly occurs to me that the bamboo barn is actually collapsing due to the weight of the rain soaked atap roof. *(Why would "the Almighty" pick a time like this for such a thing to happen?)* I can hardly move and feel like an elephant with painful, heavy, swollen feet and legs. Crash! ... the barn suddenly folds up towards the entrance which I am desperately struggling to get to. Without warning, my legs give way and for a second all I can see are the splintering bamboo leaves of the roof hurtling down towards me. Convinced they are about to plunge through my body, I manage to muster as much energy as I am able and gambol feet first in a backward direction. Such a close shave! The toes of my bare left foot are grazed by the splintering bamboo which proceeded to plunge into the rain sodden earth about two or three feet from my head. Still in shock from my narrow escape, I struggle to stand up on my sore, bleeding feet and I thank God for rescuing me from what could have led to a slow and painful death.

The torrential rain continues to pour down on us. A large number of comrades are trapped under the collapsed building crying out in agony and shouting for help. There are others like myself who have luckily escaped and we know that we must act very quickly to try and rescue our comrades. I must point out here that the guards give no help whatsoever! We spend quite a time in the continuous downpour of rain frantically attempting to free both the badly injured and those lucky enough to escape unscathed. We carry the injured to a designated point where they can be treated but, as always, any medical treatment is very sparingly given by the Nips. I will mention again here that the Nips, throughout the whole of the rescue operation, have done nothing but shelter from the rain!

My toes are red raw and bleeding but I have found a piece of old mosquito netting in my salvaged kit to bind them. I spend the last hour or two of the night trying to sleep under the nearest tree with two or three pals but sleep is nigh on impossible as I am in agony with the pain from my injury *(a cut from bamboo is more painful than a cut from a knife owing to the stinging sensation it leaves).* I must add here that I am very conscious of other men who are having to endure a lot more pain from far worse injuries. We are relieved to hear that no-one has been killed.

Still feeling exhausted, at last the break of the new day arrives. It is so good to see the sun shining and feel the warmth which helps to dry out our scantily clothed, frail and starved bodies. I cannot recollect having eaten anything since our arrival. It seems like an eternity since we landed here yesterday with the traumatic experience of the collapse of the rice barn. We tried in vain to help and rescue as many comrades as we were physically able in such torrential rain, not to mention the lack of sleep from having no bed or shelter. My water bottle is still about a third full with water as I am still trying to condition myself not to drink too much as it has a dramatic effect on my swollen feet and legs from the wet beri-beri disease.

It is not long before two Nip lorries arrive. Survivors of last night, including myself, are bundled onto the open backs of the lorries and we are accompanied by two armed-escort guards. I must say there is a noticeable difference in their attitude and expression as they appear to be worried and agitated! Squatting in the back of the truck with my comrades, our particular Nip driver revs the engine and drives off like a maniac. It turns out to be a journey from hell which I shall never forget (amongst many other experiences).

This journey from hell takes us across the Western leg of the Celebes (Sulawesi), approximately seven miles, non-stop to **Macassar**. During our journey and after some considerable distance both myself and a few others ask the guard if we can stop for toilets, which we know will be in the bush! The driver refuses to stop and we are ordered to urinate over the side of the truck – an impossible work of art travelling on jungle roads, round sharp bends and at a reckless speed! We decide that it's better to try and hold on rather than be flung off the truck in our efforts to relieve ourselves and be left for dead.

Early August 1945 – It's towards evening when we finally reach **Macassar** and taken to **a former Dutch Naval Barracks,** which has been taken over by the Nips and used as a prison camp. After a short while, the inmates of the camp come over to our billets when there are quite a few very emotional reunions of friends who have been separated since the fall of Singapore and Dutch East Indies.

It is very noticeable that our physical appearance is considerably different to the other resident prisoners – we certainly look a poor lot. It is unmistakeable from the appearance of our frail, starving bodies that our tour of the island camps has certainly left its mark upon us. Something quite simple I know but we are fascinated by the fact that the resident prisoners have the normal service style type of haircut whereas we have always been shaved with the clippers from the front to the back of the head. *(We later learn that they no longer have to conform to clippers all over).*

We're soon to find out during our brief stay that life on the prison camp in Macassar is to be quite different to prison camp life that we have become accustomed to. Not sure why but the Nips appear to have mellowed slightly!*(I can only think it's because they must by now realise that they are in a difficult position being cut off from their homeland. Needless to say, there are still one or two with that evil look of hatred across their faces!).*

We have been advised that our work from now on is no longer connected with the Jap's intended invasion of Australia (the Jap's unsuccessful goal) and we have been allocated duties such as the tending of the vegetable gardens. The produce from the gardens now ends up not only in the Nip cookhouse but also our own, which takes some getting used to as it's certainly never happened before!

Chapter 34

"GENTLEMEN ... THE WAR IS NOW OVER"

16th August 1945 – *We are sitting in the billets, having just finished breakfast, waiting for the bugle to sound for the fit men to muster on the Padang for work. Unusually, this wait lasts for the best part of an hour and eventually our section officer comes to the billet to announce that there is to be no work today! But ... we must hold ourselves in readiness to assemble on parade at any time (he is unable to tell us the reason). We remain seated in our usual friendly groups chatting and speculating ... some suggest it could be time for us to board yet another "hell ship" and some reckon we're about to be subjected to some form of Nip treachery in a way of seeing us all off? I have my own view in mind as to what could happen but I don't get chance to share it as the bugle sounds and we're immediately ordered out of our billet.*

Standing to attention on the Padang, each prisoner is issued with one straw hat, one pair of white cotton shorts, a cotton shirt and a pair of plimsoll type rubber boots which we are all ordered to change into, along with our colleagues in the sickbay.

We are informed that a large amount of Nip medical supplies will now become available. *(It crosses my mind that this could be the start of the Nips trying to soften us up to help clear their conscience after subjecting us to such brutality for three plus years at their mercy).*

Still in a trance like state, the first thing I give away is the straw hat as **I am still proudly wearing my RAF peaked cap.** It is by now a little worse for wear but I am proud to say that it is still bearing the polished badge!! *(My comrades have so many times pulled my leg about this).* I decide to stuff the cheap cotton shorts into my kitbag as I am comfortable wearing a pair of Dutch army green shorts which are still in reasonable condition. The plimsoll-type rubber boots are welcome as they are far more comfortable than the home-made, or should I say camp-made wooden 'clompers' as we call them.

In no time at all the bugle sounds again. *(It's such a familiar sound, I can still hum it to myself after all these years and I can also remember a few of the Nip tunes. I am able to pick up and remember most tunes, which regrettably include those that I connect to some obscenities).*

We are all lined up in the presence of our Senior Officers, plus Nip 'Shokos' (Officers); one of whom looks very important! We've never seen these Officers before and there's something else different ... the words of command are in English! We have become so accustomed to our drill being delivered in Nip language. Our Senior Officer announces that we're shortly to be addressed by the Senior Nip on a matter of great importance. The Senior Nip, rather short in stature, is helped up to stand on a large wooden box, *(this certainly causes a few stifled titters amongst the ranks!)* and he proceeds to gabble away in Japanese. His speech concludes and to our astonishment he actually salutes all present. Our Senior Officer then proceeds to give us the news (without the aid of the box I might add!).

"Gentlemen, the War is now over. Peace has been signed between the Allies and Japanese in South East Asia. You will still remain under the discipline of the Japanese and they will do their best to get us all back to Java as soon as possible".

AN AIR OF DISBELIEF!! ... I am sure that any "normal" human being, as they read on, would expect a loud uproar of cheering and throwing of caps into the air but this certainly is not the case where I'm standing!! We are in a state of shock, numb with bitterness! This news is impossible to take in after the years of torturous hell we have suffered at the hands of these oriental animals. How can we forget our dead comrades who died in agonising pain inflicted upon them through the indescribable ill treatment, torture, starvation and slavery of the Japanese. We still have such hatred and loathing running through our veins! How can we shout or cheer ... we do not have the strength! Our poor emaciated and listless bodies have been stripped of any spirit! I am personally finding it difficult at this point in time to focus on anything else other than 'if only I could lay my hands on just one or two of those evil guards, particularly the evil guard that booted me in the guts with his hobnailed boot' *(It's just as well that I never lay eyes on him again!).*

We are ordered to return to our billets where there is a lot of talk amongst us. It takes a while to adjust and gradually come round to the idea that it is good news and we should be feeling joyous and triumphant.

We do question the reason why we must continue to be subjected to the discipline of our captors even though the War is over! *(We later learn the truth of how the Nips have been beaten).* Aware that 'Peace has been signed', we are still under the orders of our own Officers. This confirms to us that we must continue to obey orders, although worryingly there are a few chaps who have been tempted to take the law into their own hands! Our Officers have been subjected to so much ridicule over such a long period of time at the hands of the Japs and in our presence, we continue to treat them with the highest regard. They too have suffered whilst carrying out some incredibly good work under intolerable conditions. A special mention here goes to the Medical Officers.

A few of the Japanese guards actually have the audacity to come round to the billets grinning in a friendly manner, trying to get into conversation and even offering to shake our hands! After a cool reception, they eventually give up and leave. All I can say is "Lucky for them that they manage to walk out without any incidents!" as to us, they are no longer terrifying, they are simply small, insignificant little men.

Chapter 35

ABOARD THE NIP SHIP
Destination ... Bicycle Camp – Batavia (Jakarta) West Java

'Cycle Camp' is a former Dutch military barracks so named because of the large number of cycles found by the Prisoners of War. Surabaya is a port City on Java Island.

Tom's story continues ...

18th August 1945 – the men from Raha are to immediately prepare for a draft and ordered to board a Nip "Hell Ship" which is to take us to Java Island. We have been told the 'War is Over' but we are still to be accompanied by Nip Guards and the conditions remain the same! The sick and frail are put on stretchers and we are crammed together in the holds with the same meagre rations of rice and seaweed soup and a few of the guards are still using their rifle butts on some of our weaker comrades. How are we supposed to make any sense of what we are witnessing?

We are allowed on deck during the day to breath in some fresh air. (Still wary of any possible attacks from Australian or American aircraft). We assume that all the aircraft activity we can hear, occasionally coming into view, has been operating from Australia. (I think about the first one lone reconnaissance plane that circled the Amboina Island back in April 1943). We now appreciate the efforts and contributions of the 'Aussies'.

After approximately four days sailing in a South Westerly direction, covering approximately three hundred and fifty miles, our destination of Surabaya Harbour on the Java Island is finally reached. We certainly have no trouble recognising it as we had sailed out of this harbour on our first hell ship the "Amagi Maru" at the beginning of April 1943.

I reflect back to the tragic event of that day when the Nip ship carrying many prisoners blew up (possibly caused by our own actions!). I remember how we purposefully damaged those sixty-gallon drums of aviation spirit destined for the airfields. These airfields were to be built later at the hands of the slave labour workforce of prisoners of war. The prisoners toiled under such horrific conditions in the terrific heat of the scorching sun, forced to cut the airstrip out on Haroekoe, all to no avail as it never actually became operational (a pleasing thought perhaps!) *(I might add here that the shrapnel wound in my leg continued to cause me pain at times – a permanent reminder!)*

21st August 1945 – We disembark at the harbour in **Tanjong Perak** in Surabaya and ordered to march, if one can call it that, to the railway station. We must appear a poor looking lot having lived in such appalling conditions during the long voyage from **Macassar**. A few of the ex-guards appear to have transformed and offer to help the sick clamber up into the trucks awaiting on the quay.

We arrive at **Sunbung railway station** and we are allowed to sit around whilst waiting for the train to arrive, which is to convey us the whole length of Java, westerly to Batavia (now Jakarta). A distance of approximately four hundred miles.

Whilst sitting and waiting at the railway station, there is a large crowd of Javanese natives looking on with a mixture of amazement, sadness and trepidation on their faces. Do they know that the War is over? Maybe they do and they can't understand why it is so apparent that we are still being dominated by the Nip guards! My attempt to get into conversation with one of these poor natives fails due to one of the guards; no doubt these actions confuse the natives even more. I can only imagine the Nips are keen to give the impression that they are still ruling the roost! (I have since reflected on this incident in my latter years and realised that the guards would not have been able to prevent me from conversing with the natives at this point! We had become so accustomed to abiding by their rigid discipline during those hard, cruel years, still suffering psychologically from the effects of brutal punishment for the least wrongdoing).

The train pulls into the station and surprisingly we are allowed to travel in carriages – what luxury! Whilst boarding the train, we receive strict orders that the roller type shuttered windows must be pulled down and remain down. Once settled aboard the train, we are given rations of rice and seaweed soup and the train slowly pulls out. Only after leaving the city, are we allowed to push up the shuttered windows which enables us to enjoy the scenery of the countryside, including the sights of paddy fields and the jungle. The train stops periodically at various stations to replenish water and wood supplies for the fire and boiler type engine. At each of these stops, we are greeted by local native traders, patiently standing and waiting offering various titbits of food for sale. The guards immediately prevent us from purchasing any of their tasty morsels by ordering us to close the window shutters in the faces of the traders (not that many of us have any money anyway!). It's absurd that even at this stage, with the War over, there is no let up from these hostile guards, they continue to be just as callous towards us (more so in the presence of the natives!). The journey is long and slow.

At last, our never-ending journey across Java from Surabaya to Batavia comes to an end.

22nd August 2945 – We are whisked away from the railway station through the city streets to what is to be our last prison camp **'Cycle Camp'.** 'Cycle Camp' is still under guard of the Nips, although the War is supposed to be over! It is very crowded with what are now 'ex-prisoners of war' and the conditions are so very different, almost alien to us. We are no longer compelled to parade for working parties each day but the Nips are still on guard duty! This we find quite distasteful but we have been informed that this is a temporary arrangement. They are there for the time being to protect us from militant bands of the native population, who are not prepared to go back to the old Dutch Colony days. We are fairly certain the Nips were at the root of this trouble. We believe they were responsible for inciting former corroborators to resist the Dutch from regaining control, as it has now become so evident that the Nips will soon be leaving.

The Nips are trying to be as friendly as they can towards us British but the majority of us are certainly in no state of mind or mood to acknowledge such behaviour! How can they expect us just to switch off and forget the years of brutality and slave labour? ... Impossible! In any case, we are well aware that their newly found type of behaviour is in no way genuine and recognising the deep resentment towards these abhorrent individuals, standing orders are posted around the camp stating that anyone attempting to molest Nip personnel will be subject to disciplinary action. We continue to adhere to the orders and remain faithful to our own Officers. Thankfully, we're not left to brood over this for long!

Today is the day we have been waiting patiently for ... a Fortress flies low over "Cycle Camp", so low in fact that the crew are clearly visible waving frantically. A magnificent sight!

After circling for the second time, the Fortress drops leaflets and we are given the good news that Allied troops will soon be arriving. We are to commandeer all motor transport in readiness for an air drop of food and medical supplies tomorrow at a given time.

Orders given are that we must proceed to the airfield, as early as possible, and mark out the runway as per instructions with whatever white material we can get out hands on. We must then stand by on the perimeter of the airfield until the drop has been completed.

All the "fittest" of the MT drivers are asked to volunteer for driving every available truck, some of which belong to the Nips, others are British and American types that the Nips have been using for over three and a half years during their occupation of Java. I am considered to be one of the so called 'fit', although my feet and legs are still painful and swollen with wet beriberi, but I am more than willing to be able to contribute and hope that I am capable of driving. The convoy sets out straight after breakfast.

Further orders are given ... there must be two Nip guards aboard each truck for escort (they are still in possession of their rifles!). The Nips co-operate by supplying most of the white material and working as swiftly as possible, bearing in mind the state of our frail and battered bodies, we are able to get the runway marked out in good time. I guess not many of us got much sleep last night as it is difficult to relax our undernourished, weak bodies which are still full of inflamed nerves, particularly in our legs and feet. Just a few effects caused by the prolonged period of slavery and brutal beatings.

During our wait for the arrival of the aircraft, we welcome the sight of some friendly natives who bring us tasty morsels of food ... as much as we can eat! Anything we are unable to eat is stuffed into our side packs for our sick friends back at 'Cycle Camp'. We are also now in possession of what we call "tailor made" cigarettes. The smokers amongst us have become quite accustomed to smoking the native tobacco rolled in a dried leaf, or perhaps a bit of 'acquired' Nip toilet paper.

We can hear the drone of the **Fortresses** coming in one by one. Supplies, attached to chutes begin to drift down; the food in wooden cases and the medical supplies in special large canisters. It does become a bit disconcerting at times when a few of the pilots fly down a little too close for comfort but I guess they are eager to make sure they drop the cargo as near to us as possible. Mission accomplished, the last kite leaves, giving us the Victory roll. We are now in possession of tons and tons of tinned meat, milk, fruit, Bovril, Ovaltine, cocoa, fish and many more items.

Top priority are the medical canisters which are loaded on to the trucks first ready to be delivered to various locations. We are by this time aware that there are quite a number of internment camps a few miles from Batavia, which are occupied by both women and children. They are located in the countryside.

On reaching one of the internment camps, the gates are thrown open for us to drive in and we are greeted by the sight of women and children overcome by our arrival, shedding tears of joy. I must say that even though we have been subjected to many distressing sights during our captivity, to witness this awful pitiful sight before us of these poor deprived women and children really is heart breaking to say the least. We immediately get to work unloading the life-giving supplies as quickly as possible; conscious that there must be a sickbay somewhere tucked away with poor unfortunates who are too far gone to enjoy the benefit of God's gifts to them.

Our work is done here and it is time to depart, leaving behind us the sound of a few feeble cheers from those frail women and children able to muster enough energy. Having to leave is quite a wrench. It is difficult to grasp that these are the same brave Dutch women we had come across when we were fit men **departing from Batavia at the beginning of 1942** – a lifetime ago!

I have now driven many difficult miles and by the time we return back at the drome, most of the supplies have been collected, although there are a few damaged goods that we are able to salvage. We park the truck and head back to our straw mats for a night's sleep. We have just done the best day's work since the beginning of our captivity ... a day to remember!

Allied Head Quarters has set up at the former Dutch hotel "Des Indies", some distance from 'Cycle Camp'. As a volunteer driver, I have made a few trips driving our Officers between the Head Quarters and the camp in a staff car which has been commandeered. During one of these trips I ascertain the reason for the extreme safety precautions taken with regard to the continuation of the Nips guarding the camps and ex-prisoners of war.

One evening I am stopped at a road block of armed militant Javanese natives. They ask whether I have any 'Hollanders' in the car and after convincing them that all occupants are "Engriss", as they called us British, I am allowed to drive on. I suddenly become to realise that this must account for the sudden disappearance of all Dutch Officers and other ranks from the various prison and internment camps. *(I later learn that they have been removed to a place of safety from the threat that now faces them in what will eventually become "Indonesia". Some poor reward for their three and a half years of suffering as prisoners and internees of the Nips).*

Reports indicate: *About only one-third of Prisoners of War returned to Java.*

Letter to Joan from Birmingham Prisoner of War Relatives Association

The BIRMINGHAM PRISONERS OF WAR RELATIVES' ASSOCIATION

72 Newhall Street
Birmingham 3
CENtral 6672

Postmark Dated: 4th September 1945

Dear Mrs Orton

Whilst we realise with regret that this Association has not through lack of official information from Japan, been able to be of much help to relatives who have prisoners of War in Japanese hands, we would like to assure you that our interest is nonetheless sincere.

As you know, official information is being given at the present time through the Radio and Press on all arrangements for your Prisoner's immediate care but we would like to add our hope that if you think we can advise or help you on his return you will contact us. We shall be only too happy to be of service.

You will have read of the Club we are hoping to start for ex-prisoners of war called 'The Birmingham and District Prisoner of War Association'. If your Prisoner is interested we shall be very glad to see him and explain the Association on his homecoming.

The Club will be run by ex-prisoners of war themselves when sufficient numbers of them are demobilised and have time to take over from the present temporary honorary committee.

Yours sincerely

NEWS HEADLINES BACK IN BLIGHTY … 5th September 1945 – "SINGAPORE RE-OCCUPIED BY ALLIES"

At least 3 of these guards were executed after the War

The news of the Japanese surrender extended over many months

Signing of Surrender 2nd September 1945

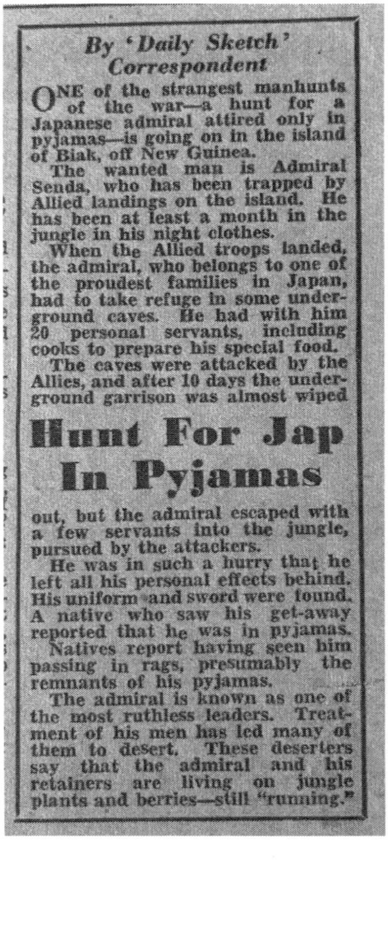

By 'Daily Sketch' Correspondent

ONE of the strangest manhunts of the war—a hunt for a Japanese admiral attired only in pyjamas—is going on in the island of Biak, off New Guinea.

The wanted man is Admiral Senda, who has been trapped by Allied landings on the island. He has been at least a month in the jungle in his night clothes.

When the Allied troops landed, the admiral, who belongs to one of the proudest families in Japan, had to take refuge in some underground caves. He had with him 20 personal servants, including cooks to prepare his special food.

The caves were attacked by the Allies, and after 10 days the underground garrison was almost wiped

Hunt For Jap In Pyjamas

out, but the admiral escaped with a few servants into the jungle, pursued by the attackers.

He was in such a hurry that he left all his personal effects behind. His uniform and sword were found. A native who saw his get-away reported that he was in pyjamas.

Natives report having seen him passing in rags, presumably the remnants of his pyjamas.

The admiral is known as one of the most ruthless leaders. Treatment of his men has led many of them to desert. These deserters say that the admiral and his retainers are living on jungle plants and berries—still "running."

Chapter 36

WELCOME ARRIVAL OF LORD MOUNTBATTEN
~ Tom's First Letter to Joan ~

We are informed that **Lord Mountbatten** has flown into Java and a date and time have been arranged for him to address all ex-Allied prisoners of war.

14th September 1945 – All men considered fit enough for Lord Mountbatten's visit are on parade ready to welcome our highly respected visitor.

Lord Mountbatten also ensures he makes it his duty to visit the poor, weak unfortunates still lying in the sick bays. A much-needed morale boost, Lord Mountbatten cheers everyone up when he delivers the news to them that they will soon be flown to the nearest military hospitals which have been prepared ready and awaiting their arrival. (*We later learn that most of these hospitals are in Australia and the patients are given the best reception and ongoing medical attention that any prisoner of war could possibly wish for).*

I shall never forget Lord Mountbatten's address to us. Those of us that are able, are standing to attention in readiness, although a little apprehensive about his arrival. I can recollect that he says something along the lines of:

"Gentlemen, you poor looking lot of specimens, I and everyone know what you have been through during your captivity and all those responsible for the atrocities you have suffered will be punished in due course".

"Write home to your loved ones in any way you are able and these messages will be top priority in despatch".

We are also told that all available transport will immediately be at our disposal to ensure we are on the road to start our safe journey home. Lost for words ... It is finally happening! A victorious outcome which we have longingly talked about so much during our three-and-a-half-year captivity. There have been so many occasions when our chips were down, feeling rock bottom when we convinced ourselves that we would never be free to return to our loved ones. Well, I can safely say that these long-awaited words result in an outbreak of the loudest cheer I have ever heard up until this memorable day. I am unable to find the right words to describe exactly how I personally feel. All I know is that in simple terms, I feel a new man! We are dismissed and I immediately go back to my bed space in the hope of finding some sort of writing material to write to my dear wife Joan.

If my memory serves me correctly, I think the last time I had been able to write to my wife Joan was from the Jaarmarkt (Surabaya) in 1942. It was on a Nip postcard using brief words selected by the Nips such as "Do not worry I am being well looked after". It is now 14th September 1945! The only writing implement I possess is a small piece of pencil which I use for my diary but I've heard that one of our Officers has managed to get hold of a number of sheets of Nip toilet paper, the dimensions of which are nine inches by six and a half inches. I am delighted as the Officer gives me a sheet to write to my dear Joan. The fact that it is toilet paper doesn't really register, all I can focus on in my state of euphoria is that I will be able to write to my loved one at last. We are told that it will be ok to put our messages in the mail without an envelope or stamp, *(which are not obtainable anyway!)*. We must, however, fold the letter and address it correctly. Suddenly feeling quite overwhelmed with emotion, I try to begin to collect my thoughts ... What can I put? I'm so desperate to put the right words down. After much deliberation, I decide to write and tell Joan that I am comparatively fit and working by driving trucks and ambulances. Most importantly, I write that I have only just received around fifty letters since my arrival at Cycle Camp. *(These letters had been stockpiling over the years – the Nips made no attempt to deliver them to us and my wife Joan later tells me that she has in fact written treble that amount!)*. My message also tells Joan that the first British War Ship is due in Batavia tomorrow. I am careful not to mention that the stationary I'm writing on is actually Nip toilet paper! *(My wife never threw this letter away. It has the* ***date of receipt of 28th September 1945*** *stamped on it, exactly fifteen days after I had written it).*

Tom's first letter to Joan – *Written in pencil on NIP toilet paper* ..."FREEDOM AT LAST!"

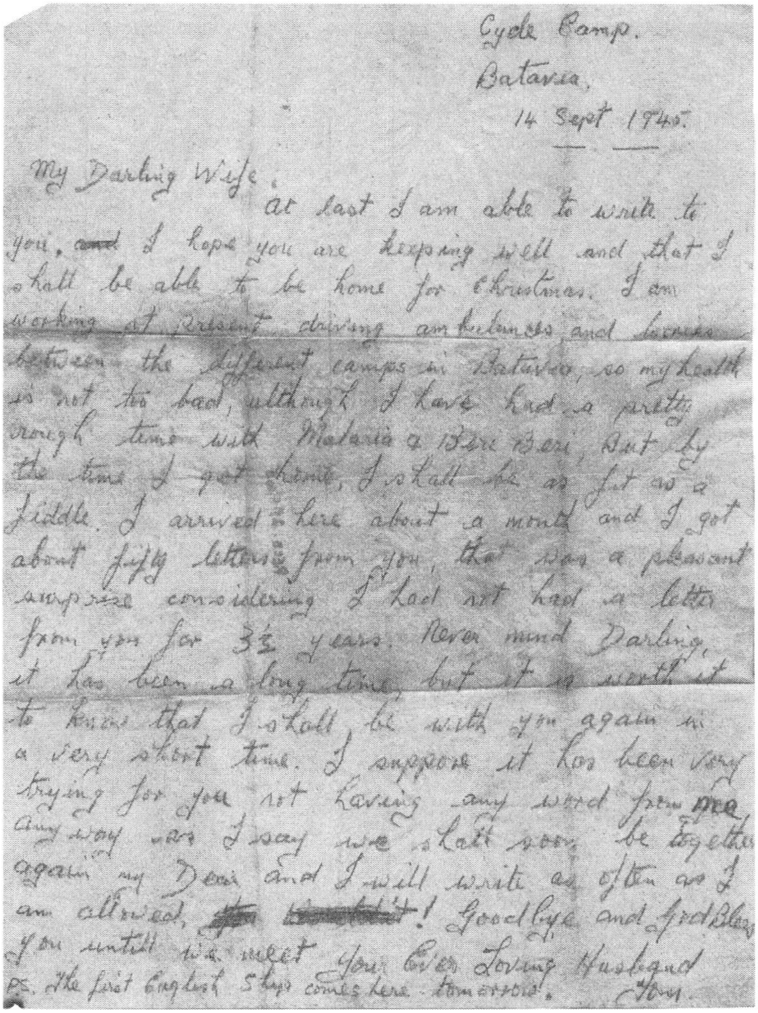

Cycle Camp.
Batavia,
14 Sept 1945.

My Darling Wife,
At last I am able to write to you, [redacted] I hope you are keeping well and that I shall be able to be home for Christmas. I am working at present driving ambulances and lorries between the different camps in Batavia, so my health is not too bad, although I have had a pretty rough time with Malaria & Beri Beri, but by the time I get home, I shall be as fit as a fiddle. I arrived here about a month and I got about fifty letters from you, that was a pleasant surprise considering I had not had a letter from you for 3½ years. Never mind Darling, it has been a long time, but it is worth it to know that I shall be with you again in a very short time. I suppose it has been very trying for you not having any word from me. Anyway as I say we shall soon be together again my Dear and I will write as often as I am allowed, [redacted]! Goodbye and God Bless you until we meet. Your Ever Loving Husband
Tom.
PS. The first English Ships comes here tomorrow.

HELPFUL COMMUNICATION FOR Joan – FAR EAST – Companion Journal to "The PRISONER OF WAR" *dated September 1945*

The Editor Writes:

The long night is ended. The grim silence is broken. Cables are streaming in to their parents and wives from prisoners and internees announcing their release after years of captivity. Soon they themselves will follow. The general rejoicing at the liberation of those held captive by the Japanese is, however, tragically married by the reports of atrocities perpetrated in some of the camps that confirm the worst anticipations. The newspapers have been filled with horrifying reports which it is not the concern of this journal to dwell upon and the statistics concerning the death roll in hospitals and working parties indicate that not a few will never return.

In offering our warm congratulations to the thousands of our readers who are soon to be reunited with their dear ones we would, then, at the same time express our deepest sympathy with those whose long-cherished hopes are doomed to disappointment.

***Homeward Bound** – a few of the repatriates will be back in this country before these lines are in print. But it must be expected that the home-coming of the prisoners will extend over many weeks. This will be of the utmost benefit to the men themselves. It would be mistaken kindness to let them make the journey before they are fit for it, nor would it be easy for their families to give them the care and attention which they at first require. This needs to be widely understood.*

***Many Routes** – it seems likely that the repatriates will come home by at least four different routes. Those from Malaya and Siam will travel via Singapore or Rangoon through the Suez Canal and the Mediterranean. In most cases they will not touch at any Indian port, but those who are flown to India or are detained in Indian hospitals may sail from Bombay or some other port according as shipping is available. Those released by the Americans from the are north of the Philippines will probably be conveyed home either by the Pacific route and across the U.S.A. or Canada and the Atlantic or, alternatively, via Australia.*

***When they arrive** – when the repatriate ships reach this country they will be met at the quayside by Red Cross representatives, who will welcome them and provide them with the first refreshments and cigarettes and newspapers they will get on British soil. The authorities have decided that it will not be practicable in the repatriates' own interests, for their relatives to meet them, as this would lead to delay in getting the repatriates to their homes.*

Service personnel, including Merchant Seamen, will be taken to reception camps, the civilians to hostels, and the necessary formalities are not likely in most cases to occupy more than 48 hours. Service personnel, if they are medically fit, will then be sent on leave. Civilians will be free to go home, and Red Cross workers will help both on their way.

***A problem of distances** – the stories of the liberation naturally tend to throw into the background the measures that were taken as soon as it became reasonable to think that Japan was on the brink of collapse. An emergency meeting of the Standing Conference of Empire Red Cross Societies was at once called to consider what should be done, what stores were immediately available. United Kingdom prisoners of war were known to be dispersed in a great number of territories and islands. Something under 30,000 P.O.W.s it was estimated were in areas south of the Philippines, something over 10,000 in areas north of them. British civilian internees numbered about 20,000.*

BRINGING THEM HOME

"In the Far East, my ministers will make it their most immediate concern to ensure that all prisoners in Japanese hands are cared for and returned to their homes with all speed" *- Extract from King's Speech at the opening of Parliament.*

Locating the Camps *– From the most northerly camp in Manchuria to the most southerly in Java is about 3,000 miles (half as far again as from London to Moscow) and from the most westerly camp in Siam or Sumatra to the most easterly in Japan about the same distance. This gives some idea of the immensity of the problem to be tackled in bringing these men home – so different from the distances involved with our prisoners in Germany. Thus from Berlin to London is 600 miles, whereas the distance from Singapore to London for instance is 7,055 miles.*

Land communications over the vast area through which the camps are scattered are generally not available and evacuation must be by sea or air from widely separated points. Sea channels must be swept clear of mines before our shipping can move freely in and out of ports. Even when our forces landed the location of some camps in such places as Java, Malaya, Borneo and Sumatra was still unknown and it may taken some weeks before all have been located.

The prisoner camps come under four different commands; in the Pacific Admiral Lord Louis Mountbatten at S.E.A.C. and General MacArthur in the South West. General Chiang Kai-Shek is in supreme command of the China mainland, while most of Manchuria is now in Russian hands.

S.E.A.C. Payments

When Allied captives are liberated from Japanese prisoner of war camps in Malaya, Burma, Siam, Sumatra, Java, French Indo-China, Hong-Kong and some Pacific islands, a S.E.A.C. paymaster will advance them £5 each.

Every man and woman in all Services, irrespective of rank, will receive ***this "Freedom Fiver".*** *Civilian internees will also be given a cash advance, said a S.E.A.C. announcement.*

While Servicemen are waiting to return home, graduated weekly advances sufficient for their immediate needs will also be made. These will be: £5 for lieutenant-colonels, £2 for other officers and £1 for other ranks.

Payment of the "Freedom Fivers" will be in local currency. *Any prisoners who hold enemy currency or token money issued by the Japanese will retain it until it can be dealt with when final adjustment of their accounts is made.*

A PRESS-CUTTING FROM A BIRMINGHAM LOCAL NEWSPAPER ~ Tom is No. 7

Glad to be free again

Here is another list of Midland men who have sent "safe and well" messages after being released from Japanese hands: (1) Gunner Thomas Mathews to his wife at 26, Hillside-avenue, Gorsty Hill, Halesowen. (2) Gordon Wade to his grandparents at 71, Belcher's-lane, Birmingham. (3) Arthur Clarke (R.N.) to his mother at 58, New-street, Erdington (in Australia). (4) Cpl. Albert Hodson (R.A.F.) to his parents at 51, Cranemore street, Nechells. (5) Cpl. Harold Shewring (R.A.S.C.) to his wife at 31, Long Acre, Aston (at Singapore). (6) Gunner George Daniels (R.A.) to his mother at 7, Eva-road, Winson Green. (7) L.A.C. Tom Orton (R.A.F.) to his wife at 432, Belcher's-lane, Little Bromwich (in Batavia). (8) Sergt. C. G. Broadis (R.A.F.) to his wife at 81, Oldbury-road, Smethwick (in Sydney). (9) Dvr. L. Parish to his father at 15, Highbury-road, West Smethwick (in Australia). (10) L./Cpl. E. Wilmshire to his wife at 2/80, Bell Barn-road, Edgbaston. (11) Joe Slater (R.A.F.) to his mother at 170, Birdbrook-road, Great Barr. (12) A.C.1 Leslie Stubbs (R.A.F.) to his parents at 72, Rocky-lane, Perry Barr. (13) Pte. William Osell to his mother at 34, Caldwell-street, Stone Cross, West Bromwich (in India). (14) Dvr. Albert Knight to his father at 140, Blakesley-road, South Yardley. (15) Pte. R. A. Wilkes (Gordon Highlanders) to his mother at 76, North-road, Harborne (in Rangoon). (16) Pte. E. W. Batsford (Royal Norfolk Regt.) to his parents at 210, St. Peter's-road, Netherton, Dudley (in Melbourne). (17) A.C. Horace Reader to his brother at 46, Wharf-road, Tyseley. (18) L.A.C. Frederick Neale, of 103, Alexander-road, Acock's Green (in Australia). (19) Dvr. Harold E. Cranmer to his wife at 61, Gleave-road, Selly Oak (in Australia). (20) Pte. Henry Pagett (R.A.S.C.) to his parents at 121, Corisande-road, Selly Oak.

Chapter 37

HOMEWARD BOUND
Leaving Batavia (Jakarta) Java aboard Passenger Nip Ship

Tom's story continues ...

16th September 1945 – we welcome the long-awaited news of the Warship sailing into dock and we're all invited aboard the ship to attend an evening concert given by the ship's entertainment group. Those of us that are able, attend the concert which is thoroughly enjoyed by all but unfortunately the mood changes when we have to disembark and reluctantly return to spending the night on straw mat beds on the floor of the camp!

Letter to Joan from Tom:

THIS LETTER IS FOR THE USE OF H.M. FORCES ONLY

Written in: English (language)

No: EX.POW 849112
Rank: LAC
Name: ORTON TW
BY AIRMAIL

Cycle Camp
Batavia

17th September 1945 *(received 28.9.45)*

My Darling wife

I wrote my first letter to you yesterday so I suppose you will get this one about the same time. There is no indication as to when I shall be leaving this place yet but according to what I can gather it may be any time. I will keep writing to you and let you know my movements as often as I can.

At this moment I am a bit peeved, I have just come in for my tiffin from work and just missed having any photo taken, a lot of the blokes got on it and the photo will be sent to their people at home with their names. Never mind I may get a chance a bit later. I am working pretty hard at the moment as I told you. I want to get myself real fit for when I get home. I am getting good food now and feel myself getting heavier and stronger every day. Yesterday allied kites came over and dropped bags of food and medicine and I fetched a lot of it in on the wagon. I am still under the same transport officer that I was in Singapore.

Well my darling I would like to let you know when I shall be home but I am almost sure it will be for Christmas so I shall be able to hang my stocking up with you. That English ship that I mentioned came in yesterday so I shall be having to get back to work as there will be more supplies to be transported from the Docks. Don't forget my darling that I will be home as soon as I can, quicker than that if poss. I hope we get the chance to fly some of the way, it will be much quicker. Anyway even if I come all the way by sea it will take only half the time it took to get out here as I came out via the Cape. That's all the gen my duck. Cheerio for a bit and God bless you.

Your loving husband Tom xxxxxx

Tom's story continues ...

September 1945 – Leaving Batavia (Jakarta) we are aboard a Nip passenger ship! The crew are commandeered by the Officers and men of the British Navy. We are heading for Singapore and set sail with as many of the sick personnel that can be accommodated. (Incredibly difficult and methodical strategic manoeuvres are required of the Officers to ensure that the worst cases are given priority). I must mention **Wing Commander Jack Carlisle** who is one of the last to leave the camp, also **Squadron Leader Pitts** who stay behind to round up the Nip criminals such as **Gunso Mori, Kasiyama** and others (see photo of them handcuffed together). These are just a few of the barbarians that exposed us to starvation, disease, brutal violence, slavery and the lowest forms of degradation. It is through these evil individuals that we have witnessed so much death. The fear of death became a daily part of our lives for so many years. The stomach-churning smell of the bamboo sickbays alive with bugs and lice will stay with us for life each time we bear to think about our experiences on the previously known "Islands of Paradise", such as Amboina, Haroekoe, Moena, Ceram and Java.

We find it difficult to adjust to such a comfortable voyage, compared with previous experiences aboard the Nip Hell Ships. (We are even allowed to buy a postcard).

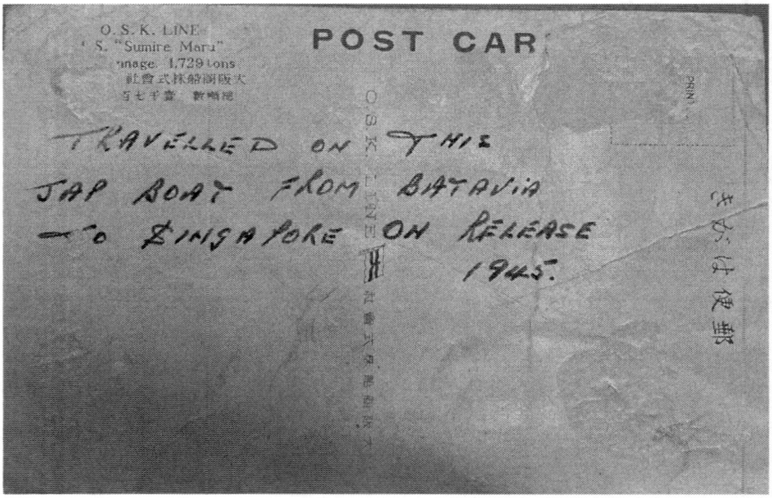

1945: M.S. SUMIRE MARU – Travelled on this Jap boat from Batavia to Singapore "Free under British Navy"

"A JAPANESE SOLDIER - World War II"

A Japanese soldier must fight to the death and never surrender. He must keep his last round of ammunition for himself or charge the enemy in a final suicidal assault. Should he be taken prisoner after being wounded, unable to move or unconscious, he would never again hold up his head in Japan. Both he and his family would be disgraced for ever.

The Japanese soldier had a feeling of utter contempt with no respect for those who surrendered to the Japanese forces.

Tom's story continues ...

We disembark at Keppel Harbour, Singapore to be welcomed by the unbelievable sight of dock sheds stacked nearly to the rooftops with Red Cross parcels. One can only guess that these parcels have been sitting here for the greater period of the Nip occupation and that they had no intention of distributing them to the many prison camps. It is tragic to think that such valuable supplies and food could have saved so many lives! It is plain enough for me to work out how long these supplies have been lying here and it is very noticeable that a lot of the contents have been pilfered.

The British and Allied Army Forces have by now taken over complete control of Singapore and I'm pleased to report that the Nips are now having a small taste of their own medicine! Pausing to watch them at work on the docks, we compare their working conditions to those we have endured. They are being treated as human beings, not "coolie slaves", being bawled at and brutally beaten as they did to us, although this does appear to change somewhat once the British guards see the poor state of the ex-prisoners of war. Poor specimens of men due to years of incarceration on the islands of South East Asia; the majority of us have lost our upright military stance, beaten out of us by these barbarians.

Arriving at a large hotel not far from the docks, which has been specially prepared, we receive a huge welcome! The kindness bestowed upon us is beyond words and we are presented with a good meal and any medical aid or assistance needed. We are also given luxuries such as razors and blades, plus all the toilet requisites needed to help us in our endeavour to clean and smarten ourselves up. Although we try our best to look presentable, the British military uniform for the three branches of the services is not yet available but there are plenty of supplies of the jungle green uniform similar to that of the Dutch issue. It is good to hear that we'll soon be kitted out properly on our way home.

I am still proudly wearing my RAF peaked cap issued back in 1939. I became married in January 1941, captured and taken prisoner, finally freed wearing the very same cap! Throughout my three-and-a-half year captivity, I concealed my precious diary in the waterproof lining. *(This tattered diary is in rather a delicate state and of great sentimental value to me).* I always vowed that I would arrive home wearing my cap bearing the highly polished RAF badge!

LETTER TO TOM FROM KING GEORGE: September 1945

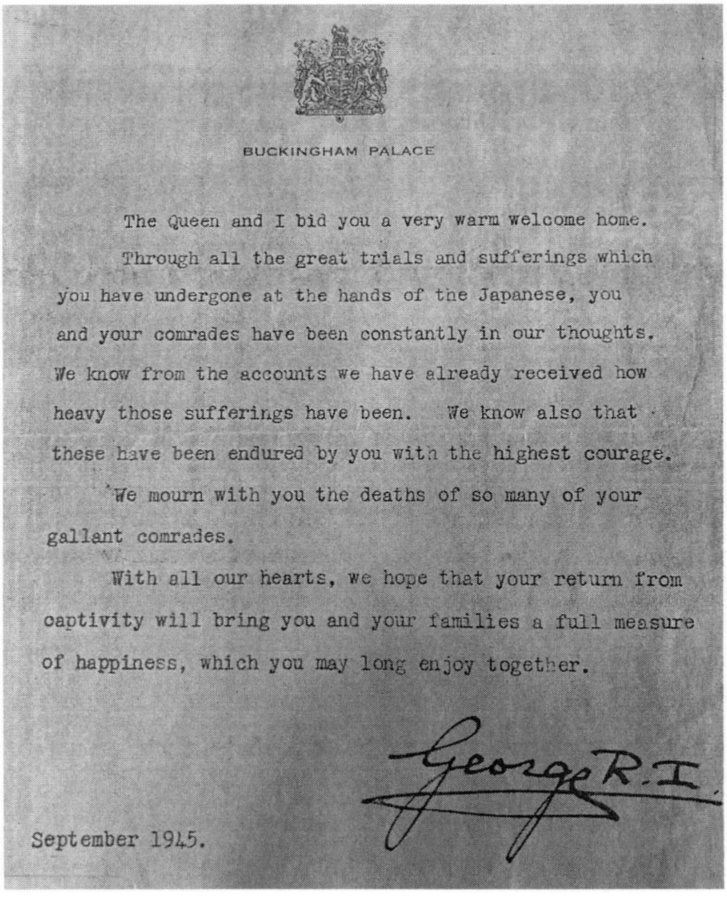

BUCKINGHAM PALACE

The Queen and I bid you a very warm welcome home.

Through all the great trials and sufferings which you have undergone at the hands of the Japanese, you and your comrades have been constantly in our thoughts. We know from the accounts we have already received how heavy those sufferings have been. We know also that these have been endured by you with the highest courage.

We mourn with you the deaths of so many of your gallant comrades.

With all our hearts, we hope that your return from captivity will bring you and your families a full measure of happiness, which you may long enjoy together.

George R.I.

September 1945.

Chapter 38

ABOARD: HMS CILICIA (Singapore - Port Said, Egypt) SS RANGITATA (Port Said, Egypt – Southampton)

Tom's story continues ...

2nd October 1945 – After receiving 'VIP' treatment in Singapore, we board the troopship "Cilicia", which to us is the equivalent of a "luxury liner" compared to the degradation of the 'hell ships' we have become accustomed to during our long captivity.

We are soon steaming west across the **Indian Ocean towards the Suez Canal** and during our voyage we are given the best of food, vitamin pills and allowed one pint of beer per day. As a malaria sufferer, I am treated with the new drug Mepaquine as Quinine is no longer being issued. I reflect back on my experiences since I was aboard the "Duchess of York" in 1941, four years ago. *(This voyage is to be much shorter and quicker for everyone except myself, the reason why I discover later).*

HMS Cilicia

It's a different route home and we are now very different men both physically and mentally. There are many still suffering with the pain of deep-rooted tropical ulcers, although many cases are beginning to heal. Weary and troubled, we certainly have no desire to partake in any sports activities such as those we enjoyed on the way out as fit and healthy men. I must add here that although we may not be physically fit, we definitely haven't lost the spirit of comradeship. (*This is to be borne out over many years to come.*)

We reach **Port Said – North East Egypt.** What a welcome? I am so very touched by the reception awaiting us as the **"Cillicia"** draws into the quayside where a large banner greets us with the words "WELCOME ON YOUR WAY HOME". A military band is playing some of the good old tunes, the tunes we have been forbidden to even whistle during our captivity on most of the prison camps.

We are instructed to disembark in mess deck order, A, B, C and I suddenly become overwhelmed! I break down and sob uncontrollably! I just cannot stop myself, whether it is the sound of the band plus the fact I am finding it so difficult to accept that we are now free men, I cannot explain!

Letter of Support to Joan from a friend:

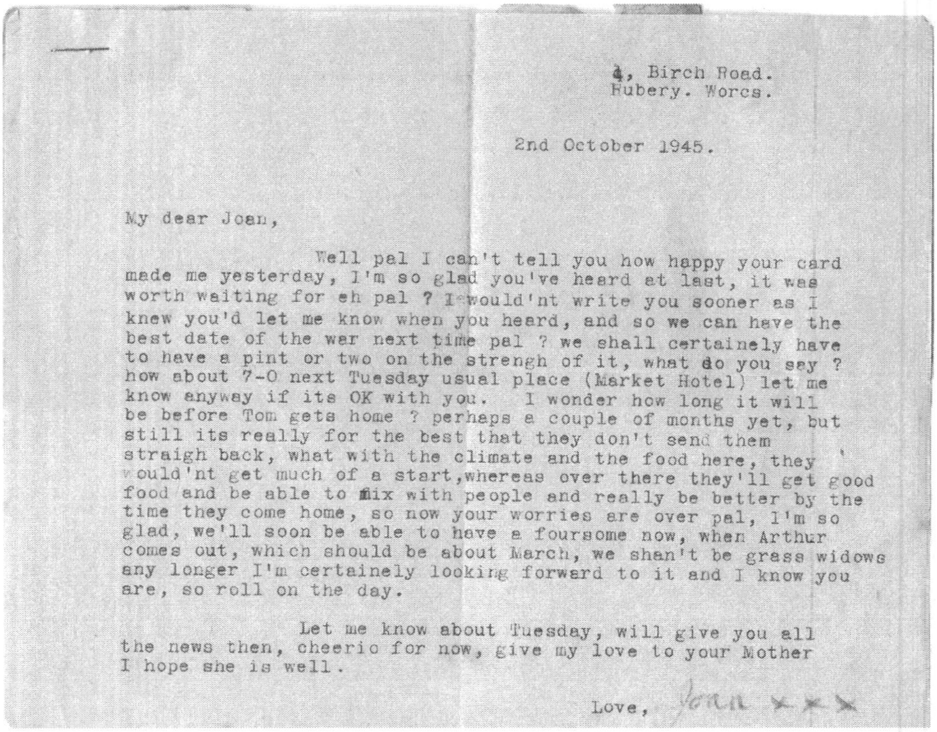

4, Birch Road.
Rubery. Worcs.

2nd October 1945.

My dear Joan,

Well pal I can't tell you how happy your card made me yesterday, I'm so glad you've heard at last, it was worth waiting for eh pal ? I would'nt write you sooner as I knew you'd let me know when you heard, and so we can have the best date of the war next time pal ? we shall certainely have to have a pint or two on the strengh of it, what do you say ? how about 7-0 next Tuesday usual place (Market Hotel) let me know anyway if its OK with you. I wonder how long it will be before Tom gets home ? perhaps a couple of months yet, but still its really for the best that they don't send them straigh back, what with the climate and the food here, they would'nt get much of a start, whereas over there they'll get good food and be able to mix with people and really be better by the time they come home, so now your worries are over pal, I'm so glad, we'll soon be able to have a foursome now, when Arthur comes out, which should be about March, we shan't be grass widows any longer I'm certainely looking forward to it and I know you are, so roll on the day.

Let me know about Tuesday, will give you all the news then, cheerio for now, give my love to your Mother I hope she is well.

Love, Joan x x x

NEWS HEADLINES BACK IN BLIGHTY ... 8th October 1945 – *"Ban on Central Heating in Shops, Offices and Places of Entertainment Lifted"*

Tom's story continues ...

Still aboard HMS Cilicia we sail into Colombo, Ceylon (now Sri Lanka) where we are able to send Post Office Telegrams to our loved ones.

Telegrams & Letters to Joan from Tom (aboard HMS Cilicia – CEYLON (Sri Lanka)

POST OFFICE

TELEGRAM

Date Stamped: 12th October 1945 **COLOMBO**

ARRIVED SAFELY BRITISH HANDS HOPE TO BE HOME SOON WRITING LETTERS AND TELEGRAMS c/o RAPWI PO BOX 164 LONDON EC1

ORTON

POST OFFICE

TELEGRAM

Date Stamped: 12th October 1945 **COLOMBO**

ARRIVED SAFELY COLOMBO HOPE BE HOME SOON WRITING LETTERS AND TELEGRAMS c/o BOX 164 LONDON EC1

T ORTON

INVITATION TO JOAN: *Joan's handwritten note "Not fit to attend"*

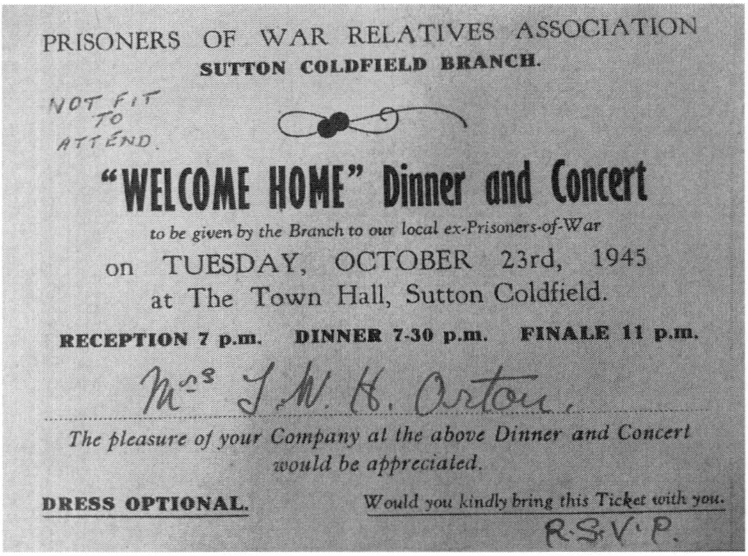
PRISONERS OF WAR RELATIVES ASSOCIATION
SUTTON COLDFIELD BRANCH.

NOT FIT TO ATTEND.

"WELCOME HOME" Dinner and Concert
to be given by the Branch to our local ex-Prisoners-of-War
on TUESDAY, OCTOBER 23rd, 1945
at The Town Hall, Sutton Coldfield.

RECEPTION 7 p.m. DINNER 7-30 p.m. FINALE 11 p.m.

Mrs J. W. H. Orton.

The pleasure of your Company at the above Dinner and Concert would be appreciated.

DRESS OPTIONAL. *Would you kindly bring this Ticket with you.*

R.S.V.P.

POST OFFICE

TELEGRAM

Date Stamped: 24th October 1945 **SINGAPORE**

AM SAFE IN BRITISH HANDS HOPE TO BE HOME SOON WRITING REPLY CARE PO

BOX 164 LONDON EC1

ORTON

Tom's story continues ...

29th October 1945 – We arrive at Port Said, Egypt and disembark.

31st October 1945 – Boarding the SS Rangitata to sail across the Mediterannean.

SS RANGITATA: Arrived Southampton 10th November 1945

Letters to Joan from British Red Cross & RAF

BRITISH RED CROSS and ORDER OF ST. JOHN
BIRMINGHAM JOINT COMMITTEE
PRISONERS OF WAR DEPARTMENT
County Representative:
Mrs. C. E. SMALLEY-BAKER

100, LIONEL STREET
BIRMINGHAM, 3

Tel. CEN. 7932

MSB/GF.

October 1945.

Dear Madam,

Will you be good enough to let us know when you receive any news concerning your ..husband........

We are very anxious to supply any necessary articles, and render any service required.

Yours sincerely,

Mary Smalley-Baker.

Prisoners of War Representative.

Please Note:-

On and after November 1st. this Department will be removed to -

72, Newhall St.,
Birmingham. 3.

Telephone:- CEN.6112.

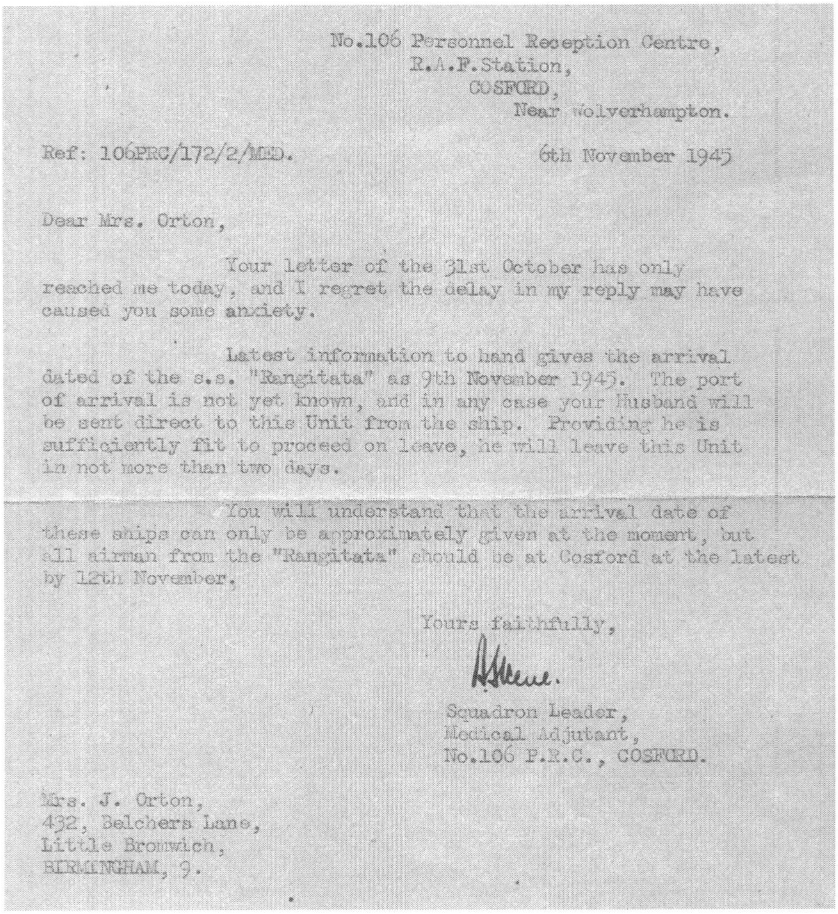

No.106 Personnel Reception Centre,
R.A.F. Station,
COSFORD,
Near Wolverhampton.

Ref: 106PRC/172/2/MED.

6th November 1945

Dear Mrs. Orton,

Your letter of the 31st October has only reached me today, and I regret the delay in my reply may have caused you some anxiety.

Latest information to hand gives the arrival dated of the s.s. "Rangitata" as 9th November 1945. The port of arrival is not yet known, and in any case your Husband will be sent direct to this Unit from the ship. Providing he is sufficiently fit to proceed on leave, he will leave this Unit in not more than two days.

You will understand that the arrival date of these ships can only be approximately given at the moment, but all airman from the "Rangitata" should be at Cosford at the latest by 12th November.

Yours faithfully,

A Skene.

Squadron Leader,
Medical Adjutant,
No.106 P.R.C., COSFORD.

Mrs. J. Orton,
432, Belchers Lane,
Little Bromwich,
BIRMINGHAM, 9.

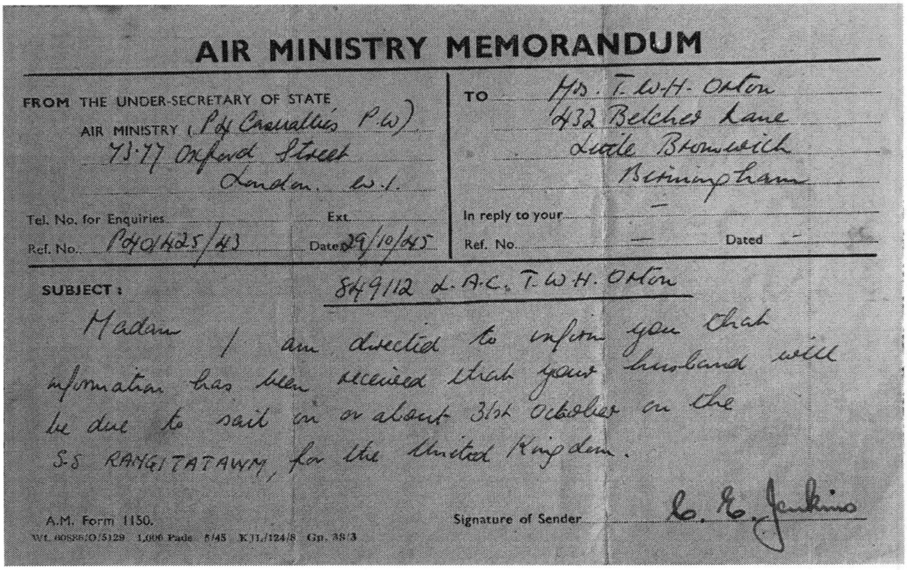

AIR MINISTRY MEMORANDUM

FROM THE UNDER-SECRETARY OF STATE
AIR MINISTRY (P4 Casualties P.W)
73-77 Oxford Street
London. W.1.

Tel. No. for Enquiries ... Ext. ...
Ref. No. P401425/43 Date 29/10/45

TO Mrs. T.W.H. Orton
432 Belcher Lane
Little Bromwich
Birmingham

In reply to your ...
Ref. No. — Dated —

SUBJECT: 849112 L.A.C. T.W.H. Orton

Madam I am directed to inform you that information has been received that your husband will be due to sail on or about 31st October on the S.S. RANGITATAWM, for the United Kingdom.

A.M. Form 1150.
Wt. 60888/O/5129 1,000 Pads 5/45 KJL/124/8 Gp. 38/3

Signature of Sender C. E. Jenkins

Letter to Joan from Air Ministry:

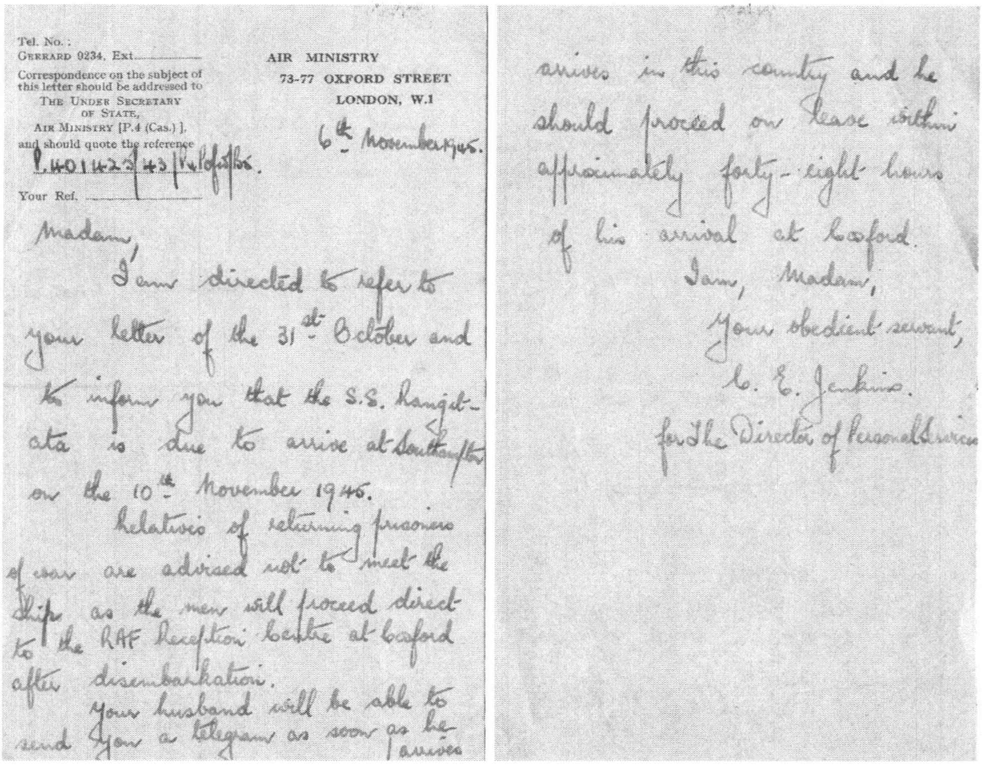

Tel. No.:
GERRARD 9234, Ext.........
Correspondence on the subject of this letter should be addressed to
THE UNDER SECRETARY OF STATE,
AIR MINISTRY [P.4 (Cas.)],
and should quote the reference P.401422/43/P4/Cas.
Your Ref. ....

AIR MINISTRY
73-77 OXFORD STREET
LONDON, W.1

6th November 1945.

Madam,

I am directed to refer to your letter of the 31st October and to inform you that the S.S. Rangitata is due to arrive at Southampton on the 10th November 1945.

Relatives of returning prisoners of war are advised not to meet the ship as the men will proceed direct to the RAF Reception Centre at Cosford after disembarkation.

Your husband will be able to send you a telegram as soon as he arrives in this country and he should proceed on leave within approximately forty-eight hours of his arrival at Cosford.

I am, Madam,
Your obedient servant,
C. E. Jenkins.
for The Director of Personal Services

LETTER FROM LORD LOUIS MOUNTBATTEN To Field Marshal Lord Chetwode, Chairman, War Organisation of British Red Cross and Order of St. John.

SOUTH EAST ASIA COMMAND HEADQUARTERS

5th November 1945

My Dear Field Marshal

The work of succouring and evacuation of the prisoners of war and civil internees from South East Asia is now complete, with the exception of those unfit to be moved and the Dutch for whom we can as yet find no home.

I wish to convey to you and to your Executive Committee the deep appreciation of myself and of my Command for the great services your Society and its willing band of workers have given to these people who were so unfortunate as to have experienced the inhumanities of the Japanese.

I would ask you to convey to the British Red Cross Society and Order of St. John the great gratitude of myself and of my Command for the services which have been so whole-heartedly placed at my disposal and to all those who have contributed so greatly to such a worthy cause.

From my own experience I can speak as to the deplorable and pitiable condition in which we found them. Notwithstanding the attention they immediately received from the Red Cross Societies operating in South East Asia Command enabled them to be restored quickly to something approaching normal physical and mental health.

It may interest you to know the following statistics:- To bring immediate relief to Allied prisoners of war and internees on the Japanese capitulation we dropped in from the air one and a quarter million pounds of Red Cross stores, medical supplies, food and clothing. The number of camps we had to cover was 229. The surrender was signed in Tokyo on September 2 and on September 3 we commenced the first movement of evacuation by sea and the first released Allied prisoners of war and internees arrived at their home countries on the following dates:-

India – September 16

Australia – September 27

U.K. – October 7 ***(Tom arrived November 10th)***

In countries where internal movement was impossible owing to destruction of communications, we had to bring out the Allied prisoners of war and internees by air, and we have moved some 16,000 in this manner. The total number we have moved in South East Asia is 104,193, including some 6,339 prisoners of war and civil internees from Hong Kong. The total number we have evacuated by sea and air to their home countries is 79,157; this figure includes 8,535 prisoners of war and civil internees from Borneo, Celebes and Shanghai evacuated from South East Asia Command.

The only people we have left are some 18,349 Dutch prisoners of war and internees whose country of domicile is the Dutch East Indies. Unfortunately, we cannot repatriate them at the moment owing to political conditions.

Yours very sincerely
LOUIS MOUNTBATTEN (signed)

Chapter 39

BACK HOME IN "BLIGHTY"

10th November 1945 – SS Rangitata – Tom *arrives safely in Southampton docks.*

RAF ex-Far East Prisoners of War were transported to RAF Cosford where a special Medical Unit had been set up.

Telegram to Joan from Tom

POST OFFICE

TELEGRAM

11th November 1945 **London**

ARRIVED SAFELY IN ENGLAND HOME SOON LOVE TOM

Extract from the **FAR EAST – Companion Journal to "The PRISONER OF WAR"** Vol. 1 No. 11 **dated November 1945**

21,000+ Prisoners of War and about 3,000 civilian internees reached England from the Far East – many more on their way. Whilst on board the Prisoner of War ships there was a 2 stone average increase in weight.

Comforts sent by the Red Cross & St Johns included 20,000 handkerchiefs, 10,000 safety razors, toothbrushes, socks, gloves, pyjamas, pullovers, 5,000 shirts, scarves, slippers, ants, vests, 2,000 dressing gowns.

Red Cross supplies had been shown to some Prisoners of War but withheld day after day by the Japanese.

Extract from the **FAR EAST – Companion Journal to "The PRISONER OF WAR" dated December 1945 – The Final Issue**

~ CLOTHING COUPONS ~

Many liberated prisoners who have arrived back in this country are applying to the Red Cross for an additional supply of clothing coupons, stating that they have been advised to do so by various local bodies and associations. We wish, once again, to emphasise that Red Cross and St. John are not authorised to supply coupons, nor can we handle claims for additional issues. Where repatriates can prove that their civilian clothing has been destroyed as a result of enemy action in this country, or where exceptional hardship can be claimed, application can be made at the local Fuel Office, usually situated in the premises of the Local Assistance Board, for a form C.R.S.C. Ia. This has to be completed and returned and is then sent to the Customs and Excise for consideration. They will decide if a special allowance of clothing coupons is justified, and will notify the result of the claim.

Article by Lady Louis Mountbatten as written in the **FAR EAST** - ***Companion Journal to*** **"The PRISONER OF WAR"** dated **December 1945** – Final Issue

"LIBERATION TEAM WORK" .... by Lady Louis Mountbatten – *Superintendent in Chief of the St John Ambulance Brigade.*

The last three months I have spent in the South East Asia Command helping with the recovery, care and repatriation of Allied prisoners of war and civilian internees, have taken me over vast areas and brought me among more than 60,000 of the prisoners themselves. By the time I return to England in a few days' time I shall have covered over 40,000 miles by air alone and visited 16 different countries.

As far afield as Siam to Morotai, and in large areas in Malaya, Indo-China, Java, Sumatra, Borneo, Labuan, Manila, Hong Kong and in many parts of India; I have visited prisoners in their actual camps in the earliest days of the liberation and also seen large numbers of them in hospital units on board ships or in transit camps.

Prisoners of war and internees had to be shipped not only to UK but to India and Australia and had to be recovered from 230 camps stretching over an area of nearly 3,000 miles.

The speed with which the operations were effected was a truly remarkable achievement and reflects the greatest credit on all those who had planned and carried out the work. Particularly those at HQ, S.E.A.C. who were initially responsible for conceiving the plans ad for the many members of the R.A.P.W.I. staff who carried out the work with such extraordinary efficiency and good will, even though at times, they were working for over 18 hours a day confronted with almost insuperable difficulties.

The R.A.F. and the R.A.A.F. who flew many hours through the worst tropical monsoon to carry out air evacuation of over 16,000 prisoners of war and internees, also deserve the highest credit. So do the many members of the medical and nursing services, British, Indian and Australian, whose care of the liberated men and women saved so many lives.

The Armies gave the fullest and most efficient support throughout, whilst the Navies afforded very fine service. In fact, the excellent team work amongst all the Allied Services was a great feature of the work.

Particular mention should also be made of the great part played by the Red Crosses, British, Indian and Australian, and later Dutch and French operating in the South-East Asia Command. One and a quarter million pounds of red Cross stores, medical supplies, food and clothing alone were dropped into the camps by air.

Great praise is also due to the welfare organisations such as W.V.S., Y.M.C.A. and to the F.A.N.Y.s who ran hostels, canteens and transports.

It was a great inspiration and joy to me to have been in so many cases the first woman to enter the actual camps and to have seen the men and women after three and a half years of imprisonment, and I was much touched at the wonderful welcome they gave me. It was also the greatest satisfaction often to find men I had seen as physical wrecks in camps in Central Sumatra or Siam, and who frequently had lost up to 4 or 5 stone in weight, sailing out of Singapore or Rangoon a few weeks later were hardly recognisable due to the improvement of their physical condition.

It has also been the greatest privilege to have worked with all those to whom was entrusted the repatriation and care of Allied prisoners of war and internees throughout South-East Asia Command, and I would like to express since admiration for what they have achieved in the Far East

~ Now back in "Blighty" Letters from Tom to Joan ~

849112 L.A.C. ORTON
Hut C8, "B" Squadron"
R.A.F.
Cosford

17th December 1945

My Darling Wife

I arrived back here at about 1.30 a.m. Tell Ernie he put me on the Bristol Road instead of the Hagley Road so I wasted about 5 miles! I reached Wolverhampton ok but someone directed me to the road to anywhere except Cosford but reached here ok having done 40+ miles from the Bullring!

I have been very busy again today, 6.30 am up and shaving, 8.30 am medical interview where I saw a familiar face. He said "I went to school with you and your brother Ray". An old school pal ***Flight Lieutenant Upton who lived in Elms Road.*** *I have had to fill in dozens of forms, give a stool and urine test, have my photo taken and cherry cherry for my Diary which I have just had returned with a thank you for the information I have given. The M.O. has arranged for me to have my teeth done at Castle Bromwich. When I am through with the medical board, I should be on my way again.*

Your Ever Loving Husband

849112 L.A.C. ORTON T.
4 M.R.U.
R.A.F.
Cosford

19th December 1945

Darling

I am afraid it will be Friday before I come home. I have more or less finished my medical and at all the stages I was passed Grade I, except the last, the President recommended me to the Medical REHABILITEE Unit as I guessed in the first place. I will send you a telegram to say what time I will arrive home on Friday.

I met my best oppo a couple of days ago, he is married and lives at Southend on Sea and he wants me to take you down for a weekend in the spring. I gave the model a good clean yesterday and kept it the billet by the side of the bed all night. The F/S asked "Has father Christmas been early?".

All my Love Tom xxx

849112 L.A.C. ORTON T.
Hut G8. 4 M.R.U. R.A.F.
Cosford

20th December 1945

My Darling Wife

I visited a Flight Sergeant I knew in the Far East today, he was properly down in the dumps recovering from pleurisy and pneumonia. I'm pleased to say I managed to leave him grinning all over his face and wanting to get out of bed. He would like to meet you sometime and Rose. When he saw the wedding group photograph, he said I was a lucky bloke and that my mother in law looks nice", so you had better tell Ernie to keep his eyes open for a big burly red faced F/S!!

Your Loving Husband Tom xxxxx

NEWS HEADLINES … 20th December 1945 – *"Labour Control Ends: People Free to Seek Own Jobs"*

849112 L.A.C. ORTON T.
Hut G8. 4 M.R.U. R.A.F.
Cosford

21st December 1945

My Darling Joan

I have been busy today drawing some pay, finding out about my promotion etc and trying to get some coupons for petrol to get home. Apparently I cannot have coupons because I am having more than 7 days leave and my promotion has not yet come from records, so I am still a common L.A.C. I.G.C!!

It is 5 days since I saw you last and it seems like 5 weeks, anyway roll on tomorrow night, perhaps I shall be there before this letter.

I shall be in kip early again tonight as there is not much to do here except go to the N.A.A.F.I. and drink beer, or go into Wolverhampton gadding about, which most of the blokes seem to enjoy.

Your Ever Loving Hubby Tom xxxx

849112 L.A.C. ORTON
Hut G8. 4 M.R.U. R.A.F.
Cosford
Staffs

Wednesday (undated) postmark 9th January 1946

My Dear Joan

I arrived back last night in record time, not getting lost this time! I have to go into dock at 4 p.m. today for 2 days. I went to get my cig & choc coupons this morning but there was a queue a mile long, so I have left it in abeyance for a time. I will be able perhaps to tell you more tomorrow, but pass or no pass, will see you Sat.

Your Loving Husband Tom xxx

849112 L.A.C. ORTON
4 M.R.U. R.A.F.
Cosford

Thursday (undated) 1946

My Darling Wife

I have managed to get the cigs & choc coupons, enough for 3 months, and I will buy as much as I can at the N.A.A.F.I. as they are much cheaper, that is if I get paid as I have missed pay parade being in dock!

I have just had my first bite since yesterday 12.30 a.m. and it is now 2.30 p.m. I had fish, peas, spuds and sweet and for breakfast I had six big capsules as big as bantams eggs and a dose of salts at 12 am, so you can imagine how I felt about 1 pm! My abdomen is now like a boiling cauldron! This is about the longest period I have been in bed as I was confined as soon as I stepped in the joint at 4 p.m. yesterday.

I shall be glad to get some pay to come home and have another holiday, it won't be long I pray, enough said. My love to Rose.

My Everything to you Tom xxxx

849112 L.A.C. ORTON
Hut G8. 4 M.R.U. R.A.F.
Cosford
Staffs

Friday (undated) postmark 12th January 1946

My Dear Joan

I am getting paid this afternoon @ 4 p.m. and see the Dental Officer at 9 a.m. tomorrow. I have put my pass in to be signed and the C.O. asked me if I would like to go to the Birmingham Hippodrome this afternoon, free seat & transport etc, but I shall not as I should miss pay again. I have just had dinner, fish, peas, spuds, and sweet with a quart of fresh milk on top.

See you tomorrow around tiffin. Goodbye for now, God Bless you.

Your Ever Loving Husband Tom xx

1**st* ***February 1946 – 3rd Class Railway ticket (Airman on leave on release) From Rugeley Railway Station to Birmingham Railway Station

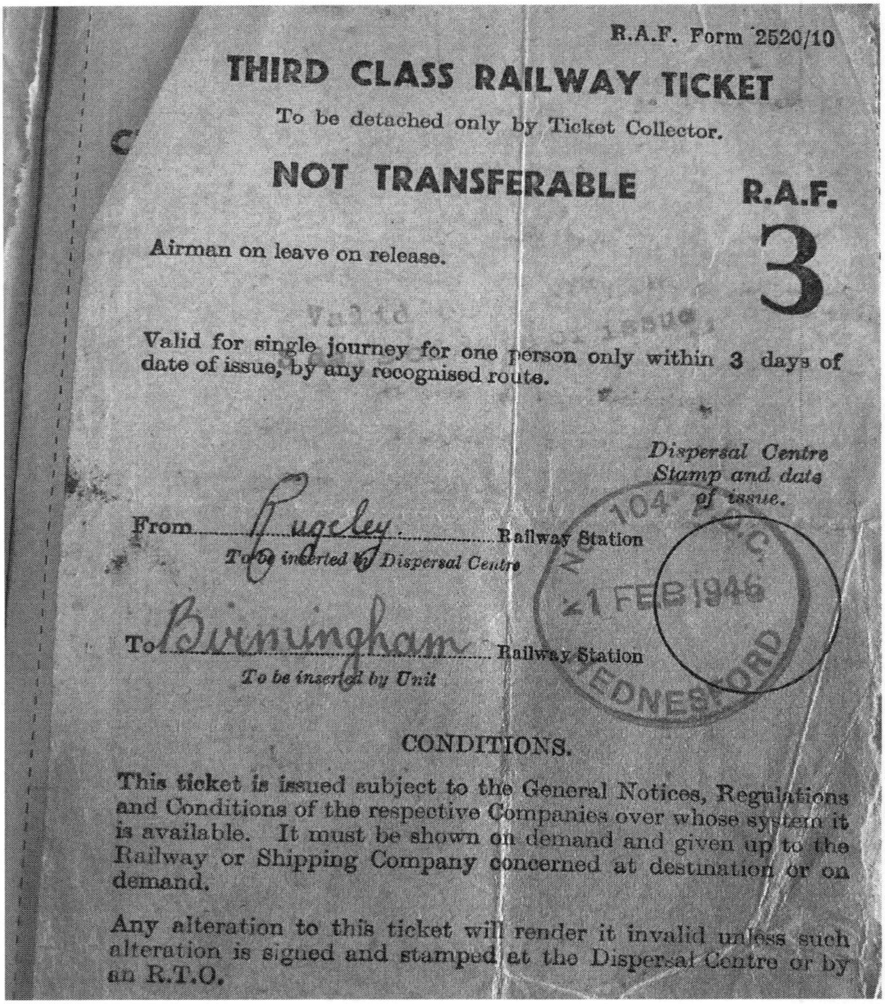
R.A.F. Form 2520/10

THIRD CLASS RAILWAY TICKET

To be detached only by Ticket Collector.

NOT TRANSFERABLE **R.A.F. 3**

Airman on leave on release.

Valid for single journey for one person only within 3 days of date of issue, by any recognised route.

Dispersal Centre Stamp and date of issue.

From Rugeley Railway Station
To be inserted by Dispersal Centre

To Birmingham Railway Station
To be inserted by Unit

No. 104 P.D.C. 1 FEB 1946 HEDNESFORD

CONDITIONS.

This ticket is issued subject to the General Notices, Regulations and Conditions of the respective Companies over whose system it is available. It must be shown on demand and given up to the Railway or Shipping Company concerned at destination or on demand.

Any alteration to this ticket will render it invalid unless such alteration is signed and stamped at the Dispersal Centre or by an R.T.O.

A printed order issued to surviving ex-Far East Prisoners of War

WARNING – GUARD YOUR TONGUE

You are free now. Anything you say in public or the press is liable to be published throughout the whole world.

You have direct or indirect knowledge of the fate of many of your comrades who died in enemy hands as a result of brutality or neglect.

Your story, if published in the more sensational press, would cause much unnecessary unhappiness to relatives and friends.

If you had not been lucky enough to have survived and had died as unpleasant death at the hands of the Japanese, you would not have wished your family and friends to have been harrowed by lurid details of your death.

That is just what will happen to the families of your comrades, who did die in that way if you start talking too freely about your experience.

It is felt certain that now you know the reason for this order, you will take pains to spare the feelings of others.

Arrangements have been made for you to tell your story to interrogating offices who will then ask you to write it down. YOU ARE NOT TO SAY ANYTHING TO ANYONE UNTIL AFTER YOU HAVE WRITTEN OUT YOUR STATEMENT AND HANDED IT IN

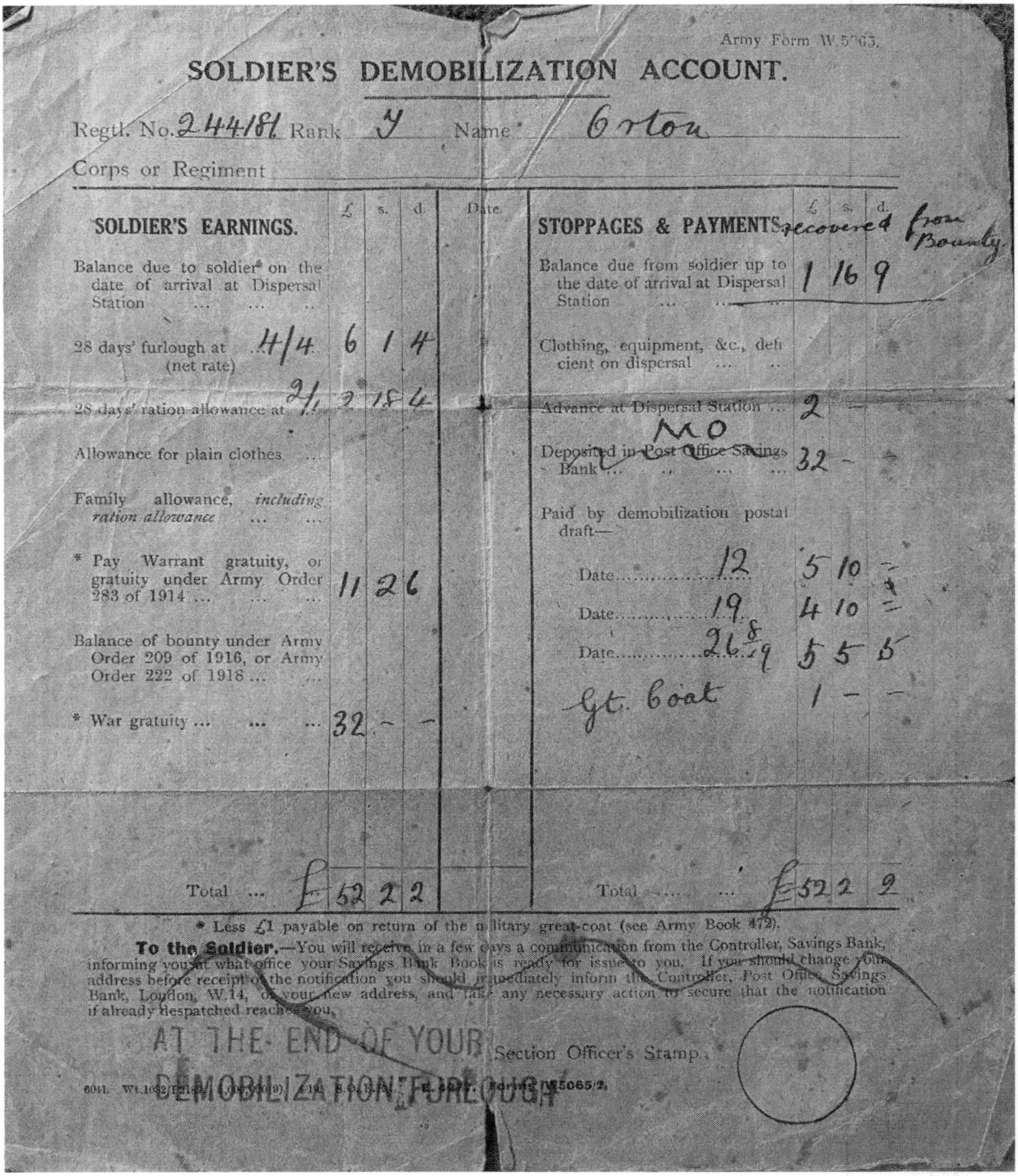

Army Form W.5065.

SOLDIER'S DEMOBILIZATION ACCOUNT.

Regtl. No. 244181 Rank Y Name Orton

Corps or Regiment

SOLDIER'S EARNINGS.	£	s.	d.	Date.	STOPPAGES & PAYMENTS recovered from Bounty	£	s.	d.
Balance due to soldier* on the date of arrival at Dispersal Station					Balance due from soldier up to the date of arrival at Dispersal Station	1	16	9
28 days' furlough at 4/4 (net rate)	6	1	4		Clothing, equipment, &c., deficient on dispersal			
28 days' ration allowance at 2/1	2	18	4		~~Advance at Dispersal Station~~ ...	2	–	–
Allowance for plain clothes ...					~~Deposited in Post Office Savings Bank~~ MO	32	–	
Family allowance, *including ration allowance*					Paid by demobilization postal draft—			
* Pay Warrant gratuity, or gratuity under Army Order 283 of 1914	11	2	6		Date 12	5	10	–
Balance of bounty under Army Order 209 of 1916, or Army Order 222 of 1918					Date 19	4	10	–
* War gratuity	32	–	–		Date 26 8/19	5	5	5
					Gt. Coat	1	–	–
Total ... £	52	2	2		Total ... ... £	52	2	2

* Less £1 payable on return of the military great-coat (see Army Book 472).

To the Soldier.—You will receive in a few days a communication from the Controller, Savings Bank, informing you at what office your Savings Bank Book is ready for issue to you. If you should change your address before receipt of the notification you should immediately inform the Controller, Post Office Savings Bank, London, W.14, of your new address, and take any necessary action to secure that the notification if already despatched reaches you.

AT THE END OF YOUR DEMOBILIZATION FURLOUGH

Section Officer's Stamp.

6041. W1.1032/T218 ... Forms/W5065/2.

Chapter 40

LIFE AFTER THE WAR ... Was it really all over?

"JAPANESE PRISONERS OF WAR DURING WORLD WAR II" *have been described as "sacrificial lambs sent to the slaughter" ... some say "Churchill's forgotten army".*

Thousands of men who lived in indescribable squalor so tragically lost their lives by slowly being starved to death in excruciating pain, whilst many were brutally beaten and tortured to death.

Numerous prisoners, who did not die whilst in the actual prison camps, perished in the holds of the atrocious "hell ships", some of which were erroneously bombed and torpedoed by Allied craft and survivors machine-gunned in the water by Japanese or Korean guards. These Japanese and Korean guards were considered to be terrified of any prisoner escaping or being rescued by the Allies, which would expose their captors to the world! The truth would then come out about the indescribable cruelty bestowed upon the prisoners as so called 'guests of the Emperor'.

Surviving Far East Prisoners of War have since spoken about their feelings relating to the bombs being dropped on Hiroshima and Nagasaki. Many believe that they not only saved their lives but possibly millions of Asian people and Allied Servicemen, who would have been killed at some point should the Japanese invasion have continued. Nevertheless, there continues to be much debate with regard to the moral and ethical implications of these nuclear attacks.

My father Tom was just one of thousands of the ex-prisoners of war eager to return home to his family convinced that life would continue as before. Reading between the lines in one of his letters to Joan in December 1945, one can sense the sheer determination to try to rise above anything that might hinder his recovery. His aim was to focus on putting all these dreadful experiences behind him and attempt to return to a life of normality. Subsequent letters detail his sudden decline in health, and as the months and years went by, it became evident that he was deeply psychologically scarred – his experience as an ex-prisoner of war with the Japanese had crawled into his mind, body and soul.

Despite his efforts and determination to try to return to normality, my father came back a different man, unable to overcome the mental torment. The months and years following were dark and brooding, with many sudden outbursts of anger; these horrific memories and experiences would remain with him for the rest of his life! As a father, he showed little or no emotion on occasion, particularly in cases of serious illness or death, but to someone who had carried and helped dispose of hundreds of corpses of tortured comrades in dire and squalid conditions, this type of behaviour would surely be inconsequential.

These brave ex-Far-East Prisoners of War were almost dehumanised, returning home as broken men and being advised by those in authority to close their mind to their past experiences!

Children, grandchildren and future generations of these ex-Prisoners of War remain in awe of their forefathers who died, or survived the horror and atrocities of the Japanese Prisoner of War Camps and continue to appreciate this important part of their heritage... a period of history which must be remembered and kept alive.

Murder, massacre, death marches, mutilation, vivisection and even cannibalism ... years of unimaginable suffering — this should never be forgotten!

On a personal note, this has been a huge deciding factor in my determination to persevere and write "My Father's Book" as a contribution to the World War II history records.

Research has shown that many ex-Far-East Prisoners of War struggled with their own personal memories until their dying day, one of whom was my father. Undoubtedly in their own minds, they believed that no one could possibly comprehend the brutal atrocities they had witnessed and endured during that long period of three-and-a-half years. Many continued throughout the remainder of their lives to suffer from severe aftereffects, such as vivid, recurring nightmares, phobias, depression and guilt, to name but a few.

By late 1945 when most of the ex-Far-East Prisoners of War had been repatriated, Britain had a new Labour government and the British people were doing their best to put the war behind them. However, it became increasingly apparent that far less was known at the time about the war in the Far East than the war in Europe, which ended much earlier on 8th May 1945. Many say that this could this have been due to an undercurrent of shame Associated with "the fall of Singapore" and the enormity of its consequences in the Far East which had been such a catastrophe for Churchill in 1942.

It is only due to the ongoing research decades later that it has become evident that all those servicemen, including my father, were sent to their fate by ill-informed and unprepared leaders responsible for Singapore's easy capture.

MORE RECENT PRESS REPORTS:

14th April 2015 (70 years on)

JAPAN WAR REMORSE – *Japanese Prime Minister, Shing Abe, expressed his profound grief for the tremendous suffering. He was full of remorse and expressed his apologies over his country's actions during World War II.*

VJ DAY Parade, London – *VJ Day is the most sombre and painful of all our commemorations of war. The terrible weapons which ended the war with Japan, and changed the world still perplex us. The unspeakable cruelty of the Japanese who captured British soldiers (and many others) remains incomprehensible and, for most, unforgivable. Yet we have survived all this, thanks mainly to the endurance and humanity of those whose last representatives movingly paraded through London. They preserved their humanity – and ours – with courage, endurance, unselfishness and a determination to save and rebuild civilisation. Let us never dare to forget them.*

SHIPS MENTIONED IN TOM's MANUSCRIPT

SS Duchess of York	Launched 28th September 1928. Originally named Duchess of Cornwall (Namesake Elizabeth Bowens-Lyon – Duchess of York) Tom aboard sailing from Liverpool to Singapore - March 1941 11th July 1943 – attacked by Luftwaffe bombers off the Spanish coast. 600 aboard. 27 killed. Left burning and sank by the Royal Navy the next day.
SS PERAK	A small coastal vessel. Tom aboard sailing from Keppel Harbour, Singapore to Palembang February 1942.
EMPIRE STAR	Tom heard attacked with troops aboard leaving Singapore
WHANG PU	Tom slept in this empty vessel overnight in holds during heavy downpour 4th February 1942.
SS ORCADES	Left Tom's convoy when split up in the Indian Ocean

MS SUMIRE MARU	Japanese ship. Tom aboard travelling from Batavia, Java to Keppel Harbour, Singapore. Free (under British Navy) September 1945.
HMS CILICIA	Tom aboard 2nd October 1945 sailing from Singapore to Port Said, Egypt. Sail into Colombo, Ceylon (Sri Lanka) approximately 12th October 1945. Arrive Port Said 29th October 1945.
SS RANGITATA	Tom aboard 31st October 1945 sailing from Port Said, Egypt to Southampton. Arrives Southampton 10th November 1945.
AMAGI MARU	Japanese "Hell Ship" built on the Clyde Tom travelled from Jaarmarkt Prison Camp to board Amagi Maru in Surabaya (North Java) 17th April 1943 - still aboard 22nd April 1943- arrive Amboina (Ambon) Island – supplies unloaded 23rd April 1943 - air-raid sirens (reconnaissance plane appears over harbour) 24th April 1943 - depart Amboina (unknown destination) 25th April 1943 - approaching large island (possibly Amahai, Ceram, North of Ambon) - no landing quay. Discover cargo is 60 gallon drums of aviation spirit + crates of bombs!! 4th May 1943 – depart from Amahi, Ceram (many comrades put ashore) 6th May 1943 – after approximately 17 days at sea, reach Haroekoe (Haruku). Taken ashore via small motor boats

NAMES & PLACES:

DUTCH EAST INDIES – Dutch Colony until December 1949. Now known as **INDONESIA** in Southeast Asia between the Indian and Pacific Oceans

AMAHAI Village (drums of aviation spirit unloaded by prisoners off Amagi Maru)

AMBON ISLAND (Amboina) – Malukan islands (or Mollucas). Site of Weijami Village. (South West Coast of Ceram)

BANDAR LAMPUNG – Port at Southern tip of Sumatra. Previously known as OOsthaven.

BATAVIA – capital of Dutch East Indies. Now known as Jakarta. North West Coast of Java.

CELEBES – One of four Great Sunda Isles. Large island now known as Sulawesi. East of Borneo with several long peninsulas. **Macassar** – largest city.

CERAM – Now known as Seram. Lies north of Ambon Island. Site of Amahai Village (60 gallon drums of aviation spirit unloaded by prisoners of the Amagi Maru).

HAROEKE Island. Now known as Haruku. (known as Nutmeg Island in the Maluku province) lies east of Ambon Island.

HARUKU Island. Previously known as Haroeke.

JAKARTA – Previously known as Batavia capital of Dutch East Indies. North West Coast of Java.

JAHMIS, Java

JAVA – Large Indonesian island. Lies between Sumatra to the West and Bali to the East. Borneo is to the north. Site of **Tjilatjap (**south coast)

KEPPEL HARBOUR, Singapore

LAMBAK VILLAGE – North Sumatra. West of Java.

MACASSAR – Port City – Sulawesi Island (formerly Celebes)

MOENA Island. Now known as Muna Island lies off the South East arm of Celebes (Sulawesi). The site of **RAHA Prison Camp.**

MUNA Island. Previously known as Moena Island.

OOSTHAVEN – Port at Southern tip of Sumatra. Now known as **Bandar Lampung.**

PADANG – Capital of Western Sumatra Province

PALEMBANG – port city and capital of South **Sumatra**.

PENANG – South of Sungai Petani, Malaysia.

PURBALINGGA – Central Java.

SELETAR, Singapore – RAF base. Housed **151 Maintenance Unit**.

SERAM – Previously known as Ceram. North of Ambon Island. Site of

SPICE ISLANDS also known as the Maluku Islands (or Moluccas) between Sulawesi and New Guinea Approximately 1,000 in total including Seram, Ambon and Sulawesi.

SULAWESI – One of four Great Sunda Isles. Large island previously known as CELEBES. East of Borneo with several long peninsulas. **Macassar** – largest city.

SUMATRA – Large Indonesian island west of Java. Palembang capital of South Sumatra. **Lambak Village** – North Sumatra. **Oosthaven** – Southern tip of Sumatra.

SUNDA STRAITS – Strait separates the Islands of Java and Sumatra.

SUNGAI PETANI – a large town in **Malaysia** in district of Kedah. North of Penang, Perak and Singapore. East of Sumatra.

SURABAYA – port city North eastern coast of Java. (Dutch East Indies Naval Base). Site of **Jaarmakt, Lyceum & Darmoc Camps.** Prisoners boarded **Amagi Maru.**

TASIKMALAYA – city west Java.

TILITJAP – harbour south coast of Java (bombed and destroyed by Japanese)

WEIJAMI VILLAGE – Ambon Island

WALIMPORE – Sulawesi

WATAMPONE – East coast of Western leg of Celebes (Sulawesi).

BAJOA (coastal village – rice barn collapsed). East of Macassar.

YOGYJAKARTA – city south central Java

REFERENCES

Father's diary

Father's rough typed manuscript [hence My Father's Book]

Original letters between Tom & Joan, brothers, parents and friends

Original Post Office Telegrams + Cable and Wireless [cables]

Original Airmail Postcards

Original letters from British Red Cross

Original British Red Cross Instructions to Joan for sending mail

Original letters from the Air Ministry

Original letters from RAF Records Office

Original letter from India Office, Whitehall

Original letter from War Organisation of the British Red Cross Society and Order of St John of Jerusalem - Prisoner of War Department

Original letter from The Birmingham Prisoner of War Relatives Association

Original Newspapers - Daily Mirror, Daily Mail, Birmingham Post

Press cuttings from Birmingham Post

Original maps from British Prisoners of War Relatives Association

Copy of original Liberation Questionnaire

Original Airman's Pay Book

Original copies of The Far East - Companion Journal to "The Prisoner of War"

My father's photographs

My father's copy of the Knights of the Bushido [Father's handwritten notes]

Spice Island Slaves [Tom's acknowledged contribution]

RESEARCH now available on-line to members:

COFEPOW [Children of the Far East Prisoner of War Association]

FEPOW [Far East Prisoner of War]

FEPOW Family

Researching FEPOW History Community

Printed in Dunstable, United Kingdom

66038275R00202